TIMMON MILNE WALLIS was born in Boston, Massachusetts and moved with his family to Scotland when his mother re-married. He studied politics and international relations at the University of Aberdeen and then moved to the peace studies course at Bradford University in West Yorkshire, where he eventually obtained a PhD.

Timmon spent several years living at a peace camp and campaigning against the building of a nuclear cruise missile base at RAF Molesworth in Cambridgeshire, England. He then went on to be international secretary of Peace Brigades International (PBI), editor of *Peace News* magazine, director of the National Peace Council, founder and director of Peaceworkers UK, training manager for International Alert and executive director of Nonviolent Peaceforce. He also had a brief stint working for the Hollywood actor, Forest Whitaker, before returning to the UK in 2014 to work for Quaker Peace & Social Witness, where he served as Programme Manager for Peace and Disarmament.

Timmon has two grown daughters, who are both artists. When he is not writing or campaigning, he spends his time singing and performing his own peace and protest songs. He has written numerous articles on peace-related issues. His first book, *Satyagraha, the Gandhian Approach to Nonviolent Social Change*, was published by Pittenbruach Press in 1984. In 2017, Timmon returned to his native Massachusetts to look after his elderly mother.

Praise for *The Truth About Trident*

I read The Truth About Trident *recently. It's really excellent: well done! I'm about to plug it on Facebook. It's so thorough (I learnt loads, despite knowing a fair bit already!), the structure is very helpful and accessible, and the writing is easy to follow despite some of the complex issues and points you explore.*

OWEN EVERETT

I have found The Truth about Trident *to be excellent – a mixture of robust common sense and well-argued philosophical principles. I have recommended it to an anti-nuclear mailing list I am on in France.*

MARC MORGAN

I feel that your book is an excellent piece of work and brilliant marshalling of all the facts. I am sure that had Theresa May read and absorbed it, she could not have given the debate the introduction she did.

DON SOUTHALL

The Truth About Trident sets out a blow-by-blow detailed analysis... of Britain's nuclear weapons' system... Laid out in a reader-friendly way, the book steers us through key headings such as, What is Trident? What is Radiation? Have Nuclear Weapons kept the peace? Is Trident Affordable? But Wallis does sum up the conclusion of the book in the introduction. 'What we are left with is a weapon system that is not powerful at all but is extremely dangerous.'
ELIZABETH INGRAMS, Peace News

With remarkable foresight, Timmon Wallis... had prepared comprehensive and powerful arguments against Trident – not just its replacement but against Trident as now – in his book The Truth About Trident: Disarming the Nuclear Argument...*Twenty-one questions are addressed [on] topics such as deterrence, insurance, legality, independence, morality and so on... each question is, helpfully, stated early in the book and the issues addressed in more detail in specific chapters.*
FRANK BOULTON, The Friend

Providing a comprehensive demolition of the case for Britain keeping nuclear weapons, this is a timely book from Timmon Milne Wallis. Methodically, he outlines the various arguments for and against and dismantles the claims of those who favour their renewal... Much of the detail provided by the author will surprise and alarm many... A must read.
PAUL DONOVAN, Morning Star

The author has done all of us who are working for a peaceful and nuclear weapons free world a great service with this book. I have not before come across such a comprehensive and easy to read critique of current nuclear weaponry and of the arguments used by the nuclear weapon lobby... Anyone hesitant about writing letters to the press will find in this book all the information that they need about Trident and its planned replacement. I recommend it without hesitation.
BRUCE KENT, CND Campaign magazine

Disarming the Nuclear Argument

The Truth About Nuclear Weapons

DR TIMMON MILNE WALLIS

Luath Press Limited
EDINBURGH
www.luath.co.uk

First published 2017
(text revised and updated from *The Truth About Trident:
Disarming the Nuclear Argument* published by Luath Press in 2016)
in association with

Quakers in Britain
Revised edition 2018

ISBN: 978-1-912147-86-1

The author's right to be identified as author of this book
under the Copyright, Designs and Patents Act 1988 has been asserted.

The paper used in this book is recyclable. It is made from low chlorine pulps
produced in a low energy, low emission manner from renewable forests.

Printed and bound by
Bell & Bain Ltd., Glasgow.

Typeset in 11 point Sabon

© Dr Timmon Milne Wallis 2017, 2018

Contents

List of Abbreviations	9
Acknowledgements	13
Author's Preface	15
Introduction: Getting at the Truth	17

PART 1: THE BASICS

Chapter 1	What are Nuclear Weapons?	26
Chapter 2	What is Radiation?	34
Chapter 3	What is Deterrence?	41
Chapter 4	What is Mutually Assured Destruction?	49

PART 2: WE NEED NUCLEAR WEAPONS FOR OUR SECURITY

Chapter 5	Did Nuclear Weapons End WWII?	56
Chapter 6	Have Nuclear Weapons 'Kept the Peace' Since 1945?	66
Chapter 7	Are Nuclear Weapons Keeping Us Safe Today?	77
Chapter 8	Do Nuclear Weapons Protect Us From Future Risks?	86

PART 3: WE NEED NUCLEAR WEAPONS FOR OUR PLACE IN THE WORLD

Chapter 9	Do Nuclear Weapons Guarantee a Seat at the Top Table?	94
Chapter 10	Being a 'Responsible' Nuclear Weapons State	98
Chapter 11	The Special Case of NATO	100

PART 4: NUCLEAR WEAPONS ARE LEGAL, SAFE, AFFORDABLE

Chapter 12	Are Nuclear Weapons Legal?	106
Chapter 13	Are Nuclear Weapons Safe?	115
Chapter 14	Are Nuclear Weapons Affordable?	124

PART 5: WE ARE DOING ALL WE CAN TO DISARM

Chapter 15	Is There a Commitment to 'Multilateral' Disarmament?	130
Chapter 16	Haven't We Already Disarmed to the Minimum?	139
Chapter 17	Would Disarmament Have Any Effect?	144

PART 6: THE BOMB IS HERE TO STAY

Chapter 18	'But You Can't Uninvent the Bomb'	152
Chapter 19	Can Nuclear Weapons be Morally Acceptable?	157
Chapter 20	Do Nuclear Weapons Fit the World of Today?	166

PART 7: WRAPPING IT ALL UP

Chapter 21   The Truth About Nuclear Weapons   172

APPENDIX I

Treaty On The Non-Proliferation of Nuclear Weapons (NPT)   178

APPENDIX II

Summary of Advisory Opinion of the International Court of
Justice on the Legality of the Threat or Use of Nuclear Weapons   184

APPENDIX III

Full text of the Treaty on the Prohibition of Nuclear Weapons   186

References   197

Endnotes   203

Quakers in Britain   213

This book is dedicated to all those politicians and diplomats from around the world who have had the courage to urge their governments to sign and ratify the new Treaty on the Prohibition of Nuclear Weapons. May your efforts help to move us towards a world free of all nuclear weapons…

List of Abbreviations

ABM	Anti-Ballistic Missiles
ABMT	Anti-Ballistic Missile Treaty
ACTS	Action of Churches Together in Scotland
AWE	Atomic Weapons Establishment
B61	Nuclear weapon dropped from planes and deployed in Germany, Belgium, Netherlands and Turkey
BAE	BAE Systems, (formerly) British Aerospace
BAOR	British Army on the Rhine (Germany)
BBS	British Bombing Survey
CD	Conference on Disarmament
CEP	Circular Error Probable = measure of how close a missile is likely to hit target
CND	Campaign for Nuclear Disarmament
CTBT	Comprehensive Test Ban Treaty
D5	Trident missile used on vanguard and successor submarines
DFID	Department for International Development
DML	Devonport Management Ltd
DOD	US Department of Defence
FOI	Freedom of Information
FMCT	Fissile Material Cut-Off Treaty
G8	Group of eight largest global economies – US, Canada, UK, France, Italy, Japan, Germany
GDP	Gross Domestic Product
GPS	Global Positioning System
HMNB	Her Majesty's Naval Base
IAEA	International Atomic Energy Agency
ICBM	Intercontinental Ballistic Missile
ICC	International Criminal Court
ICJ	International Court of Justice (World Court)
IISS	International Institute of Strategic Studies
IMF	International Monetary Fund
INF	Intermediate Nuclear Forces
ISIS	Islamic State in Iraq and Syria, also known as Isil, IS, Daesh
KT	Kilotonne, or 1,000 tonnes of TNT equivalent

MAD	Mutually Assured Destruction
MDA	Mutual Defence Agreement
MIRV	Multiple Independently-targeted Re-entry Vehicle
MOD	Ministry of Defence
MORI	Ipsos MORI, a market research organisation in the UK.
MP	Member of Parliament
MSP	Member of Scottish Parliament
MT	Megatonne, or one million tonnes, 1,000 KT, of TNT equivalent
NATO	North Atlantic Treaty Organisation
NDA	Nuclear Decommissioning Authority
NFZ	Nuclear Free Zone
NGO	Non-Governmental Organisation
NNWS	Non-Nuclear Weapon State
NPG	Nuclear Planning Group
NPT	Non-Proliferation Treaty
NSS/SDSR	National Security Strategy and Strategic Defence and Security Review
NWS	Nuclear Weapons State
OECD	Organisation for Economic Cooperation and Development
OEWG	Open-Ended Working Group of the UN General Assembly
OSCE	Organisation for Security and Cooperation in Europe
P5	Permanent five members of the UN Security Council
PRIO	Peace Research Institute Oslo
PSA	Polaris Sales Agreement
PSI	Pounds Per Square Inch
PTBT	Partial Test Ban Treaty
RAF	Royal Air Force
RN	Royal Navy
RNAD	Royal Navy Arms Depot
RV	Re-entry vehicle on a nuclear missile
SDP	Social Democratic Party, later merged with Liberal Party to become Liberal Democrats
SNP	Scottish National Party
SIPRI	Stockholm International Peace Research Institute
SSBN	Strategic Ballistic Missile Submarine
START	Strategic Arms Reduction Talks
STUC	Scottish Trades Union Congress
TNT	Trinitrotoluene, a standard explosive
UNESCO	UN Educational, Scientific and Cultural Organisation
UNGA	UN General Assembly
UNSC	UN Security Council

USSR	Union of Soviet Socialist Republics
USSBS	US Strategic Bombing Survey
VSE	Vickers Submarine Engineering Ltd.
W177	UK-made nuclear weapon
W76	US-made nuclear warhead used on Trident Missile
WMD	Weapons of Mass Destruction
WTO	World Trade Organisation
WWI	World War I
WWII	World War II

Acknowledgements

Special thanks to the following experts and advisors, without whom this book could not have been written: John Ainslie, Martin Birdseye, Frank Boulton, Elizabeth Chappell, Janet Fenton, Steve Hucklesby, Paul Ingram, Bruce Kent, David Lowry, Steven Schofield, Rae Street, Jane Tallent and Phil Webber. As author, I of course take full responsibility for any remaining errors or omissions in the text. Thanks also go to Nora Catlin, Haifa Rashed and Holly Wallis for typing up drafts, and to Ellis Brooks, Izzy Cartwright, Stephen Clement, Roslyn Cook, Helen Drewery, Naomi Engelkamp, James Grant, Claire Poyner, Andrew Rigby, Chris Venables, Emily Wallis and colleagues at the Norges Fredsrad for reading and commenting on earlier drafts, and to Gavin MacDougall, Marigold Bentley, Juliette King, Teddy Milne, Vicki Elson, Louise Dickie and Lotte Mitchell Reford for getting the book into final shape for publishing.

Author's Preface

YOU HAVE in your hands the 'international edition' of a book published originally for a UK audience under the title, *The Truth About Trident: Disarming the Nuclear Argument*. Since it was originally written for a British audience and is published by a British publisher, the spellings and punctuation remain British in this edition. Nevertheless, the content is universal. My hope is that readers in the United States, Canada and elsewhere are able to see beyond the language differences to the common arguments being made in favour of nuclear weapons in all these different countries.

Trident is the UK's (only) nuclear weapon system, and it was of great concern to me in writing the original book that the arguments in favour of retaining, and then upgrading, the UK's Trident system were rarely challenged, or even questioned, by Members of Parliament, the mass media or the general public.

The Truth About Trident was an attempt to look in detail at each and every argument in favour of maintaining the UK's Trident system in order to understand a) what these arguments are really saying; b) on what basis these arguments are made and why people believe them; c) how well they stand up to the historical evidence and the tests of logic; and finally d) whether we are able to reach anything remotely resembling the 'truth' of the matter.

I was prepared for the likelihood that most of these arguments would be found wanting, but that at least some of them would stand their ground as sensible, rational reasons for having nuclear weapons. I thought that, on balance, I would be able to make the case that the arguments against Trident slightly outweighed the arguments in its favour. As I wrote in the preface to the UK book, I was rather surprised to find that *none* of the arguments used to justify the Trident system were able to withstand even the most basic scrutiny.

The truth, as I found it, is that nuclear weapons may be the most powerful weapons ever invented, but the arguments in favour of having them are exceedingly weak. It therefore takes relatively little effort to effectively disarm whatever force those arguments may have been thought to have. If only the pride and machismo that underlie these arguments could be so easily disarmed, the world would be free of them by now.

While there are some unique features about the UK's nuclear weapons and the UK's circumstances in the world, the arguments made in favour of nuclear weapons in the UK are not substantially different from the arguments being used in the US, in France, or in the other countries which supposedly rely on the US nuclear 'umbrella', such as Canada, Australia, Japan, South Korea and the many European members of NATO.

In Russia and China there is less open debate about nuclear weapons, but it is unlikely that where the arguments are made, they are substantially different to what are presented here. The situation is not dissimilar in India and Pakistan.

Israel is a special case because its government does not publicly admit to *having* any nuclear weapons, even though the rest of the world believes they do. Apart from anything else, this at least means the government of Israel is under no obligation to explain or justify why they have them. Nevertheless it is difficult to believe that Israelis would use arguments any different to the ones used here to justify their possession of nuclear weapons if or when they were called to do so.

And then we come to North Korea. North Korea's reasons for wanting to develop nuclear weapons are exactly the same as those which have motivated the US government to develop theirs. So while we may be a long way away from any kind of public discussion about nuclear weapons in North Korea, the reasoning in this book still applies.

This book, while drawing heavily on the UK version, attempts to bring in some of the differences and nuances to the arguments that apply to some of these other countries. The US, in particular, has a much more entrenched commitment to nuclear weapons than probably any other country. As the first country to develop nuclear weapons, the only country to have ever used them in war, and the initiator of more or less every technical advancement in the field of nuclear weaponry since then, the US is clearly in the lead when it comes to justifying why it must have these weapons.

At the same time, the US is the most open about its nuclear weapon programme. Of all the nuclear weapons states, we know the most about what goes on in the US. Indeed, most of what we know about the UK's nuclear weapons programme comes not from the UK government but from documents freely available in the US or obtained through Freedom of Information requests in the US.

It is therefore in the United States more than anywhere else that a thorough and proper public debate about nuclear weapons is both needed and possible. My only hope is that this book can make a small contribution to that debate, and that the people of the United States, along with the people of many other countries, will 'arm' themselves with the information and the arguments needed to disarm the nuclear argument and rid the world of nuclear weapons.

INTRODUCTION

Getting at the Truth

ANY BOOK WITH the word 'truth' in its subtitle is bound to attract a certain amount of scepticism if not downright ridicule. The idea that there is a single, knowable 'truth' about anything is rightly to be questioned. Even if such a concept exists in any objective sense, perhaps we are each bound by our own set of circumstances to see only our own truth and to claim anything beyond that as a delusion.

And yet, the reality is that none of us would be able to go about our daily lives without some concept of truth as a reference point. Being able to distinguish truth from lies, facts from opinions, evidence from hearsay is part of what makes us human. We all need to be able to establish for ourselves what is true and what is not.

Every witness in a court of law promises to tell 'the truth, the whole truth and nothing but the truth' before giving their testimony. That is a very exacting bar to meet, but if you are caught lying in court, you will go to prison for it. This book attempts to tell the truth, the whole truth and nothing but the truth – as best we are able to ascertain it – about nuclear weapons. It is a tall order, and not without its challenges.

The nuclear secret

For a start, we are faced immediately with the difficulty that what we are talking about is, at its core, a secret. Julius and Ethel Rosenberg were US citizens accused of passing atomic secrets to the Soviet Union, given the death sentence, and executed by electric chair in 1953. Today, vastly more information about the design and construction of nuclear weapons than was available to the Rosenbergs is freely available on the internet and accessible to anyone in the world. Yet the nuclear weapons states (NWSS) remain highly secretive about key aspects of their nuclear weapons programmes.

This is not just because these are horrifically dangerous weapons that governments don't want falling into the 'wrong hands'. It is also because, as we shall see, the whole doctrine of nuclear deterrence depends upon convincing a potential opponent that a government with nuclear weapons is deadly serious about this business. Deterrence is all about presentation and perceptions rather than about the reality that may lie beneath these.

It is precisely *because* these are such horrifically dangerous weapons and because governments are deadly serious about them that there also needs to be much more public discussion about nuclear weapons than there is. We need to know why we have these weapons, under what conditions would they ever be used, what would be the impact of their use, how safe are they in the meantime, are they really necessary, can we afford them, are there better alternatives? These are right and proper questions which ought to be discussed openly and publicly in any country relying on such weapons. And in order to discuss these questions, we need to know a certain amount about the subject matter.

The approach of this book

This book attempts to dig out the truth about nuclear weapons by examining the arguments *for* nuclear weapons and putting those to the test. Do these arguments hold up under scrutiny? What assumptions are being made and are these justified? What are the facts as best we know them and where are they coming from? What is the logic of the argument and is it valid and reasonable?

This book looks at 20 key arguments that are regularly used to present the case in favour of nuclear weapons. In each case, the argument in favour is explained, along with the assumptions and logic behind it. The arguments are then unpicked and examined in more detail, revealing in most cases cracks in the logic, gaps in the evidence and inherent contradictions in what is being asserted. This analysis then forms the basis for summarising the argument *against* nuclear weapons in each case. The arguments in favour of nuclear weapons are given a fair and sympathetic hearing. But this is not a book aiming to present a 'balanced' view, in which each side of the argument is given equal weight and neither turns out to be more 'right' than the other. This is a book about the truth of the matter and trying to seek out and determine what that is.

It will become obvious to the reader, if it is not already, that this book comes down clearly opposed to nuclear weapons. Whether this is justified on the basis of the arguments and the evidence presented is up to the reader to judge. What most people hear, however, are the pro-nuclear weapons arguments. These are presented to us every day by politicians of major political parties, the vast majority of journalists and broadcasters, academics, think tank experts, admirals and generals, business leaders, trade unionists, teachers and parents. It is hard to imagine another issue of such importance that is presented in such a one-sided, unbalanced way. This book is one small attempt to redress that balance.

Who this book is for

This book is intended for the general reader who may know little about the subject beyond what they hear on the news. It is also for those who have followed this issue closely over the years, but may now wish to refresh their memories in order to more confidently join in the current discussions. While covering in some detail the 20 arguments for and against nuclear weapons, this book does not need to be read from cover to cover. Some may want to dip into chapters that are particularly relevant to them or to the discussion at hand. Others may want to review the different arguments for and against nuclear weapons by looking at the beginnings and/or endings of each chapter.

The aim of the book is to get beyond the soundbites, headlines and slogans that tend to dominate the debate about nuclear weapons. The issues are complex and nuanced. They require more thought and attention than they are normally given. But for people who have neither the time nor the patience to read through a full-length book, there are plenty of short-cuts at hand.

Structure of the book

This book is divided into seven parts. Before looking at the arguments in favour of nuclear weapons, the four chapters in part one summarise what it is we are talking about. What are nuclear weapons (Chapter 1)? What is the fundamental difference between a *nuclear* weapon and any other kind of weapon (Chapter 2)? What is meant by 'deterrence' (Chapter 3)? And what does nuclear deterrence mean when other countries *also* have nuclear weapons (Chapter 4)? Following on from this introductory section, the arguments in favour of nuclear weapons are grouped into five parts.

Part two looks at the arguments that centre around the claim that we need nuclear weapons for our security. Did nuclear weapons end WWII (Chapter 5)? Have they 'kept the peace' since 1945 (Chapter 6)? Are nuclear weapons protecting us here and now (Chapter 7)? And are they needed to protect us from future risks (Chapter 8)?

Part three looks at the arguments which focus on the nuclear weapons states themselves and their 'place in the world'. Do nuclear weapons guarantee a seat at the 'top table' of world affairs (Chapter 9)? What does it mean to be a 'responsible nuclear weapons state' (Chapter 10)? Does the US (or the UK) need nuclear weapons to fulfil their obligations to the rest of NATO (Chapter 11)?

Part four looks at the arguments relating to nuclear weapons in terms of some more basic practicalities. Are they legal (Chapter 12)? Are they safe, even if never used (Chapter 13)? Are they affordable and what are the opportunity costs of maintaining nuclear arsenals today (Chapter 14)?

Part five then addresses the arguments that claim the states which have nuclear weapons are doing all they can to disarm. How committed are they to 'multilateral' disarmament (Chapter 15)? Have they already disarmed as much as they can (Chapter 16)? And even if we got rid of nuclear weapons, would it have any effect on other countries acquiring them (Chapter 17)?

And finally, in part six, we address the set of arguments that say you can't 'disinvent' the bomb, so we need to learn to live with it, however awful that may be (Chapter 18). This includes the moral arguments (Chapter 19) and the claim that opposing nuclear weapons is not living in the 'real world' (Chapter 20).

In brief, the main arguments for and against nuclear weapons and the chapters in which they are covered are as follows:

The main arguments made for and against nuclear weapons:

Chapters 1 and 2

FOR	The awesome destructive power of nuclear weapons is what makes them effective as a deterrent.
AGAINST	They are Weapons of Mass Destruction with unacceptable humanitarian consequences.

Chapters 3 and 4

FOR	They are a deterrent and will never be used as a weapon. Having them prevents others using them.
AGAINST	A deterrent is a weapon that will sooner or later be used as a weapon.

Chapter 5

FOR	Nuclear weapons forced Japan to surrender and ended WWII, saving lives as a result.
AGAINST	The bombing of Hiroshima and Nagasaki was unnecessary and unjustified.

Chapter 6

FOR   Nuclear weapons have kept the peace since 1945 and prevented WWIII.

AGAINST   There is no hard evidence that they have ever 'worked' as a deterrent.

Chapter 7

FOR   Nuclear weapons are essential to national security in the 21st century.

AGAINST   Nuclear weapons serve no military purpose and do not defend us from 21st century threats.

Chapter 8

FOR   Nuclear weapons are an insurance policy against future unknown risks.

AGAINST   Nuclear weapons will be increasingly vulnerable and only make the world less safe.

Chapter 9

FOR   Nuclear weapon gives the NWSS a seat at the top table and status in the world.

AGAINST   The major powers do not need nuclear weapons to be key players in the world and would be more respected if they gave them up.

Chapter 10

FOR   Being a 'responsible' NWS means making sure that nuclear weapons cannot get into the 'wrong hands' or be used except as the ultimate 'deterrent'.

AGAINST   There is no such thing as a 'responsible' NWS. Possessing these weapons is the height of irresponsibility.

Chapter 11

FOR   We have a duty to share the nuclear burden and to protect other countries in NATO.

AGAINST   US nuclear weapons do not protect NATO countries either. NATO nuclear policy makes the world less safe.

Chapter 12

FOR — The NWSS can maintain nuclear arsenals without reneging on international commitments.

AGAINST — Nuclear weapons are illegal under international law and maintaining them indefinitely violates NPT obligations.

Chapter 13

FOR — Nuclear weapons are kept safe and out of harm's way with little risk.

AGAINST — There is a large and increasing risk of accident, miscalculation or unauthorised use.

Chapter 14

FOR — The costs are affordable and justified, and do not adversely affect other government spending.

AGAINST — The costs are huge and take funds away from other much-needed government programmes.

Chapter 15

FOR — The NWSS are committed to a multilateral approach to nuclear disarmament.

AGAINST — The NWSS continue to block multilateral disarmament because they are not really serious about it.

Chapter 16

FOR — The NWSS have already disarmed to the barest minimum needed for deterrence.

AGAINST — The NWSS have removed obsolete weapons but continue to upgrade their nuclear capabilities.

Chapter 17

FOR — There's no point in the NWSS disarming further because it will have no effect on other states.

AGAINST — If any one of the NWSS took a lead it could break the deadlock on disarmament and speed up the process towards elimination.

Chapter 18

FOR — Nuclear weapons are here to stay and they cannot be 'uninvented'.

AGAINST — Eliminating nuclear weapons is doable and there is no need to hold onto things that are no longer needed.

Chapter 19

FOR — Nuclear weapons prevent war, which is a greater evil, so they are morally justified.

AGAINST — Nuclear weapons are morally indefensible.

Chapter 20

FOR — Nuclear weapons are part of the real world and those who think otherwise are living in La-La land.

AGAINST — The real world is one in which the majority of countries oppose nuclear weapons. No country can be secure unless all are secure.

Each chapter investigates these issues in detail and at the end of each chapter is a summary of the conclusions reached. At the end of the book is a summary of all the chapters (Chapter 21). For anyone looking for even more information, there is a detailed bibliography of relevant books and other materials, including websites with vast amounts of relevant information. These can be accessed through the dedicated website for this book: www.disarmingarguments.com.

PART ONE

The Basics

CHAPTER 1

What are Nuclear Weapons?

NUCLEAR WEAPONS use the physics of 'fissile materials'[1] to create a very large explosion. The smallest possible nuclear explosion is similar in size to some of the largest possible conventional (ie non-nuclear) explosions,[2] but most nuclear weapons involve explosions many thousands or even millions of times larger than that.[3] As with any large explosion, the heat and blast effects kill and injure people, topple buildings and cause other widespread destruction. Unlike any other type of explosion, however, nuclear weapons also release radiation, which is uniquely harmful to humans in a range of different ways (see chapter 2).

The early 'atom bomb' was based on nuclear fission – splitting the atoms of uranium or plutonium in a chain reaction that rapidly creates temperatures hotter than the interior of the sun. At those massively high temperatures, other elements can also break apart to 'boost' the fission process and atoms of hydrogen can fuse together to create helium, causing an even larger explosion. This is where the term 'hydrogen bomb' came from, although the latter process is called nuclear fusion.

Today, most nuclear weapons incorporate all three stages into a single weapon: a fission bomb is detonated first, to create the temperatures needed for fusion, a neutron 'booster' then multiplies the impact of the fission process, and finally a fusion bomb is exploded, using hydrogen to create the maximum blast for the minimum quantity of fissile material.

When we talk about nuclear weapons we are mainly talking about the nuclear warhead, where the explosion takes place. To be used as a weapon, the warhead must be made into a free-fall bomb or put onto a missile so it can reach its target. Bombs and missiles also require some form of platform, or 'delivery vehicle', to launch the weapon. Delivery vehicles include aircraft, submarines, missile silos, mobile missile launchers and other delivery systems.

Nuclear weapons have been produced in all shapes and sizes since 1945. The smallest nuclear weapons ever deployed had a destructive capacity equivalent to around 10 tonnes of TNT, or 0.01 Kilotons (0.01 KT). The largest nuclear weapons ever deployed were in the 20–25 MT (25,000 KT) range. Most nuclear weapons today are between 100–1,000 KT (or 0.1 – 1 MT) in size.

Nuclear weapons capable of reaching targets many thousands of miles away are considered 'strategic' weapons. These are delivered by long-range bomber aircraft, ballistic missile submarines or inter-continental ballistic missiles (ICBMs). Nuclear weapons with a shorter range, measured in hundreds rather than thousands of miles, are considered 'intermediate' nuclear forces, and normally these are defined in terms of the shorter range of bomber aircraft or missiles.

Nuclear weapons with a very short range, measured in miles or tens of miles, are considered 'battlefield' or tactical nuclear weapons. During the Cold War, tens of thousands of battlefield nuclear weapons were facing each other in Central Europe. These included nuclear weapons fired from artillery pieces, dropped from helicopters, fired from trucks and jeeps, dropped as depth charges from ships, fired from torpedo tubes and even nuclear weapons designed to be carried into battle strapped onto the backs of soldiers and then detonated from a distance.

Who has nuclear weapons?

As of 2018, only nine states are producing and deploying their own nuclear weapons: The United States, Russia, China, UK, France, India, Pakistan, Israel and North Korea. South Africa developed and tested a nuclear weapon but then gave up its nuclear programme. Eleven other countries toyed with the idea of developing their own nuclear weapons and gave up their programmes before actually testing a nuclear device.[4] At least 37 other countries are considered economically and technically capable of producing nuclear weapons if they chose to do so.

According to the US Bureau of Arms Control, Verification and Compliance, reporting in April 2017 under the terms of the NewSTART Treaty,[5] the US currently has a total of 1,411 deployed nuclear warheads on 673 delivery vehicles and Russia has 1,765 deployed nuclear warheads on 523 delivery vehicles. These numbers do not include nuclear warheads which are considered 'stockpiled' or 'retired'. Both countries have approximately 4,000 warheads in the first category and 2,500 in the second category, bringing the total warhead count up to around 7,000 nuclear warheads each.[6]

The UK claims to have 120 warheads operationally deployed on its Trident submarines, with another 95 'stockpiled', for a total of 215. France and China both have close to 300 warheads in total. France is considered to have nearly all its warheads 'deployed' while China is not considered to have *any* of its warheads deployed.⁷ India and Pakistan currently have between 100–150 each, although again these are not considered to be deployed. Israel is believed to have around 80 nuclear warheads and North Korea around eight.

That makes for a grand total of just under 15,000 nuclear warheads in the world as of early 2018, of which around 4,000 are 'operationally deployed'. Many of these are, in turn, on hair-trigger alert, ready to be fired at a moment's notice.

At the height of the Cold War in the mid-1980s, there were more than 60,000 nuclear warheads in the world. More than 45,000 nuclear warheads have been successfully taken out of service and dismantled since then, meaning a reduction by three-quarters in the total number of nuclear weapons.

Virtually all of the largest nuclear weapons in the multi-megaton range have been removed since the height of the Cold War. Ironically, perhaps, so have most of the smallest nuclear weapons in the 1–10 Kiloton range and smaller. Currently, the smallest nuclear warhead in the US arsenal is in the 50 Kiloton range and the largest is in the 1,200 Kiloton (1.2 MT) range. While it is difficult to know for sure, the largest nuclear weapon currently deployed by Russia is probably in the 1,000 Kiloton range (1 MT) and the smallest is probably in the 10 Kiloton range.

The UK has only one type of warhead, and that is believed to be in the 100 Kiloton range, although they have at times claimed to also have a smaller yield option. All of France's nuclear warheads are now in the 150–300 KT range, while China is believed to still have nuclear weapons in the 3,000–4,000 KT (3–4 MT) range, as well as weapons as small as 20 KT.

The impact of a nuclear detonation

The Hiroshima bomb was estimated to be in the range of 12,000–18,000 tonnes of TNT (12–18 KT), or roughly 1,000 times as powerful as the largest conventional bomb in the US arsenal today.⁸ The total number killed by the Hiroshima bomb is not known. The original estimate of 68,000 dead and a similar number injured was based on a random survey of households in 1946. However this did not take into account up to 20,000 Korean prisoners of war and an unknown number of refugees from other Japanese cities known to be in the city at that time.

Many of those who were injured by the Hiroshima blast died subsequently from radiation sickness and fatal injuries, in part because medical facilities were destroyed and very little was known about the dangers of radiation poisoning. It is difficult to know how many of the subsequent deaths in Hiroshima should be attributed to the atomic bomb as opposed to other causes. Most sources now use the figure of 140,000 as the total number killed by the Hiroshima bomb, although the city of Hiroshima maintains an official register of deaths from the atomic bomb right up to the present day, and that register now has more than 200,000 names.[9]

The atom bomb which was dropped on Nagasaki was of a different design and estimated to be slightly more powerful at 20 KT. The total death count was initially estimated at 60,000, or slightly less than at Hiroshima. A much larger number were injured but more of these people survived than in Hiroshima. Other differences between the death tolls in the two cities had to do with weather conditions, terrain, the type of buildings, the population density of the city and where the bomb was dropped in relation to where people were at the time.

A modern nuclear warhead with a yield of 100 KT is 6.6 times the size of the Hiroshima bomb. The scale of the destruction and the number of people who would be killed or injured from such an explosion is difficult to determine and depends on many factors, including those just mentioned above. There is not a linear relationship between the size of a nuclear explosion and the numbers killed or area destroyed. The biggest factor has to do with whether the bomb is detonated at, or near, the ground or higher up in the atmosphere (see next chapter). Nevertheless, based on what we know about Hiroshima, it is clear that the effects of a single nuclear weapon today, detonated on, or above a city, would be devastating.

The nuclear fireball

The detonation of a nuclear weapon creates a massive fireball as the nuclear chain reaction, or 'fission', breaks down the atoms of uranium and/or plutonium that are the initial fuel of the bomb. The temperature inside this fireball rises to tens of millions of degrees Centigrade. This is hotter than the interior of the sun and thousands of times hotter than a conventional explosion.[10] Inside the fireball, these temperatures trigger the thermonuclear 'fusion' reaction that creates even more destructive energy as atoms of hydrogen are fused into helium and other by-products. The fireball of a 100 KT warhead is a sphere approximately 500 metres (1,500 ft) across in all directions.

If the fireball is 500 metres across and the centre of it is more than 250 metres above the ground, this is called an 'airburst'. With the whole of the fireball in the air, very little else is consumed by the fireball other than the nuclear fuels contained in the bomb and small quantities of oxygen and other gases in the air. If the fireball is detonated below this height, this is considered a 'groundburst'. Everything within that sphere is then turned into radioactive by-products as a result of the explosion, and this is a critical factor which we shall explore in greater detail in the next chapter.

From a basic airburst explosion, already more than 300 different radioactive isotopes are created from the exploding uranium and/or plutonium.[11] Many more varieties of radioactive material may be additionally created from a groundburst explosion, depending on what was on the ground at that precise time and place. If the target of a groundburst explosion was a nuclear missile silo, nuclear weapons store or other nuclear facility, any nuclear warheads or other nuclear materials – as well as living creatures – that end up within reach of the fireball are themselves going to be irradiated and added to the total fireball and subsequent release of radioactive by-products.

Heat and blast effects

Conventional explosives cause death, injuries and destruction of property from the heat and blast of the explosion. This rips through buildings, sets fire to anything that burns and throws shrapnel, bits of building and other debris through the air, all of which is highly dangerous to anything or anybody that may be nearby. A nuclear explosion causes all these same effects, in addition to the unique effects of radiation, which are discussed in the next chapter.

At a distance of 4 km from a 100 KT nuclear explosion, temperatures are still hot enough to set papers and other flammable materials alight.[12] Therefore fires are an enormous hazard in the aftermath of a nuclear explosion even at great distances from ground zero. In Hiroshima, the entire city centre was burnt to the ground and many of the injuries suffered by the inhabitants were the result of burns.

Blast is normally measured in pounds per square inch (psi) of 'overpressure.'[13] Ten psi of overpressure is enough to damage lungs and cause widespread fatalities and 20 psi is enough to pull down a heavily reinforced concrete building.[14] Near the nuclear fireball, the shock wave which is created by the explosion reaches 200 psi of overpressure, with winds of more than 2,000 mph, enough to flatten and kill anything, even the most heavily reinforced concrete bunker.[15] At 1 km (0.6 miles) from a 100 KT blast, the overpressure is 20 psi, which is lethal for human beings and still capable of considerable damage to buildings. At 2 km, the overpressure still reaches 5 psi, with windspeeds over 100 mph and up to 50 per cent fatalities.[16]

Nuclear winter and nuclear famine

Another product of a nuclear explosion is the dust and soot that rises up as a result of fires and the intense heat created. Most atmospheric tests took place on Pacific islands, barren atolls or in the deserts of western US, central Australia or Siberia. Under these conditions, even groundburst explosions would not be expected to cause major fires and therefore the soot content has been minimal. If a nuclear explosion took place over dense forest or a densely populated city, however, fires could be expected to burn out of control for some days over a large area. This happened in Hiroshima and Nagasaki as well as in places like Dresden and Tokyo where conventional explosives were used in huge quantities to create 'firestorms'.

During the 1980s there was concern that an all-out nuclear war between the Soviet Union and the West could push so much soot into the atmosphere that it would lead to a 'nuclear winter' – a lowering of global temperatures, causing widespread famine, disease and death of large numbers of people not already killed by the nuclear weapons themselves or the after-effects of radiation.

The US and Russia each had an estimated 2,500 MT worth of TNT in their nuclear arsenals at that time and climate scientists calculated that an all-out nuclear war would therefore put about 150 million tonnes of soot into the atmosphere. Using complex computer modelling of the earth's climate, they estimated that that much soot could lower the earth's average temperature by as much as 8.5 degrees C and reduce annual rainfall globally by as much as 1.4 mm. This in turn would reduce growing seasons worldwide and mean that some key grain-producing regions like Iowa and Ukraine would remain below freezing even in the height of summer and thus unable to grow anything for up to two years.[17]

Using the same modelling techniques, scientists then tried in the 1990s to estimate the climatic effects of just 100 Hiroshima-sized bombs, for instance in a regional war between India and Pakistan.

Given the population densities in those two countries and the vulnerability of crops to radiation damage, it was concluded that even a 'small-scale' nuclear war in that region would have hugely devastating consequences for all the countries across the whole Northern Hemisphere and could lead to the death of over two billion people.[18]

Further studies have looked at the effects of 'limited' forms of nuclear warfare, for instance the launching of nuclear weapons from a single UK Trident submarine. Dr Philip Webber, chair of Scientists for Global Responsibility, has estimated that the simultaneous detonation of 4 megatonnes of TNT, roughly the total firepower of one UK Trident submarine, could produce between 10 and 38 million tonnes of soot, sufficient to cause a cooling of the earth by 1.5–3 degrees C and a shortening of growing seasons by 10–30 days over a five-year period.[19]

How this might affect global food supplies is hard to estimate, but the implications are clear. Even a comparatively 'limited' nuclear war could cause devastating and long-lasting climactic effects, while a major all-out nuclear war would endanger the entire planet.

Targeting nuclear weapons

At the end of WWII, the US was the only country with nuclear weapons. Although there was talk of getting rid of them at that point, the US began to rapidly build up its arsenal of nuclear weapons as well as the means to deliver them. By 1946, the US had a total of nine atomic bombs, but had already identified a list of 20 major cities in the Soviet Union to drop them on. By 1948, the US had about 50 nuclear weapons. Their targeting plans at that point still involved dropping them on those same 20 cities, only by this time they would be hit by at least two nuclear weapons each.

By 1950, the Soviet Union had acquired about five nuclear weapons of its own. The US by this time had about 300, and their target list began to expand very rapidly. In addition to cities, the US military began to focus on targets that would 'blunt, retard and disrupt' the Soviet Union's nuclear weapons capability. This meant targeting industrial infrastructure, such as chemical factories, power plants and shipyards.

By 1955, the US had over 5,500 targets in the Soviet Union, Eastern Europe and China assigned to its arsenal of about 2,500 nuclear warheads. And by 1960, the target list was growing exponentially as the US nuclear stockpile increased to over 20,000 nuclear warheads. The US target list was so large at this point it was incorporated into a 'Bombing Encyclopedia' which eventually listed over 80,000 targets to be hit in case of nuclear war with the Soviet Union and/or China.

During the 1960s, there was so much 'overkill' built into the US nuclear war planning that Moscow, for instance, was expected to be hit with 23 separate multi-megaton nuclear weapons. Kaliningrad would be hit with 18 nuclear weapons and Leningrad with four. Recently de-classified documents from this period show that the US military expected the death toll in the event of war with the Soviet Union to be in the region of 285 million dead across the Soviet bloc, with up to 40 million injured.

During the 1970s and '80s, US nuclear targeting plans were reviewed and revised a number of times. The specific targeting of cities ('counter-value' targeting) became more controversial, not least because it became illegal under international law following the signing of the Additional Protocols to the Geneva Convention in 1977 (see chapter 12). However the specific targeting of the other side's nuclear weapons ('counter-force' targeting) was also highly controversial, since it increased the risk of one side launching a first strike.

If one side can destroy the other side's nuclear weapons in a surprise first strike attack, that other side is under great pressure to fire their weapons before they are destroyed. This increases the likelihood that either side will try to be the first to launch a surprise attack, but it also increases the pressure to 'launch on warning', ie to launch nuclear weapons at the very first indication that an attack is underway, rather than waiting to verify the attack. Waiting for confirmation that an attack is underway might mean it is too late to fire back with weapons that have already been destroyed.

We now know from the historical record that faulty radars, technical glitches and human error led either the US or the Soviets to believe an attack was underway at least 11 times in the last 50 years (see Chapter 13). Only luck saved the world from all-out nuclear war on those 11 occasions. With 'launch on warning' the world might not be so lucky.

Summary

Nuclear weapons are capable of causing death and destruction on a scale unparalleled in human history. A single 100 KT nuclear warhead can produce temperatures of tens of millions of degrees Centigrade and a shock wave sufficient to flatten skyscrapers, together with everything else that may be standing, or alive, within 500 metres of the blast.

At a distance of 2 km, the blast is still sufficient to bring down buildings and cause many casualties, with wind speeds at over 100mph. At a distance of 4 km from an exploding 100 KT warhead, the heat is still intense enough to set newspapers on fire.

The US and Russia each have more than 1,500 warheads many times this size, ready to launch if given the order, 24 hours a day, 365 days a year. Altogether, there are nearly 15,000 nuclear weapons in the world today. Launching just one of these warheads, by accident or by design, would cause a humanitarian catastrophe of unparalleled proportions. Launching a handful of them could push millions of tons of soot into the atmosphere and seriously affect global food supplies for billions of people, on top of all the other destructive effects of those weapons. An all-out nuclear war between the US and Russia would almost certainly mean the end of modern civilisation as we know it, and could well lead to mass global extinctions, including of our own species.

All of this is a risk we face with weapons whose destructive power is out of all proportion to any cause we could possibly have for their use. And yet, we have not even taken into account the most serious by-product of nuclear weapons – the radiation effects.

CHAPTER 2

What is Radiation?

THE BLAST AND heat effects of a nuclear explosion are very similar to those of a conventional weapon, just multiplied many times in scale because a nuclear explosion is so much more powerful than a conventional explosion. Even the environmental effects are not qualitatively different, since extensive fire-bombing of cities with conventional weapons would also push equivalent amounts of soot into the atmosphere, potentially affecting global climate in a similar way.

But nuclear weapons also produce short-term and long-term effects from ionising radiation which are qualitatively different to any effect produced by other types of weapon. These have huge importance in terms of the impact of nuclear weapons beyond the immediate point of detonation, not only in terms of spreading death and injury far and wide geographically, but also spreading it across time to future generations.

The main forms of ionising radiation are alpha, beta and gamma rays, and also neutrons. These are all produced in large quantities from a nuclear explosion. All ionising radiations increase the chemical reactivity of the materials they irradiate, by altering the electrical charge of (or 'ionising') their atoms. In living things, these chemical effects can be very damaging.

Alpha radiation comes from helium ions (with two protons and two neutrons) released during the decay of uranium and many of its decay products. Alpha particles penetrate matter very poorly – a single sheet of paper can provide effective shielding – so external exposure has very little effect on health. But any alpha particles that are swallowed or inhaled can reach body tissues where they can seriously damage cells in the immediate vicinity.

Beta rays are electrons formed during radioactive decay. They penetrate more than alpha particles but are still most damaging if the radioactive source materials are inhaled or swallowed.

The most penetrating and damaging external forms of ionising radiation are the gamma rays. Gamma rays are a form of electromagnetic radiation. They can behave either like waves or like particles (when they are referred to as 'high energy photons'). Unlike alpha particles and beta particles, gamma rays will travel through metal, rocks and concrete. Depending on the strength of the gamma rays, a certain thickness of any given material will reduce the gamma rays by a certain percent. Six feet of concrete, for instance, will reduce typical gamma rays by a factor of one billion, although a small fraction of the rays will still get through.

When ionising radiation is absorbed by a given mass of material, the received 'dose' can be measured in physical units called 'Grays' (Gy).[1] But the amount of biological damage varies widely according to the type of radiation (alpha, beta or gamma), and the various organs affected, because these all have different rates of sensitivity to radiation. A Gy of alpha rays inside the body (for example from inhaled uranium or radon) is reckoned to be 20 times more dangerous than the same dose of external gamma rays.

A different measurement, the 'Sievert' (Sv)[2] is therefore used to indicate the biological effect of a given radiation dose. One milli-Gray of gamma rays, for instance, is 'equivalent' to 1 milli-Sievert, and one milli-Gray of alpha rays is equivalent to 20 milli-Sieverts. For humans, the consequences of most concern from even relatively low doses (below 0.1 Sv) are the increased risks of cancer, and of inheritable changes affecting offspring.

Effects of radiation on the human body

Acute radiation poisoning can result from sudden exposure to doses of 1 Sv or more – for example from the first flash of a nuclear detonation. The clinical effects are predictable and depend on the dose and whether the whole or only part of the body was exposed. As the main form of radiation will be high-energy photons (gamma rays), shielding in the hollows of hills (which occurred at Nagasaki) or inside buildings which remain standing can be partially effective in reducing exposure.

All those receiving more than 8 Sv will die, and progressively higher doses will kill more quickly. About half those exposed to 4 to 5 Sv will die after a month or so. The symptoms are progressively of bone marrow failure (anaemia and bleeding), severe diarrhoea and vomiting, to severe brain damage at very high doses resulting in seizures, coma and rapid death.

Up to half the people exposed to between 1 and 2 Sv will develop relatively mild nausea and slight headache after a few hours, lasting a day or so; but after a week to a month their blood cell counts fall giving them temporarily a tendency to bruise and bleed easily after mild injury, and to get infections more readily. About five per cent may die of complications. Doses of less than 1 Sv are likely to cause short-term hair-loss or long-term eye cataracts.

Certain radioactive isotopes have particular effects on certain organs of the body. Bone-marrow and lungs are particularly vulnerable to ionising radiation, as are the reproductive organs and thyroid glands.

Strontium-90 is taken up selectively by bones as strontium is chemically very similar to calcium. This has a half-life of 28.8 years and emits beta particles which, being more penetrating than alpha particles, can reach the blood-cell forming tissues of the bone marrow. A large-scale study of baby teeth in the US in the 1960s found that children born in 1963 had 50 times as much strontium-90 in their teeth than children born in 1950. This was attributed to the atmospheric nuclear testing which took place during the late '50s and early '60s.[3]

Following the Partial Test Ban Treaty of 1963, which ended most atmospheric testing, the levels of Strontium-90 began to drop. Children born in 1968 thus had 50 per cent less strontium-90 in their teeth than those born in 1963. Although further studies of baby teeth have not been conducted since, they should continue to show a steady decline in levels of strontium-90 as it continues its radioactive decay.

What has been studied more recently is the incidence of cancer among adults whose baby teeth had varying levels of strontium-90 in the 1960s. Those who later died of cancer before reaching the age of 50 were found to have had twice the level of strontium-90 in their baby teeth at an early age as compared to those who had not died of cancer by the same age. This suggests that the strontium-90 from nuclear fallout in the 1950s that had found its way into children's teeth in the 1960s had also increased their likelihood of getting cancer by the 2010s.[4]

Iodine-131 (half-life eight days) gets into milk from cows grazing on contaminated land, and represents a thyroid cancer risk to children drinking it. Adults appear to be at much lower risk. Administering normal (non-radioactive) iodine can provide some protection but has to be given very early. Ironically, a standard treatment for thyroid cancer is high-dose radio-iodine.

Caesium is chemically very similar to potassium, so its radioactive isotope caesium-137 – half-life 30 years – is also of biological and clinical significance. Most of it decays by beta emission but it also emits gamma rays. It gets deposited on the soil and taken up by plants and crops, entering the human food chain. Potassium and caesium are widely distributed through the body and are integral minerals essential for all cells. They get washed out of the body in a matter of days but can still cause a great deal of damage to cells in that time.

Other radioactive isotopes produced by nuclear fission include uranium-237, neptunian-239, sodium-24, manganese-56, silicon-31, aluminium-28 and chlorine-38. Tritium (H-3) has a half-life of 12.3 years and is produced in very large quantities by the fusion process used in modern nuclear weapons.

Airburst and groundburst

The bombs dropped on Hiroshima and Nagasaki were both detonated at an altitude of about 1,500 feet above the ground. As was mentioned in the last chapter, this is known as an 'airburst' and it causes the maximum death and destruction over the widest possible area. If the bomb is left to reach the ground (or nearly reach the ground) before exploding, more or less half the impact goes into the ground rather than being spread out across a wider area.

If the target is a city and the aim is to cause maximum damage, the weapon is most likely to be exploded above ground as an airburst. A large amount of initial radiation is released by an airburst explosion, but the amount of radioactive fallout downwind of the explosion is much less than for a groundburst explosion, because less earth and other materials from the ground are consumed by the nuclear fireball.

A groundburst detonation means that large quantities of earth and whatever else happens to be on the earth (ie buildings, people, etc) are engulfed in the nuclear fireball and become irradiated. This additional matter creates many more radioactive particles of many more types and these are carried up into the mushroom cloud where they are dispersed with the wind and eventually come down as radioactive fallout.

While a nuclear strike against a city is likely to be an airburst and thus have comparatively less radioactive fallout, a nuclear strike against a military target such as a hardened nuclear missile silo or command bunker is likely to be a groundburst and thus involve much higher levels of fallout.

Radiation effects from a 100 KT groundburst

Anyone within 1,500 metres of a 100 KT nuclear detonation is likely to receive an immediate dose of radiation well in excess of 100 Sv as a result of the 'initial' radiation effects of the nuclear explosion.[5] This is much more than a lethal dose of radiation but anyone that near will have been killed already from the heat and blast of the explosion. Within a radius of 2,500 metres, the instant dose of radiation is still in excess of 3 Sv, but this then falls off quickly to levels of 0.3 Sv at 3,000 metres. This is the initial, or 'instant' dose of radiation.

At distances further than 1,500 metres from the fireball, the *accumulated* dose of radiation starts to have the greater effect on human health. A dose of 3 Sv in one hour may not be fatal, but over a 4-hour period, the continued exposure to that level of radiation, even though it is rapidly diminishing in strength, almost certainly will be fatal. A dose of 0.3 Sv at a further distance may not be fatal, but again, if the dose is sustained over 24-hours or even longer, it can nonetheless prove deadly.

At even further distances, there is the 'delayed' radiation which travels with the wind and comes down as rain or snow at some distance from the nuclear fireball. In the case of a groundburst explosion, the radiation from this fallout can still be at lethal levels even hundreds of miles from the explosion. During one of the largest nuclear tests in the Pacific, islanders 330 miles from the detonation of a 15 MT hydrogen bomb received accumulated doses of radiation that caused birth defects, leukaemias and other fatal cancers.[6]

Then there is the global radioactive fallout resulting from the smallest of radioactive particles making their way into the upper atmosphere where they may traverse the globe for years before coming back down to earth. By this time, the levels of radioactivity are much lower, but alpha particles of very long-lasting isotopes can still get into the food chain and be ingested into the human body.

Some 26 years after the Chernobyl nuclear accident in 1986, more than 250,000 sheep in Wales and northern England, more than 1,000 miles away from where the accident happened, were still considered unfit for human consumption because of the levels of Caesium-137 they contained.[7] Caesium-137 contamination is now a major problem in the areas of Japan affected by the Fukishima accident in 2011.

Impact of small doses of radiation

The main risk from lower doses of radiation, which may have no immediately apparent effects, is the delayed onset of leukaemia (especially in children and occurring up to ten years after exposure); or of cancers (the onset of which starts after about five years but the risks are life-long). Even very elderly survivors have an increased risk of cancer, a prospect which may have haunted them throughout their lives. The psychological effects of knowingly being exposed even to relatively low doses of ionising radiation can be profound – and are rarely taken into consideration.

While it is impossible to predict whether an individual person will get cancer or other complications as a result of sudden exposure to a dose of 0.1 Sv, more people within a given population exposed to 0.1 Sv will get cancer than in a similar population *not* exposed to 0.1 Sv. This implies that *any* increase in exposure to radiation will increase the likelihood of cancer and other diseases.

According to one study, as many as 2.4 million people could eventually die worldwide from cancers and leukaemias as a result of the atmospheric testing in the '50s and '60s – ten times as many as died from the bombs on Hiroshima and Nagasaki themselves.[8] That is a hugely controversial figure if it is true. It would mean that the numbers killed from cancers and leukaemias as a result of the normal radioactive discharges from civil nuclear power stations would also be correspondingly large and create huge insurance problems for the nuclear industry.

What we do know is that the cancer rates in Hiroshima and Nagasaki are higher than the average for Japan as a whole even today, 70 years after the bombs fell and long after both cities have been re-built into the thriving cities they are today.[9]

Summary

Nuclear weapons are not just very large conventional weapons. They produce effects which no other type of weapon has ever produced. It is the ionising radiation that potentially causes the most serious and long lasting effects of a nuclear explosion. This is especially the case if it is a groundburst explosion aimed at a hardened military or government target.

Mild radiation poisoning destroys blood cells and damages the genetic material in human cells. More severe forms of radiation poisoning destroy the linings of stomach and intestines, cause internal haemorrhages, loss of electrolyte balance, and heart failure. Death from radiation poisoning can take from a few days to several weeks, and beyond a certain dose of radiation, even the most modern medical treatments are unlikely to be effective.

Groundburst nuclear explosions produce large amounts of radioactive fallout which can travel hundreds of miles downwind. The smallest radioactive particles rise up into the upper atmosphere and are dispersed across the entire globe. These small radioactive particles can still be fatal if they enter the food chain and are ingested by humans.

Radioactive isotopes produced by atmospheric nuclear testing in the Pacific in the 1950s were found in the teeth of children as far away as the USA. There are no definitive scientific conclusions on the effects of relatively small doses of radiation, however some medical professionals have suggested that as many as 2.4 million worldwide will have died from leukaemia and other cancers as a direct result of radiation from those nuclear tests.

This means that if nuclear weapons were ever used as a weapon of war, they would not only cause cruel and unnecessary suffering to those immediately affected by high doses of radioactivity near to, and downwind of, the explosions. They would also, especially if used as a groundburst weapon to target hardened command and control bunkers, cause large amounts of radioactive materials to enter the earth's upper atmosphere and cause leukaemias and other cancers to people hundreds and thousands of miles away.

CHAPTER 3

What is Deterrence?

IN HER STATEMENT to the Third International Conference on the Humanitarian Impacts of Nuclear Weapons, held in Vienna in December 2014, the official UK spokesperson, Susan Le Jeune d'Allegeershecque, told delegates from 158 other countries that the devastating humanitarian consequences that could result from the use of nuclear weapons was 'not new' but was indeed the reason why these weapons were so effective as a deterrent. In fact, the most common response to the humanitarian concerns raised in the previous chapter is 'of course nuclear weapons would never be used, they are merely a deterrent'.[1]

> The UK's nuclear weapons are not designed for military use during conflict but instead to deter and prevent nuclear blackmail and acts of aggression against our vital interests that cannot be countered by other means... ('The Future of the UK's Nuclear Deterrent' White Paper, 2006)

The British government indeed prefers to refer to its own nuclear weapons, not as a weapons system at all, but as 'the deterrent', as if this categorically defines what a nuclear weapon is. But a nuclear weapon is not 'a deterrent' in and of itself. Even the BBC acknowledges that in its internal guidance to journalists.[2] Any government possessing nuclear weapons *hopes* these weapons will act as a deterrent and will never actually be used as weapons. Whether there is evidence that nuclear weapons have acted as a deterrent up until now is the subject of following chapters. The question at this stage is what does deterrence actually mean?

According to the US Department of Defence, deterrence is 'the prevention from action by fear of the consequences. Deterrence is a state of mind brought about by the existence of a credible threat of unacceptable counteraction.'[3] In other words, deterrence is a psychological term, not a military term. It is about trying to create a sense of fear that you hope will convince someone that they don't actually want to do something they might otherwise choose to do.

As a strategy for controlling someone else's behaviour, deterrence relies on threatening that person with some form of punishment if they do something you don't want them to do. Leaving aside whether coercion through fear is morally palatable, 'successful' deterrence means the punishment never has to be carried out because the mere threat of it is sufficient to control the behaviour. 'Unsuccessful' deterrence is when the threat has to be carried out in order to control the behaviour in question.

Deterrence in everyday life

As any parent knows, deterrence as a strategy for controlling the behaviour of small children is rarely successful – and with older children even less so. Children are not easily deterred from doing what they want to do at that moment, even when they know they will have to suffer the consequences later. When deterrence *does* (apparently) work as a strategy for managing the behaviour of children, it normally does so only when:

1. The actual punishment has been carried out recently enough or frequently enough for the experience of that punishment to be vividly present when the threat is made.
2. The threat is able to be carried out then and there with immediate effect.
3. There is no possibility of evading responsibility for the behaviour in question or of getting away with it undetected.

In the absence of these pre-existing conditions, parents find themselves inflicting punishments to 'teach a lesson' for the next time – assuming there *is* a next time. Whether or not the subsequent punishment is effective, the deterrence has clearly failed by that point.

These same principles also apply to the use of (legal) threats to deter criminals. Deterrence is a well-known, but highly controversial, concept in the field of criminal justice. Although the primary function of arrest and detention is to punish criminal behaviour, it is secondarily aimed at deterring further criminal behaviour. There is an extensive body of evidence to suggest that people are less likely to engage in criminal activity if they know they will be caught. However there is an equally compelling body of evidence to suggest that very few criminals are deterred by the severity of the punishment they can expect to get, much less by the mere threat of being punished.

Even the threat of death apparently does little to deter murderers. One has only to compare the murder rates of countries which still have capital punishment with those which do not to see that the correlation is entirely opposite to what the theory of deterrence would suggest.[4] Almost without exception, countries with capital punishment have *higher* murder rates, higher rates of crime generally, and higher prison populations than those countries which have abolished capital punishment. This is even the case within the United States, where some individual states retain the death penalty while other states have abolished it.

These correlations, it should be pointed out, do not prove that the death penalty increases the likelihood of murder. However, it certainly does not provide evidence to support the theory that murderers are deterred from committing murder or other crimes by being threatened with their own death.

Indeed, reoffending by people who have already served a prison sentence for an offence is commonplace. In the US, 43.3 per cent of released prisoners are sent back to prison for another offence. In the UK, some prisons report a reconviction rate of more than 70 per cent, with an overall national average of 53 per cent – even higher than in the US.[5]

What this means for the criminal justice system is beyond the scope of this chapter. But what it means for deterrence theory is that criminals who know exactly what it means to be incarcerated for committing a crime appear nonetheless undeterred by the threat of being incarcerated again.

Military forms of deterrence

Deterrence in warfare is nothing new. The existence of standing armies are in and of themselves a form of deterrence, meant to warn off any potential invader by making it clear that the country stands ready and willing to inflict serious damage on any invading army. All manner of armaments and fortifications merely add to the deterrent value of being able to threaten retaliation for any attack.

Switzerland, a country of EIGHT million people surrounded on all sides by much larger and more powerful countries, was last invaded in 1813. Since that time, Switzerland has had mandatory conscription for all males aged 19–34 years of age as a deterrent against any possible aggressor.

Although Hitler never invaded Switzerland, it is doubtful it was the existence of the Swiss Army that deterred him. It is even more doubtful that the Swiss Army would have deterred an invasion, let alone a nuclear attack, from the Soviet Union during the Cold War. And yet the Swiss have carried on with their universal conscription in the belief that they are deterring their enemies from attacking them.

In 1914, the deterrent that was designed to prevent war in Europe took the form of a massive network of military alliances that threatened to drag the whole of Europe into a suicidal war if any one country were so foolish as to attack another one. The deterrence in that case failed spectacularly and Europe was quickly locked into a devastating war which took many millions of lives.

Following the devastation of WWI, the French began construction of the most advanced set of fortifications ever known – designed to inflict heavy damage on any advancing armies from Germany and thus hoping to deter them from attacking. The Maginot Line consisted of 22 underground fortresses, tank traps, tunnels, rail links and 500 smaller buildings constructed along the 280 mile border with Germany. One quarter of France's entire army was stationed along this line and yet it turned out to be completely useless against Hitler's invasion as he simply went around it in May 1940.

The one certainty that can be gleaned from all these examples of real-life deterrence at all these different levels right up to international war is that deterrence, even if it may appear to work in some cases, is never guaranteed to work in all cases. In fact, if history is anything to go by, deterrence is guaranteed *not* to work at some point or other.

Nuclear deterrence

The theory of nuclear deterrence depends upon it working not just most of the time but *all the time* – and *for* all time. There is no room for a margin of error if the consequence of nuclear deterrence not working is an all-out nuclear war that destroys the whole of human civilisation.

The 'credibility' of US nuclear deterrence furthermore rests completely on the fact that two atom bombs were dropped on Japan more than 70 years ago. While subsequent nuclear tests have shown how enormously devastating the consequences of a nuclear weapon would be, they do not in themselves demonstrate a willingness by the US to use such a weapon. The other nuclear powers meanwhile have never used a nuclear weapon against another country in anger. This makes it exceedingly difficult to argue that their threat to use a nuclear weapon is a credible one.

This credibility 'gap' is a dangerous one when it comes to nuclear deterrence, because it increases the likelihood that sooner or later a nuclear weapon *will* be used, if only to send a clear signal to some future adversary that the deterrent is backed up by real intention and willingness to use it.

The logic of nuclear deterrence gets more and more convoluted the deeper one goes into it. It is assumed, for instance, that the leaders of Russia, in contemplating an attack on the US, would be sufficiently sane and rational as to weigh up the consequences of a possible retaliatory nuclear strike from the US and decide on that basis to refrain from attacking. On the other hand, it is assumed that those same leaders would base their sane and rational decision on the likelihood of their counterparts in the US acting so insanely and irrationally as to be willing to launch nuclear weapons against Russia that would almost certainly bring about their own total self-destruction (see next chapter on Mutually Assured Destruction).

Furthermore, the theory demands that 'we' must be willing to use our nuclear weapons if necessary and that willingness must be sufficiently convincing to our opponent that they believe we really *will* actually use our nuclear weapons if they dared to attack us. On the other hand, if we are willing 'if necessary' to use our nuclear weapons against another country which also has nuclear weapons, then at some level we are not 'deterred' by *them* having nuclear weapons. That other country is likewise not deterred by the fact that *we* have nuclear weapons if it is to be believed that they also would use their nuclear weapons 'if necessary' against us.

Ultimately, nuclear deterrence rests on the assumption that no ordinary, sane person would choose to bring death and destruction down upon family and friends and loved ones, and would therefore choose some alternative route other than to invite nuclear retaliation. The problem with this line of thinking is that nuclear deterrence does not operate at the level of ordinary, sane people who care about their loved ones. It operates at the level of generals and politicians who make their decisions according to quite different criteria. It was the logic of those same generals and politicians who sent millions to their certain death in the trenches of WWI and authorised the saturation bombing of German and Japanese cities and the dropping of atom bombs in WWII.

The actual use of nuclear weapons would cause wholescale slaughter on an unimaginable scale, but there is no evidence that such a result would necessarily 'deter' generals and politicians from embarking on such a course should they decide the circumstances 'justified' it. Indeed, they have been ready to launch nuclear war on several occasions and it is luck, more than 'deterrence', which has kept us from having a nuclear war up to now (see Chapter 13).

General MacArthur wanted to drop atom bombs on China during the Korean War. President Nixon was considering the use of nuclear weapons during the Vietnam War. Mrs Thatcher apparently threatened to use nuclear weapons during the Falklands War.[6] Plans were readied for the use of nuclear weapons during the first Gulf War. And President Trump has threatened to rain down 'fire and fury' on North Korea in order to stop North Korea from firing its nuclear weapons.

Pressing the button

In her first full speech as British Prime Minister on 18 July 2016, Theresa May was asked in parliament if she was personally prepared to authorise a nuclear strike that could kill hundreds of thousands of innocent men, women and children. Her answer was an unequivocal 'yes'. 'And I have to say,' she went on, 'that the whole point of a deterrent is that our enemies need to know that we would be prepared to use it.'

Nuclear weapons as a 'deterrent', therefore, are not somehow distinct from the intention to use nuclear weapons as a weapon.

In the words of the late Sir Michael Quinlan:

> We cannot say that nuclear weapons are for deterrence and never for use, however remote we judge the latter possibility to be. Weapons deter by the possibility of their use and by no other route.[7]

We do not know whether any President or Prime Minister really would press the button in the event that Russia or another potential opponent called their bluff and launched an attack anyway. Saying that they would does not by itself make the threat credible. A Russian leader might calculate that actually, if push came to shove, a US president wouldn't actually press the button even though he said he would. It all comes down to psychology and there are so many unknowns it is impossible to know what anyone would do under any number of possible scenarios. That is what makes the whole theory of deterrence so fanciful.

Deterrence and defence

In the case of nuclear weapons, if and when deterrence 'fails', all you can do is launch nuclear weapons at the other side – or not. In neither case is anyone being 'defended' from attack as such by having nuclear weapons. This is an important distinction. What would normally be thought of as 'defence' are the strategies and resources need to fend off or resist an attack as opposed to merely retaliating against the aggressor after an attack has already happened.

During the 1930s, Britain's air and sea power was strengthened in the hope of deterring Hitler from invading Britain. When this did not work as a deterrent, those military resources were used to actually defend Britain from the impending invasion. The planes and ships were not just a deterrent, they were a form of defence. Nuclear weapons do not work in the same way. It would be literally suicidal to start launching Trident missiles at ships crossing the English Channel, let alone at planes flying over London. Nuclear weapons cannot defend the UK or any other country even against incoming nuclear weapons.

If any country were really threatened with attack or invasion by a foreign power, their only defence against the actual incoming nuclear weapons themselves would be an anti-ballistic missile system, and even that would have limited effect. The only real defence against advancing troops or invading ships are conventional forces, sea defences and other kinds of fortifications. Nuclear weapons may or may not function effectively as a deterrent. But if the deterrent fails, nuclear weapons cannot then function as a form of defence. They are quite literally useless in that sense. While it is often assumed that somehow nuclear weapons are going to 'defend' the country which has them from being attacked by some other large and powerful enemy, the truth is they cannot.

Summary

The theory of nuclear deterrence suggests that nuclear weapons are so effective in preventing war that they are unlikely ever to be used. Their function is to deter aggression, and the more powerfully destructive they are, the more effective they are as a deterrent.

Deterrence is commonly used as a strategy in all sorts of circumstances short of nuclear war. In all these other cases, it can be seen that deterrence is not effective 100 per cent of the time, and can only be effective if the intention to follow through with the threat is credible, immediate, and realistic. These same principles apply to nuclear deterrence.

Nuclear weapons cannot be said to act as a deterrent unless there is a credible, immediate, and realistic intention to use them as a weapon. Thus it is a contradiction in terms to say that nuclear weapons will never be used 'because they are only a deterrent'. Nuclear weapons are designed and deployed as weapons of mass destruction. It is hoped that they will never be used, but that can only remain a hope.

Successive Presidents and Prime Ministers have claimed publicly that they would press the nuclear button if the circumstances required it. But would they? Is it credible, immediate, and realistic that any country would launch nuclear weapons in self-defence of their homeland, let alone in defence of some distant ally?

Since the bombing of Hiroshima and Nagasaki, no country which has had nuclear weapons, has ever used one in war, even when they were on the verge of losing that war.[8] That is not to say that they will never be used, because the theory of deterrence merely increases the risk that they *will* be used. However, the fact that they have not been used so far is not itself evidence that deterrence has worked. The fact that wars have continued to be fought and that nuclear weapons have *not* been used actually undermines the theory that these weapons are an effective and credible deterrent.

CHAPTER 4

What is Mutually Assured Destruction?

WE HAVE LOOKED in chapters one and two at the human, physical and environmental consequences which using nuclear weapons might have on a country that has been targeted with attack as well as on the rest of the world. But what about the consequences to *that country itself* of using nuclear weapons? We have already seen that radioactive fallout could end up coming down thousands of miles from the intended target, as did the fallout from the Chernobyl meltdown. Are there other likely effects on the country launching a nuclear attack, as opposed to the country at the receiving end of such an attack?

Mutually assured destruction, or 'MAD', is the logical outcome of attacking with nuclear weapons a country capable of striking back with nuclear weapons. It means that despite the enormous amount of death and destruction which one country may be able to inflict on another country with its nuclear weapons, if that second country also has nuclear weapons, it may still be able to inflict an enormous amount of death and destruction on the first country in retaliation.

In the 1960s, both the US and the Soviet Union had enough nuclear weapons, and the means to deliver them, to utterly destroy each other many times over. US Defence Secretary Robert McNamara made it US policy that such a balance of terror should be maintained, as the best guarantee against either side attacking the other.

The MAD balance of terror was strengthened by the introduction of ballistic missile submarines like Polaris and later Trident. This meant that no matter what one side might do to destroy the planes or missiles of the other, they would still be able to launch nuclear weapons from secret locations under the sea in a devastating retaliatory strike.[1]

The Anti-Ballistic Missile Treaty (ABM), which was signed in 1972, is perhaps the best example of the US and Soviet Union cooperating with each other during the Cold War to maintain the situation of mutually assured destruction. The ABM Treaty limited the numbers and types of anti-ballistic missile defences that each side could maintain. The purpose was very specifically to ensure that one side could not protect itself against incoming missiles to such an extent as to feel it could survive such an attack. If ABM systems became too effective, that might encourage one side to think they could launch a nuclear war without fear of retaliation, upsetting the balance created by the situation of MAD.

To reinforce the concept of MAD and to be confident of overwhelming even the most sophisticated anti-ballistic missile defences, the US, quickly followed by the Soviet Union, developed a whole range of devices designed to ensure that the nuclear weapons would always get through. The most important of these was the development of the MIRV, or 'multiple independently-targeted re-entry vehicle'. MIRVs meant that several warheads could be launched from a single missile and land on different targets, making it impossible for radar systems monitoring the trajectory of the missile to know where the warheads were going to end up.

The ABM Treaty was officially abrogated by President Bush in 2002 and both the US and Russia have invested heavily in anti-ballistic missile defences since then. Both sides have significantly reduced the total numbers of nuclear weapons in their stockpiles as well, but they still retain more than enough to utterly destroy each other. The development of technologies designed to defeat and overwhelm the other side goes on.

How does MAD apply to a smaller country like the UK?

The development of MAD as a reality and then as a policy applied in the 1960s to the US and the Soviet Union, who had then and still have now the vast majority of the world's nuclear weapons, vastly more than needed to utterly destroy each other. MAD carried with it the implication of *total* destruction, against which there was no defence except to ensure that nuclear weapons would never be used.

MAD, as a concept however, does not depend on total destruction of two countries with nuclear weapons aimed at each other, but only on the *assured* destruction of those two countries. Another term which could be used here is 'unacceptable damage', since this is the term most often used by governments to describe the purpose of nuclear deterrence.

Nuclear weapons are designed to cause unacceptable damage to another country, and thus in theory to, deter that country from attacking oneself. But every country with nuclear weapons must itself have a level of unacceptable damage which it would not want inflicted on its own people and infrastructure. If, by attacking another (nuclear weapon possessing) country a government were to bring about its own destruction – or a level of unacceptable damage to its own country – one might presume that it would not attack that country in the first place. And if attacking that said country is the 'threat' being made by the possession of nuclear weapons, that threat is not very credible.

We cannot easily define what level of destruction counts as unacceptable, but successive UK governments, for instance, have considered 40–50 per cent of the population of Moscow killed, together with 40–50 per cent of the buildings destroyed, to be an unacceptable level of damage to Russia. If we were to apply the same criteria to London we would have to assume that 40–50 per cent of the people killed and 40–50 per cent of the buildings destroyed in London might count as 'unacceptable damage'.

Alternatively, we can look at a number of different possible targets in the UK that could be hit in a retaliatory strike by Russia in the event of a nuclear war. Instead of destroying only London, perhaps we would consider destruction of Britain's 40 largest towns and cities as sufficiently devastating to count as 'unacceptable damage'? Alternatively, perhaps unacceptable damage in military terms, or in terms of 'centres of state control' would mean destruction of major airfields, submarine bases, NATO command and control bunkers, nuclear facilities, parliament, etc.

How much nuclear firepower would it take to inflict unacceptable damage on the UK under these different scenarios? As we have seen, one 100 KT nuclear explosion can have a devastating impact on a large city, killing tens of thousands instantly, physically destroying an area of several square miles, and depending on whether it is airburst or groundburst, depending on the wind speed and other weather conditions, fatal levels of radioactive fallout could spread over a much larger area.

A study produced by Article 36 in 2013 examined the effects of a single 100 KT nuclear detonation (the size of one UK Trident warhead) over Manchester. This concluded that 81,000 people would be killed directly and more than 212,000 would be injured. With the destruction of vital infrastructure, including hospitals and emergency services, the injured would not stand a high chance of surviving. Everything up to 1.8 km from ground zero would be completely destroyed and fires would cause severe destruction out to a distance of 3 km. People up to 7 km from the explosion would still receive severe second degree burns and most buildings would be damaged.[2]

The equivalent of one UK Trident submarine of nuclear weapons, or 40 × 100 KT, striking the UK would cause 'unacceptable damage' to the UK under any of the above definitions. Russian submarines, like their US counterparts, carry much higher yield weapons and they have many more of these submarines than the UK has. One modern SSBN Russian sub is normally believed to have 16 missiles, each containing eight warheads of 400 KT each. That is equivalent to 51 MT, or more than ten times the firepower of a UK Trident submarine. In other words, no matter what Russia may have already done or threatened to do to the UK, if the UK were to launch nuclear weapons at Russia, Russia could still retaliate from under the sea with sufficient ferocity to cause 'unacceptable damage' to the UK by any definition of that term.

It's a MAD, MAD world

It should be obvious from the above discussion that were a smaller country with nuclear weapons (say UK or France) to attack a larger country with nuclear weapons (say Russia or China), the concept of MAD would certainly apply: no matter how much damage might be inflicted on a country with a large number of potentially 'survivable' nuclear weapons, that country would almost certainly be able to inflict an 'unacceptable' level of damage in return.

The Russian government, therefore, can hardly be threatened by the nuclear weapons of countries like the UK or France, knowing that it can utterly destroy those countries in retaliation, no matter what they may do to Russia. Why would a UK Prime Minister or a French President ever take that risk?

The reverse is of course true in the case of a country like North Korea. The leadership of North Korea may believe that by threatening the United States with nuclear weapons, they are somehow protecting themselves from possible attack. However, since no matter how many nuclear weapons or advanced delivery systems they may acquire, North Korea will still face the risk of unacceptable damage from a US retaliatory strike, why would they ever take such a risk?

Perhaps there are people who *would* be prepared to take such risks. Perhaps it is being too generous to apply the principles of logic to such decisions. Or perhaps there are other calculations at play which outweigh what we might consider to be an 'unacceptable' level of damage to one's own country. The reality, however, is that from a rational point of view, threatening another country with your own country's destruction is not a very credible threat.

What about the larger nuclear weapons states attacking the smaller ones? Surely, the US could launch a massive nuclear attack against North Korea, for instance, without much risk of triggering unacceptable damage in return.[3] The real risk here is that even a small nuclear weapon state like North Korea *could* inflict unacceptable damage on a third party, for instance South Korea or Japan in this case. This still qualifies as MAD since a nuclear attack on *any* other nuclear weapons state runs the risk of causing catastrophic and unknowable consequences and is therefore irrational.

Extended deterrence

So-called 'extended' deterrence, or the 'nuclear umbrella' is the idea that if Russia, or another country, were to attack another NATO country, say for example Estonia, then the US or the UK would retaliate with a nuclear attack against Russia. Russia, knowing this would be the result, would therefore supposedly be deterred from attacking Estonia in the first place.

This threat, however, could be perceived by Russia as lacking credibility, since it would seem unlikely that either the US or the UK would risk launching their nuclear missiles at Russia merely for the sake of a third country like Estonia, knowing that Russia would retaliate by launching nuclear missiles against *them*. Why would a UK Prime Minister, let alone a US President, invite the nuclear destruction of their own country for the sake of Estonia, or Poland, or Turkey, or even France?

Indeed, these were the very concerns which led in the 1970s and '80s to the concept of 'flexible response' and to the deployment of a whole range of intermediate nuclear weapons in Europe. These were designed to provide a nuclear response to any invasion by the Soviet bloc without, it was hoped, inviting an all-out nuclear attack against the US mainland. Without this intermediate level of nuclear response, it was felt that the Soviet Union might not be deterred by the threat of a nuclear strike from the US for the very reason that such a strike was not credible if merely for the defence of European allies. A US President is not, and never was, likely to order an all-out nuclear attack for the sake of its allies if such an attack is sure to invite a response in kind against the United States itself.

Summary

The use of nuclear weapons against Russia or China would almost certainly result in a devastating nuclear counter-attack on the US and/or any of its nuclear allies, whether or not a nuclear attack on the US or one of its allies had already taken place. The use of nuclear weapons against one of the smaller nuclear weapons states might avoid the risk of an immediate counter-attack, but risks nuclear weapons being used in retaliation on some other country.

With thousands of nuclear warheads pointing at each other in the US and Russia, it is unlikely in the extreme that there would be none left to launch a counter-attack in the event of one side or the other pressing the nuclear button, no matter how many may have already been launched prior to that. Therefore one can only assume that neither side is actually 'deterred' by the nuclear weapons of the other side as much as they are deterred by possible use of their *own* nuclear weapons. Furthermore, it is accepted NATO policy not to rule out the possibility of a 'first use' of nuclear weapons against a conventional attack on a NATO member state. A conventional attack by Russia against the west, for instance, would mean they still had a considerable arsenal of nuclear weapons in reserve. Therefore if NATO were seriously to consider launching nuclear weapons against Russia in response to a conventional attack, they would be doing so in the full knowledge that they were inviting a nuclear retaliation and in such a case they are not 'deterred' by that possibility.

The concept of Mutually Assured Destruction, or MAD, means that to launch nuclear weapons, in most cases, against another country with nuclear weapons is to invite the assured destruction of your own country in return. Such a prospect makes a mockery of the idea that having nuclear weapons somehow 'deters' those other countries from attacking. If anything, it is the likelihood of nuclear retaliation against the countries which have nuclear weapons that ought reasonably to deter those countries from ever using *their own* nuclear weapons.

PART TWO

We Need Nuclear Weapons for Our Security

CHAPTER 5

Did Nuclear Weapons End WWII?

THE THEORY OF nuclear deterrence rests on the notion that no country would attack a nuclear weapons state (NWS) if it meant the certain destruction of their own cities and civilian populations. This in turn rests on the widely held assumption that it was the atom bombs dropped on Hiroshima and Nagasaki that caused Japan to surrender at the end of WWII. If just two atom bombs, small in comparison with today's nuclear arsenals, could force Japan to surrender unconditionally, then surely today's nuclear arsenals are sufficient to prevent any would-be aggressor from ever considering an attack on a NWS. These are the premises on which the whole theory of deterrence has been built. But are they true?

'The bomb saved lives'

Bill Westwood, the late Bishop of Peterborough, was a strong proponent of nuclear weapons. In the summer of 1945, he was a 20-year-old paratrooper in the British Army, stationed in Sri Lanka and awaiting the orders to invade Japan. He remained convinced to his dying day that more lives were saved by the dropping of the Atom Bomb than were lost, and he was by no means alone in holding that view.

To be fair, Bishop Bill was concerned not only with the lives of British and American servicemen, but also with the lives of the countless Japanese military as well as civilians who would have surely died had there been an invasion of the Japanese home islands. The estimates vary widely and there is no way of knowing how many would have died.[1] However, nearly 150,000 Japanese civilians were killed during the invasion and occupation of the island of Okinawa in the spring of 1945, together with as many as 77,000 Japanese soldiers and 14,000 Allied soldiers.[2]

President Truman had already given the go-ahead for 'Operation Olympic' to invade the Japanese 'home' island of Kyushu on 1 November 1945 with a force of more than 750,000 troops. Although the Allies were unaware at the time, the Japanese military had already deployed nearly one million of their soldiers to Kyushu by August 1945, ready to fend off the invasion. With nearly 2.5 million civilians living in the southern part of Kyushu at that time as well, there is no doubt that an Allied invasion would have resulted in a very large number of casualties on all sides, with possibly four times as many as were killed on Okinawa, given the numbers involved. Four times the number of deaths as in Okinawa would have meant as many as 60,000 Allied soldiers, 300,000 Japanese soldiers and 600,000 civilians killed.

By the summer of 1945, WWII had been going on for six years. Nearly every country in the world was involved, hundreds of cities were in ruins and at least 40 million people were already dead. Everyone wanted the war to be over. When President Truman announced that the atom bombs had been dropped on Hiroshima and Nagasaki, there was a huge sense of relief – even jubilation – from people like Bill Westwood, whose chances of surviving the war were otherwise probably less than 50–50 at that point.

When the Japanese surrendered one week later, both President Truman and the Japanese Emperor Hirohito claimed it was because of the atom bomb. Every newspaper and radio the world over (with the possible exception of those in the Soviet Union) reported that the war ended because of the atom bomb. Nearly every history textbook and academic historian tells the same story. Why would anyone disbelieve it?

Questioning the impact of the atom bombs

The Japanese surrender in August 1945 meant an end to the most violent war in human history. For that we can all be very grateful. But do we know that it was the dropping of the atom bombs that caused Japan to surrender? What is the evidence to support this, apart from the statements mentioned above and other similar assertions? The media do not always know what is going on behind the scenes and public statements by politicians do not always tell us the whole truth either.

Even before the bombing of Hiroshima and Nagasaki, some senior politicians and military figures in the US were already convinced that Japan was on the verge of surrendering. Others were questioning the need to use the atom bomb out of concern over the potential consequences of unleashing such a deadly weapon. Immediately after the war, there was an increasing realisation that Japan had indeed been thoroughly defeated by this point in the war:

> Based on a detailed investigation of all the facts and supported by the testimony of the surviving Japanese leaders involved, it is the

Survey's opinion that certainly prior to 31 December 1945, and in all probability prior to 1 November 1945, Japan would have surrendered even if the Atomic Bombs had not been dropped...[3]

That was the official view of the US Strategic Bombing Survey (USSBS), which conducted an extensive examination into the effects of US and Allied bombing in both Germany and Japan immediately following the war. The editorial board of USSBS can hardly be considered a neutral source of information, since their main intention was to prove the effectiveness of US bombing as justification for creation of a separate US Air Force with equal status to the US Army and US Navy.[4]

Indeed there are many contradictions between the evidence provided in the 330 reports and annexes of the USSBS and the conclusions drawn by the report's editors. Their opinion that the Atom Bombs may not have been necessary to secure the surrender of Japan is all the more significant precisely because this goes against the general presumption of the report that winning future wars will hinge on the quantity and quality of the bombs dropped by American fighting forces.

What else was going on at that time?

Before the bombing of Hiroshima and Nagasaki, the US had already bombed 67 other Japanese cities, killing as many as 300,000 civilians, wounding 750,000, rendering 1.7 million people homeless and utterly destroying more than 50 per cent of Japan's urban centres. The firebombing of Tokyo alone cost as many as 130,000 lives and incinerated 16 square miles of the city centre.[5] In terms of the number killed outright, Tokyo ranks above both Hiroshima and Nagasaki (although the effects of radiation meant many more were killed from the atom bombs in the months and years to come). In terms of area destroyed, Hiroshima ranks sixth among all the cities bombed and in terms of the destruction as a percentage of the total size of the city, Hiroshima ranks 17th if we look at all the cities in Japan affected by Allied bombing.

What does this mean in terms of the impact of the atom bomb? It is of course hugely significant that a single bomb could be developed to have such devastating consequences as the one which was dropped on Hiroshima. Hydrogen bombs more than a thousand times more powerful than the Hiroshima bomb have since been developed. But apart from the radiation effects, dropping one bomb with the power of 15,000 tonnes of TNT is roughly equivalent to dropping 1,000 bombs which each have the power of 15 tonnes of TNT or dropping 15,000 bombs which each have the power of one tonne of TNT.

As far as the Japanese military were concerned in August 1945, it probably made little difference whether it was one big bomb or 15,000 little bombs that were dropped on Hiroshima. The effect was the destruction of a city and the deaths of many civilians and in terms of the overall conduct of the war, neither of those appeared to be of major concern to Japan's war leaders.

What we now know about Japanese military thinking at the time

From the historical records and archives of the Japanese military and interviews with Japanese political leaders after their surrender and the accumulated evidence of the effects of aerial bombing both in Germany and in Japan, we now know a lot more about what was going on in the summer of 1945 than Bill Westwood or anyone else at the time knew or could have known.

Japan was ready to surrender

We know, for instance, that even before the fall of Germany, many in the Japanese government were looking for an honourable way to surrender and that as early as February 1945, the Japanese premier, Kantara Suzuki, submitted an official memo to the emperor saying 'I regret to say that Japan's defeat is inevitable'.[6] This was on the basis of military assessments definitively indicating that Japan was no longer in a position to be able to win the war.

With Germany defeated, the US could now turn its entire resources to the war against Japan. The Japanese economy was in rapid decline due at least in part to the Japanese being surrounded by Allied ships cutting off its supply lines. Rationing was now very severe, well below the average required intake of energy for a healthy diet; meals rarely included staples, even rice, and consisted mainly of watered down miso soup and substitute foods. Government advice included the eating of grasshoppers, plants and even sawdust. Children were falling sick, coal was used in car engines as it was impossible to obtain fuel and it was clear to much of the population that Japan was on its knees.

Japan was willing to negotiate

We know that among those running the Japanese war effort at the time there were those who wanted to sue for peace and those who wanted to continue fighting to the end. As is almost always the case in war, and was certainly the case in the US as well at that time, the strength of the 'war party' relative to the 'peace party' depends to a large extent on the behaviour of the enemy – in this case the US, who were right up until the dropping of the Hiroshima bomb not prepared to accept anything except unconditional surrender.

In fact, the Japanese had as their leader at this point Prince Fumimaro Konoe, who as Prime Minister had originally attempted to avoid war with the United States. In February 1945, he advised the Emperor Hirohito to begin negotiations to end WWII. Konoe's recommendation was to sue for peace with the Soviet Union to find a negotiated settlement to end the war and save Japan from unconditional surrender. Although the Japanese never in fact received an audience with Stalin, this didn't deter the 'peace party' and the Emperor from holding out hope against hope that a bargain would be struck, even as far as to offer to give various contested islands back to them, lease out ports, railways and fishing rights that they were asking for. We know there were daily phone calls to the Soviet embassy during this period and a telegramme on 28 June in which Japan said 'we are prepared to make considerable sacrifices... and to settle all the problems the Soviet Union was interested in settling'.[7]

We also know that Japanese experts in the US State Department were advising President Truman that 'Japan would never accept unconditional surrender'.[8] Even as Churchill, Truman and Stalin were meeting in Potsdam to issue what became the final 'ultimatum' to Japan at the end of July 1945, the emperor himself sent a message that he 'desires from his heart that [the war] may be quickly terminated'.[9]

The allies' insistence that the Japanese give up the Emperor system was particularly insensitive. Although the emperor system had been manipulated by the military regime to enforce unity on the nation through for instance the adoption of the imperial state religion symbol to be worn on all outer clothing, the Japanese emperor symbolised the Japanese race and ethnicity itself. For instance the unbroken lineage of Japanese emperors stretching back 2,600 years had recently been celebrated on the Emperor's birthday in 1940. When finally the Japanese did capitulate to the Potsdam declaration on 10 August 1945, the Americans quickly agreed that they retain the Emperor, indicating perhaps that they could have been less hawkish with the Japanese before, had they not been intent on using the atomic weapon in any case.

The Soviet entry into the war

We know that in May 1945, the Supreme War Council agreed that 'Soviet entry into the war will deal a death blow to the Empire'.[10] We know that Truman informed Stalin that he had a working atomic bomb at the Potsdam conference on 27 July 1945 (the Trinity test in the US had just proved successful), and that Stalin did not react to this game-changing news at the time. But by August 1945, we know that the Soviet Union had secretly moved more than 1.5 million soldiers, 5,400 planes and 3,400 tanks from Eastern Europe to the Far East, ready for a surprise attack against Japan on three fronts, air, land and sea.

We know that when the Soviets declared war on Japan on 8 August (Soviet time) and followed with an invasion by land, sea and air, this triggered the scheduling of a Japanese war council meeting for 9 August – the meeting was scheduled *before* the news of the dropping of the atomic bomb on Nagasaki the next day at 11.14 am. The dropping of the bomb on Hiroshima had triggered no such high-level meeting. Thus the invasion of the Soviet Union had a much greater impact on the behaviour of both the peace party and the war party in Japan than did the bombs dropping on Hiroshima or Nagasaki.[11]

It is not difficult to see that the invasion by the Soviet Union would have dashed the hopes of the peace party whose strategy was to use the Soviets as a mediator to end the war. The invasion equally dashed the hopes of the war party to retain some semblance of dignity in a final showdown with the Americans on the southern island of Kyushu. Since they had already moved so much of their manpower and military assets down there, they could not hope to stem the advance of the Soviets coming down from the North and West. It would only be a matter of time before the Soviets would reach Tokyo. One Japanese General estimated it would take them only ten days.[12]

Alternative explanations

Perhaps the atom bombs offered the perfect excuse to enable Japan to save face and avoid the humiliation of defeat at the hands of the Soviets? Perhaps, in a sense, the atomic bomb played into the Japanese military government's hands as it offered them the chance to blame the need for surrender on this terrible new 'cruel' weapon, thus exonerating them from the blame by a war-weary nation of having brought ruin on Japan and leaving the country vulnerable to invasion on all sides (the US and the Soviets).

We will, of course, never know what *might* have happened had history turned out differently, but we are obliged, at the very least, to *question* the accepted version of events and to weigh up the pros and cons of alternative explanations. There are now at least three alternative explanations for why WWII came to an end in which the dropping of the atom bombs barely feature:

According to the first theory, Japan already knew it was losing the war long before August 1945. Its economy was in ruins, millions of people were homeless and destitute, its ports were at the mercy of US warships and its cities were at the mercy of US warplanes. Its ability to wage war was severely curtailed and its only allies (Germany, Italy and Turkey) already defeated. It was only a matter of time before it would have surrendered.

According to the second theory, if there had been any serious attempt by the Allies to respond to Japanese overtures for peace, negotiations might have ended the war months earlier on terms more or less identical to what was finally agreed by the US. The main obstacle to Japanese surrender was their insistence on retention of the emperor, which in the end the US gave them, despite the 'unconditional surrender'.

According to the third theory, it was the Soviet invasion of Japan on 9 August, rather than the second atomic bomb dropped on Nagasaki that same day, which led the Japanese to realise all was lost and to accept unconditional surrender.

The effects of aerial bombing in WWII

The atom bomb was – and is – uniquely powerful and many thousands of times more powerful than the largest conventional bombs. However, the result of dropping many thousands of conventional bombs on a single city is just as devastating (apart from the effects of radioactive fallout). To understand the effects of dropping the atom bombs on Japan, we need to understand the effects of dropping conventional bombs on cities up to that point.

The deliberate bombing of cities is generally considered to have begun with the bombing of Guernica during the Spanish Civil War in 1937. In that case, the destruction of the 'spiritual capital' of the Basque country appeared to aid the advance of Franco's forces along the north coast of Spain, although the Republican forces fought on for two more years.

The bombing of Warsaw by German forces in 1939 and then the bombing of Rotterdam in May 1940 seemed to be much more decisive militarily, lending support to the myth that bombing of cities was somehow a 'successful' military strategy in WWII. In the case of Warsaw, although it was being bombed by the *Luftewaffe* from day one of the German invasion, the most extensive bombing took place on 'Black Monday', 25 September 1939. German bombers flew 1,150 sorties on that day, dropping 500 tonnes of high explosives and 72 tonnes of incendiaries, causing widespread destruction of the city centre.

Although fighting continued for another week or two in some other parts of Poland, Warsaw capitulated the day after Black Monday. But by this point, German and Soviet forces already occupied most of the country and were already fighting within the city. It is debatable therefore whether the bombing of Warsaw ended the war in Poland or was merely a part of the ongoing destruction that was taking place there.

The Netherlands surrendered to the Nazis the day after the bombing of Rotterdam and the German threat to bomb Utrecht next. A fuller analysis of the conditions which led to both Poland and the Netherlands surrendering to the Nazis is beyond the scope of this book; however it must at least be questioned whether the bombing of those two cities played as large a part in the decision to surrender as has been widely assumed.

The Netherlands, a small, neutral country hoping to stay out of the war, was invaded on 10 May 1940 from the north, south and in several places on the east by a country ten times its size, with a very powerful and fully mobilised war machine which had already invaded several other countries. Half of the Dutch air force was destroyed by a surprise attack on the first day. By 13 May, the German army had already occupied three-quarters of the country and was preparing to enter Rotterdam. In fact the Dutch commander of Rotterdam was already negotiating the terms of surrender with his German counterpart on the morning of 14 May, but the planes had already set off with their instructions to bomb the city.

Sixty-one cities in Germany and 67 cities in Japan were bombed extensively during WWII in addition to Warsaw, Rotterdam and of course London and other cities in England. As many as 1,000 planes were involved in some of the biggest bombing raids, dropping as many as 650,000 bombs in one raid. A total of 500,000 tonnes (500 KT) of TNT was used by the RAF to attack German cities between October 1939 and May 1945. Some 3,600,000 dwellings were destroyed, 7,500,000 people were made homeless, 300,000 civilians were killed and 780,000 injured in Germany alone.[13]

This bombing went on for six years and the destruction was relentless, and yet there is no evidence to suggest that either Germany or Japan were closer to surrendering as a result of it. In fact both the US Strategic Bombing Survey and the British Bombing Survey that was conducted in parallel following the end of the war found to the contrary that war production actually *rose* in Germany throughout the war, despite the bombing.[14]

According to the British Bombing Survey Unit, which devoted a whole separate chapter to the 'Reasons Underlying Failure of Primary Strategic Aim of Offensive Against Cities':[15]

> Hitler himself paid little apparent attention to the destruction of German cities... (p. 164) Area attacks against towns were undoubtedly overdone, in the sense that however successful they were in terms of material destruction and in pinning down defensive forces, they had little effect upon the trend of German war industry. (p. 166)

The unit concluded that:

> The several lines of evidence that have been discussed thus *put it beyond question that in spite of the widespread physical devastation they caused, area attacks against German cities had little effect* either upon the trend of production or upon the morale of the German worker. (p. 97)

And again:

> In so far as the offensive against German towns was designed to break the morale of the German civilian population, it clearly failed. (p. 79)

Given what John Kenneth Galbraith called in his memoirs 'the disastrous failure of strategic bombing'[16] it is somewhat surprising that the US continued with the same policy in the war against Japan and indeed in the many wars it has fought since.

Drawing from other experience

How could it be that such devastating destruction as was wrought on Germany and Japan by conventional bombing of cities as well as by the atomic bombs could have so little effect on the morale of the population or the willingness of the leaders to continue fighting? If we look at the effect of the Blitz on the British people and British government, we can perhaps get a better understanding of this.

During the Blitz, at least 40,000 and perhaps as many as 60,000 civilians were killed[17] in London and 15 other UK cities. One million homes were destroyed, large areas of London devastated, the population was terrorised night after night and forced to sleep in London Underground stations. Certainly there was fear. But was there defeatism? Did the British people rise up and demand that Britain surrender rather than endure any more of this devastation? Of course not.

Did Churchill ever suggest that Britain should give up under those difficult circumstances? Or did Britain plough on, more determined than ever to beat back the Nazi war machine?

What happened when the planes hit the Twin Towers of the World Trade Centre in New York on 9/11? Did Americans cower in fear and demand that all US forces be withdrawn from Saudi Arabia? No, what happened was that the US immediately went onto a war footing. American flags started appearing all over the country on cars, houses and on people's clothing. Bush's approval rating soared to 90 per cent, the highest of any US president in modern times.[18]

Summary

The deliberate and targeted bombing of civilian populations is most likely to result in a desire for retaliation and a redoubling of efforts to fight back rather than in resignation and surrender on the part of the targeted population.

The evidence from Germany and Japan in WWII as well as from Vietnam, Iraq and other countries which have suffered huge losses from conventional bombing, is that bombing of cities does not significantly reduce the ability or willingness of people to fight back. It is not the response of the civilian population that matters in terms of willingness to wage war, however, so much as the response of political and military leaders. Here the evidence is crystal clear: massive bombing of cities does not deter states from waging war and therefore there is no reason to suppose that the threat of massive bombing of cities would deter them, either.

Japan surrendered shortly after the atom bombs were dropped and the Soviet Union entered the war. It was preferable for the Japanese military to surrender to the US and say it was the atom bombs that made them do it, but it is more likely that it was the Soviet invasion, together with many other factors, which forced them into that decision at that particular time. Many lives could have been saved and the war could have ended months earlier if the Allies had been willing to negotiate the terms of surrender.

Nuclear weapons have enormous power to destroy whole cities and kill large numbers of civilians. However, destruction alone does not win wars.[19] There is no evidence to support the belief that nuclear weapons, any more than conventional weapons, can bring a country to its knees and force it to surrender. Therefore it is a weak argument to suggest that the *threat* of such destruction, ie so-called nuclear deterrence, actually deters anybody from doing what they would otherwise be determined to do, whether that be another Hitler or a more benign opponent that might be expected to be somehow more concerned about their own civilian population.

CHAPTER 6

Have Nuclear Weapons 'Kept the Peace' Since 1945?

IT IS PROBABLY the most common argument used in favour of nuclear weapons to say that they have 'kept the peace' since 1945. This argument claims that the nuclear weapons of the US (and to a lesser extent those of the UK and/or France), prevented a Soviet invasion of western Europe during the Cold War and prevented that war from becoming 'hot' and turning into WWIII. The more universalist claim of this argument is that the possession of nuclear weapons, not just by the UK, France and the US but also by Russia and China, has somehow created a 'stable' situation in Europe and the world and prevented war between the major powers from breaking out.

'Be careful above all things not to let go of the atomic weapon until you are sure and more than sure that other means of preserving peace are in your hands,' said Winston Churchill.[1] This has been the mantra of US Presidents and British Prime Ministers ever since. If nuclear weapons are the reason we have had a period of relative and sustained peace since WWII, why would anyone wish to destabilise such an arrangement?

We have already looked in Chapters 3 and 4 at the concept of nuclear deterrence. We now need to look at the historical record. Has it actually worked or hasn't it? Do we have irrefutable evidence to back up either claim? And if so, what are the implications of this?

The long peace

It is certainly the case that Western Europe, at least, has had a prolonged period of relative peace since WWII and of that we can all be very grateful. There has not been a nuclear war between the superpowers, for which we can be even more grateful, since if there had been we would probably not be here now discussing it. It is hardly the case, however, that there have been no wars at all during this period.

Throughout the world, there have been well over 100 wars since 1945 and depending on what you count as a 'war', as many as 250 of them.[2] Of these, a few have been civil wars or border wars with no involvement of the major powers. However, the military forces of one or more of the nuclear states have been directly involved in nearly half the wars fought since 1945.[3] Many of the civil wars which did not involve any of the nuclear powers directly have nonetheless involved armed groups militarily supported openly or covertly by one side or other of the Cold War.

Within Europe, there have been violent and long-running conflicts in Northern Ireland and the Basque Country, the war in Cyprus, the wars in former Yugoslavia, the invasions of Hungary and Czechoslovakia, military coups in Poland, Greece and Spain. Outside Europe, there have been major wars and military confrontations involving one or more of the superpower blocs in Korea, Vietnam, Angola, Mozambique, Iraq, Afghanistan, Egypt, Lebanon and all across Africa and South America.

The claim that nuclear weapons have prevented war in the wider sense does not stand up to much scrutiny. More people have been killed in wars since 1945 than were killed in the whole of WWII, so the world has hardly been cleansed of war as a result of nuclear weapons. Perhaps if we look at the more narrow claim, we will find that nuclear weapons have prevented war between the major European powers?

Have there been fewer wars in Europe than there were previously?

In addition to the 'long peace' that we have seen in Europe since 1945, there is an assumption in the 'nuclear weapons have kept the peace' argument that Europe was in a constant state of warfare between the major European powers *before* 1945. It is certainly the case that Europe went through two devastating world wars in the first half of the 20th century, but prior to that was almost a century of relative peace since the Napoleonic Wars of 1803–1815. This was broken by a number of smaller wars in the Balkans and elsewhere, but the only war involving more than two European countries having a brief spat during that period was the Crimean War of 1853–1856.[4]

From the close of the Crimean War to the start of WW1 was 58 years. From the end of the Napoleonic Wars to the start of WW1 was 99 years. Either way, it is hardly an astounding fact that Europe has not had a major war for the last 70 years.

The fact that there has not been a war between the major powers in Europe since 1945 is no more in need of an explanation, statistically speaking, than the fact that there has not been a major earthquake in Europe since 1945 either, or a major famine or a major outbreak of the plague. In other words, there have *not* been so many wars in Europe prior to 1945 that the absence of war since then requires a historical explanation.

Changing face of Europe

The wars of the first half of the 20th century were fought mainly between Germany, Italy and Turkey on one side and Britain, France and Russia on the other. Why has that configuration of countries ceased fighting each other since 1945? The Cold War created a different configuration of warring parties, pitting Britain and France together with Germany, Italy and Turkey against the Soviet Union. But even more importantly, the central divide in Europe, between France and Germany, was re-engineered so as to make war between them less likely if not impossible.

The European Coal and Steel Community, which eventually became the European Union, consciously and deliberately fused together the economies of Germany and France to such an extent that war and the preparations for war would not be possible for one without implicating the other. Whether the European Union deserved the Nobel Peace Prize in 2012 or not is another matter, but the EU has without doubt been a significant factor in making war less likely between the major powers in Europe since 1945.

Did nuclear weapons prevent a Soviet invasion of Western Europe?

Prior to the 20th century, imperial Russia had invaded Finland and Poland and fought various wars with Sweden, Turkey, Prussia and Serbia. However neither Russia nor the Soviet Union has ever invaded Western Europe, despite being invaded twice by Germany in the 20th century and once by France in the 19th century.[5]

The Soviet Union used its military forces to crush uprisings against puppet regimes in Hungary (1956) and Czechoslovakia (1968) and attempted to do that in Afghanistan (1979–1989), but there is no evidence that it intended or wished to invade other countries not already within its 'sphere of influence'. Unlike Napoleon and Hitler, who had clear and undisguised ambitions to conquer Europe, no Russian or Soviet leader ever claimed such ambitions.

> The Soviet Union had no interest in overrunning Western Europe militarily and would not have launched an attack on Europe in the decades after the Second World War even if nuclear weapons did not exist.[6]

This is according to George Kennan, former US Ambassador to Moscow during the 1950s and a key architect of Cold War 'containment' policies of the US at that time. What he and many others knew at the time, though the general public did not, was that numerous formal and informal discussions between Roosevelt, Churchill and Stalin during the war had thrashed out agreed 'zones of influence' between the three leaders. These discussions, consolidated at Yalta in February 1945, gave Stalin the green light to create a permanent 'buffer zone' between Germany and Russia after the war, comprising the countries of Eastern Europe which would later become the 'Warsaw Pact'.[7]

We do not need the existence of nuclear weapons to explain why the Soviet Union did not invade Western Europe if the Soviet Union or its predecessor had never invaded Western Europe prior to 1945 and showed no intention of doing so after that date.[8] It is certainly possible that had there been no nuclear weapons in Western Europe, the Soviet Union *might* have invaded during that period. But there is certainly no reason to believe that they *would* have invaded under those circumstances and therefore there is no justification for claiming that the existence of nuclear weapons prevented them from doing so.

Post-war world

In fact, the world has changed dramatically since 1945 in so many ways that the existence of nuclear weapons cannot be the only explanation for the absence of a major war in Europe since then. The United Nations came into existence in 1945 and with it a whole body of international law and international institutions that have totally transformed the way nation-states relate to each other, handle disputes and conduct warfare.

For all their flaws and failings, the UN Security Council, the Universal Declaration of Human Rights, the World Court, the Geneva Conventions and a whole host of other treaties have been created to govern and regulate the use of certain weapons, the conduct of war, the laws of the sea, and even the use of outer space. Global trade agreements, global institutions like the IMF and World Bank, and the humanitarian and development agencies of the UN as well as the thousands of civil society organisations have sprung up to address and respond to humanitarian and development needs across the world. UN peacekeeping missions, international diplomacy and mediation efforts, the international protection of civilians and of human rights, the monitoring of early warning signs of war and genocide – all these and many, many more factors have transformed the way conflicts are handled in the post-war world. Perhaps most important of all has been the growth and spread of democracy and the civilian control of military forces, making war between states less likely.

Everyday changes since 1945, like the development of air travel, television, mobile phones, computers and the internet make the world a much smaller and more closely interdependent place. Warfare is a hideously barbaric and increasingly outmoded means of managing disputes in a world in which people can see what is happening in other countries right across the world, where they trade with each other and interact with each other and even make friends with each other transcending countries and continents on a daily basis.

Steven Pinker, in his 2012 book *The Better Angels of Our Nature* takes a broad sweep at the trends in human behaviour over the centuries and millennia of human history and concludes that human beings have been becoming less and less violent with every passing generation. His methodology may be disputed,[9] but his conclusions are inescapable: just because we saw two world wars and untold numbers dead in the first half of the 20th century does not mean that we need an explanation as to why an even more deadly third world war has not occurred by now.

The logical fallacy of this mindset

Imagine for a moment that your home was burgled on a regular basis until one day when you decided to get a cat. Since having that cat, you have not been burgled once. Is it the cat that is protecting you from the burglars? And if everyone had a cat, would all burglary cease?

It *could* be the case that your former burglar was afraid of cats (or allergic to them) and the cat really *is* the reason you are no longer being burgled. But there are quite a lot of other possible explanations, in fact an *infinite number of them*!

In terms of logic, to argue from correlation to causation is known as *post hoc ergo propter hoc* (followed by therefore caused by) and it is one of the most common of all logical fallacies. The fallacy is assuming that if two things are linked chronologically, the former must have caused the latter. But this is rarely the case and the logic is inherently faulty.

This can easily be seen with the common example of the cock and the sun: Every morning without fail, the cock crows just before sunrise, ie the cock crows, *then* the sun rises. *Therefore*, according to the logic of *post hoc ergo propter hoc*, the crowing of the cock causes the sun to rise. Wrong!

If we break down the claim that nuclear weapons have kept the peace since 1945, what this is arguing is that:

1 There have been wars for centuries [between the major European powers].
2 In 1945 the nuclear weapon was invented.

3 Since 1945 there have been no wars [between the major European powers].
4 *Therefore* nuclear weapons must be the reason there have been no wars since 1945 [between the major European powers].

The conclusion that nuclear weapons are the reason for there being no wars between the major European powers since 1945 is a *post hoc* fallacy and therefore logically incorrect. There are an infinite number of other possible explanations for why there have not been any such wars since 1945.

If we go back to the cat-deterrent analogy, we could rule out the cat hypothesis if we were to find that other people *with* cats were still being burgled or that people *without* cats were also not being burgled. These are called 'counterfactuals' and with an infinite number of possible explanations for why anything may or may not happen, it helps enormously if we can rule out some of the obvious explanations by finding examples which would disprove them being the cause in question.

*Is there evidence that nuclear weapons have **not** prevented invasions?*

In 1945 only one country had nuclear weapons (the USA) and that number has by now increased to nine.[10] If, while having nuclear weapons, any of those countries have still been attacked, that would negate the theory that nuclear weapons are the cause of them not being attacked. Similarly, if other countries which do not have nuclear weapons have also not been attacked, that too makes nonsense of the theory that nuclear weapons are what prevent a country from being attacked.

Let's look at the second proposition first. Are there countries and situations in which one might have expected those countries to have been attacked because they were 'defenceless' in the face of nuclear weapons and yet they did not get attacked? In other words, if nuclear weapons were protecting the NATO countries from being attacked by the Soviet Union, for instance, what about the countries not similarly protected by NATO nuclear weapons? Presumably these *would* have been attacked by the Soviet Union.

During the Cold War, countries located in western Europe but not members of NATO included Finland, Sweden, Austria, Switzerland, Yugoslavia, Spain[11] and Ireland. There is no particular reason why the Soviet Union should have invaded or threatened or 'blackmailed' any of these countries, but the fact is that it did not – despite them not being at all 'protected' by nuclear weapons.

Other countries bordering the Soviet Union and/or China during the Cold War but also without the 'protection' of nuclear weapons included Iran,

Pakistan, India, Nepal, Bhutan, Burma and Laos.[12] None of these countries were invaded or threatened or blackmailed, despite not being likewise 'protected' by nuclear weapons. As we have already noted, Afghanistan was invaded by the Soviet Union in 1979 to prop up a pro-Soviet regime that was at risk of falling into the hands of Islamic 'mujahideen' militants, themselves heavily funded and supported by the US.[13]

What about the countries *with* nuclear weapons; what is the evidence that these weapons have 'kept the peace' for all these years? The US has had nuclear weapons since 1945. Its military forces have fought, and lost, wars since then in Vietnam (1955–1975), Cambodia (1967–1975), Cuba (1959), Nicaragua (1979), Iran (1980), Angola (1975–2002), Laos (1975–2007) and Somalia (1992–1993). Nuclear weapons played no part in helping the US prevail in any of those cases. US nuclear weapons did not stop the Soviet Union from directly attacking US troops during the Korean War nor did they stop the Chinese from entering that war at a time when only the US and Soviets had nuclear weapons.

The UK has had nuclear weapons since 1952. The UK's possession of nuclear weapons did not stop Egypt from taking over the Suez Canal in 1956, they did not stop Iceland from seizing British fishing vessels in 1974 or Argentina from invading the Falklands/Malvinas in 1982.[14] They did not prevent the bombing of the plane which crashed on Lockerbie in 1988 or other attacks which have taken place on British soil.

Possessing nuclear weapons did not save any British or American lives in Iraq or Afghanistan nor did they in any way affect the outcome of military interventions in Kosovo, Libya, Sierra Leone or anywhere else where British or American troops have been deployed. UK nuclear weapons did not stop the Provisional IRA from carrying out any of its bombings nor did they have any impact or affect the outcome of the Good Friday agreement. Nuclear weapons did not stop suicide bombers from attacking New York and Washington on 9/11 nor did they stop them blowing up trains and buses in London on 7/7.

France acquired nuclear weapons in 1960, but that did not stop Tunisia from blockading their naval base at Bizerte in 1961. Although French forces overpowered the Tunisians and re-took the city, they were forced to finally abandon it in 1963. Meanwhile, in 1962, France was forced to also abandon Algeria after a long and bloody war fought on territory which the French insisted was French soil. Nuclear weapons were no help in that case. Nor were they any help in the case of Chad, where France attempted to intervene during various phases of the civil war there between 1965–1979.

We will look at the case of India and Pakistan below, but it is worth noting that in the case of the Soviet Union, the above example of Afghanistan illustrates the failure of Soviet nuclear weapons to protect its own client states, as was also the case with a great number of US client states during the Cold War. And although Russia eventually prevailed in Chechnya, they only reclaimed their break-away province after many years of fighting and it was again no thanks to the possession of nuclear weapons that they eventually succeeded.[15]

Israel is presumed to have had nuclear weapons since 1966, which would mean it has been directly attacked since possessing nuclear weapons. Even if it did not have a fully deployable nuclear weapon by the time of the Six-Day War of 1967, it almost certainly did at the time it was attacked by Egypt and Syria during Yom Kippur, 1973. It could be argued that wars involving Israel since then have all been initiated by Israel rather than in response to an attack on Israel. Nevertheless there is no evidence that possessing nuclear weapons has deterred other countries or armed groups from fighting Israel. During the Gulf War of 1991, Iraq fired a number of Scud missiles at Israel which at the time no one was sure did not contain chemical or even nuclear warheads on them.

The case of India and Pakistan

India and Pakistan have fought four wars and engaged in a number of military confrontations short of war since they became independent countries in 1947. Three of these wars took place (in 1947, 1965 and 1971) when neither country had any nuclear weapons. The fourth took place after both had officially acquired them.

Serious incidents between India and Pakistan that could have escalated into full-scale war but did not, have been taking place throughout this period, particularly in Kashmir, where armed clashes took place in 1984, 1985, 1987 and 1995. Military stand-offs as a result of heightened tensions between the two countries took place after the terrorist attack on the Indian parliament in 2001 and following the Mumbai attacks in 2008. Other border skirmishes have taken place in 1999, 2011, 2013 and 2014–15.

Between India's first nuclear test in 1974 and Pakistan's first nuclear test in 1998, India had a monopoly of nuclear weapons in South Asia.[16] Interestingly, this period coincides with the longest period of relative peace between the two countries. Does this mean that India's monopoly of nuclear weapons gave it such a military advantage over Pakistan that the latter was 'deterred' from engaging with India's military during this period?

The problem with that theory is that India has always had a military advantage over Pakistan, being a much larger country with a much larger military force. The period of relative peace between 1974 and 1998 also means that India's military did not engage with Pakistan's military, either. In any case, how do we account for the fact that military confrontations – including a full-scale war – resumed after both states had acquired nuclear weapons?

The Indo-Pakistani War of 1999 (the 'Kargil War') was comparatively limited and short-lived. This was primarily a result of the intense international pressure, especially from the United States, to end the war before it could escalate into a nuclear confrontation.[17] Nevertheless the fact remains that a dangerous, full-scale war took place between two countries possessing nuclear weapons. Neither India nor Pakistan were apparently deterred by the prospect of nuclear retaliation from the other side.

Cuban missile crisis

During the Cuban Missile Crisis in 1962, President Kennedy threatened Khrushchev with nuclear war if he did not turn around his ships loaded with Soviet nuclear missiles heading for Cuba. At the 11th hour, with all US nuclear forces on full alert and ready to launch, Khrushchev backed down and nuclear war was averted.

Proponents of nuclear deterrence showcase this as an example of when deterrence 'worked'. President Kennedy threatened the USSR with nuclear weapons and the USSR backed down. But as Ward Wilson points out in his insightful book, *Five Myths About Nuclear Weapons*, the real story here is that deterrence did *not* work in this example. What worked was behind-the-scenes diplomacy and the American promise to remove nuclear missiles from Turkey which were aimed at the Soviet Union. It was the proximity of those missiles to Russia which almost certainly prompted the reciprocal Soviet placement of missiles in Cuba in the first place.[18]

What worked was also the good sense of Premier Khrushchev not to engulf the world in a nuclear holocaust over a relatively minor incident like this. Was Khrushchev 'deterred' by the threat of American nuclear weapons raining down on his country, or was he simply the more sane of the two? President Kennedy was apparently not deterred by the threat of Soviet nuclear weapons raining down on *his* country, because if he had been, he would not have made ultimatums to Khrushchev that brought the world to the brink of nuclear war.

In order to be able to say that nuclear deterrence 'works', it is necessary for the threat of nuclear annihilation of one's own country to be sufficient to prevent one from attacking or threatening to attack another country. In the case of the Cuban Missile Crisis, the US President threatened the USSR to the point of being willing to initiate nuclear hostilities despite the clear and unmistakable risk that nuclear annihilation of the US could result from that.

Summary

The first half of the 20th century was by most accounts the bloodiest in human history, with two world wars claiming the lives of at least 50 million people worldwide. Thankfully, there has not been a third world war in the last 70 years. But neither was there a full-scale confrontation between the major powers of Europe for nearly 100 years prior to WWI.

We need to go back to the Napoleonic Wars of 1803–1815 to witness battle deaths on a scale equivalent to WWI or WWII. There was the Crimean War of 1853–1856, but most historians consider the 19th century to be one of the most peaceful periods in European history. From a historical perspective, therefore, there is no need to explain why a third world war did not take place in the second half of the 20th century.

The major European and Asian powers fought smaller wars and skirmishes with each other throughout the 19th century, as indeed they continued to do throughout the 20th century. The so-called 'peace' of the last 70 years has in fact been punctuated with more than 250 wars, many of them involving one or more of the nuclear weapon states – including wars which those states lost, despite having nuclear weapons.

Immediately following WWII, the Soviet Union installed puppet regimes across Eastern Europe and maintained tight control over them, blockading Berlin in 1948, crushing the revolt in Hungary in 1956, invading Czechoslovakia in 1968, and imposing martial law in Poland in 1980. These were all seen as signs of Soviet 'aggression' and an intent eventually to invade Western Europe. Yet it was Churchill and Roosevelt who defined the post-war 'spheres of influence' and in effect gave Stalin 'permission' to maintain Eastern Europe as a permanent 'buffer zone' between Germany and Russia.

Following the collapse of the Soviet Union in 1991, it has become increasingly clear that despite all the cold war propaganda at the time, no Soviet leader had any plans, or any intentions, to invade Western Europe. The nuclear arms race, which brought the world to the brink of nuclear war on several occasions, was fuelled by unfounded fears on both sides.

There is, in fact, no real evidence to support the common belief that it was nuclear weapons, rather than any other reason, that prevented the Soviet Union from invading Western Europe or kept the Cold War from turning 'hot.' Indeed, if nuclear weapons were the only thing preventing countries from being attacked by the Soviet Union, one would expect countries without nuclear weapons to have been attacked or invaded during that time, such as Finland, Sweden, Austria, Switzerland, Yugoslavia, Ireland or Spain. None of these countries were protected by the NATO nuclear 'umbrella' and yet they suffered no adverse consequences.

Similarly, if nuclear weapons were as effective at deterring attacks and preventing war as they are believed to be, one would reasonably expect that those countries which have had nuclear weapons not to have been attacked or to have suffered defeat in wars, and yet this is also not the case.

There are many plausible reasons why a third world war has not taken place and there is no need to believe in the theory of nuclear deterrence to explain this fact. For a start, all countries agreed in 1945 to renounce war except in self-defence and to rely instead on peaceful means of settling disputes, especially through the mechanisms of the United Nations. Other explanations include the increasingly interdependent nature of the world economy: this means that attacking another country invariably damages one's own economic interests. We are also an increasingly cosmopolitan world in which people interact with, befriend, and marry each other across national and cultural boundaries as never before. All these and many other factors are what have most likely 'kept the peace' since 1945.

CHAPTER 7

Are Nuclear Weapons Keeping Us Safe Today?

IT IS COMMONLY believed that nuclear weapons put an end to WWII and prevented WWIII. Both of these beliefs must at least be questioned, since there are other plausible explanations for both results (see Chapters 5 and 6). The Cold War ended nearly 25 years ago but we still have nuclear weapons. Have they been keeping us safe since then and are they keeping us safe today?

Britain's highest serving general, Chief of Defence Staff General Sir Nicholas Houghton, is concerned that people understand how important nuclear weapons are to the defence of the realm. He refers to the UK's Trident system as 'the deterrent' and said on the *Andrew Marr Show* in November 2015, 'when people say you are never going to use the deterrent, what I say is that you use the deterrent every second of every minute of every day'.[1]

There is a confusion of language here between 'using' the deterrent (ie the weapon), in the sense of pressing the button and firing a nuclear missile at somebody and 'using' the deterrent (ie the policy), in the sense of preventing somebody from attacking you by the threat of striking back at them with a nuclear missile. General Houghton is obviously not suggesting that he fires nuclear missiles every second of every minute of every day, but he is implying that his government is successfully preventing potential aggressors from attacking the UK because he is threatening every second of every minute of every day to fire nuclear missiles at them if they do.

Is that meant to mean that *without* nuclear weapons acting as a deterrent every second of every minute of every day, the UK or any other NWS would face an ever-present threat from potential aggressors trying to attack them here and now? Are we, at this present moment, faced with such a threat? According to the UK government's own 2015 National Security Strategy, 'there is currently no immediate direct military threat to the UK mainland.'[2] This has been the assessment produced by successive UK governments for at least 25 years.

The US is in an even more unassailable position and has been for most of its 240 year history. Despite the Japanese attack on Pearl Harbor in 1941, does anyone realistically think that the Japanese planned to, or could have, actually invaded and occupied the US mainland?

Neither Russia nor China nor any other country is at this precise time threatening to attack and invade either the US or the UK. Perhaps General Houghton believes that during the Cold War, the Soviet Union did pose such a threat. Perhaps he believes that Russia or some other country could, in future, pose such a threat. These are issues we look at in some depth in other chapters. But the claim that nuclear weapons are here and now 'being used' as a deterrent every second of every minute of every day is difficult to understand and if true, highly dangerous – since it implies the 'deterrent' could also fail at any second of any minute of any day.

Current threats facing the West

If neither the US, nor the UK, nor any other major power in the world today are facing a direct military threat at the moment, what are the threats that they *do* face and in what ways, if any, can nuclear weapons address these more direct threats to national security? The UK's national security risk assessment for 2015 lists six 'tier one' risks that the UK is likely to face over the next five years.[3] These are not dissimilar to the threats facing any other Western power, and include:

1. Terrorism
2. Cyber warfare
3. International military conflict
4. Instability overseas
5. Public health
6. Major natural hazards

Nuclear weapons and terrorism

Let us first of all distinguish 'terrorism' as a tactic that is used by certain groups to achieve their objectives and 'terrorist groups' who use this tactic. Terrorism as a tactic, at least as it has been most often used in modern times, is a means by which a relatively weak party attempts to use the strength of their adversary to their advantage. They do this by goading their adversary into committing acts of (indiscriminate) violence and repression which they hope will sufficiently anger and antagonise the victims of that violence and repression as to bring themselves (ie. the terrorist group) more support and more recruits.

It is not difficult to see how this vicious cycle works in the case of a terrorist organisation such as ISIS, for instance. First, a so-called ISIS terrorist beheads a British tourist, guns down holiday-makers on a beach, or blows up a restaurant in Paris. Next, western governments step up their attacks on so-called ISIS strongholds in Syria or Iraq and in the process, kill women and children, destroy homes and disrupt whole communities trying to survive. Those communities then rise up in anger and indignation, vowing to avenge the death of their loved ones. They join ISIS, give money, provide shelter and otherwise support the ISIS cause more than they did previously. And the cycle continues, with ISIS growing in power and support all the while.

In the case of terrorism of this kind, the concept of deterrence does not and cannot apply, since the whole purpose of using terrorism, by a group like ISIS, is to push the US, UK and other Western powers to bring down more violence on their own communities. Imagine that the US decided the only way to stop ISIS was to launch a nuclear attack on their headquarters in Raqqa, Syria. The whole world would probably recoil in horror and there would be a huge outpouring of sympathy for ISIS, accompanied by a huge flow of funds, weapons and volunteer fighters to avenge the attack, leaving ISIS many times stronger than it was before.

When it comes to terrorist groups like ISIS, it must be remembered that they do not only employ terrorism as their weapon but may also fight their enemies in a more conventional fashion, with armies, weapons and battles over territory. In this sense, a terrorist group is like any other adversary, especially if they hold large amounts of territory, have large amounts of cash and weaponry, operate as a government over their territory and do business with the outside world, even if only on the black market.

ISIS, as a quasi-government controlling large areas of Syria and Iraq was, in this respect, similar to the Taliban when they were in control of Afghanistan. Perhaps they could be defeated and dislodged by other rebel groups with the support of outside powers like the US and the UK. But would nuclear weapons likely be of assistance in this kind of scenario? Apart from antagonising the local population and driving them further into the hands of ISIS, nuclear weapons are unlikely to be of much use in guerrilla warfare settings where the fighting groups are agile and dispersed and where the fighting takes place house to house, neighbourhood to neighbourhood, with fighters intermingling with the civilian population.

Nuclear weapons are utterly useless as weapons for fighting terrorism, and for that reason they are just as ineffective as a deterrent against terrorist groups. However, these weapons are themselves weapons of terror, raining down death and destruction like no other weapon on earth. Nuclear weapons are therefore a prize which any terrorist group in the world would be glad to get their hands on. Imagine the impact globally, if instead of destroying the Twin Towers and killing 3,000 people, Osama bin Laden had been able to detonate a nuclear bomb, however crude, in the centre of New York.

As we shall see in Chapter 13 the risk of a nuclear detonation, whether by accident or by design, is a very real one and it is our own politicians and generals who pose that risk to the world, not terrorists. Nevertheless, the fact that terrorist groups exist and are forever seeking more lethal forms of terrorism is a sober reminder that nuclear weapons or fissile material getting into the hands of a terrorist intent on using it against random civilians in any city in the world is a very real risk.

Nuclear weapons and cyber warfare

As modern societies become more and more dependent on computer systems for every aspect of daily life and especially for control of political and military processes, the more at risk we become to the possibility of cyber attacks which might not only inconvenience people but put lives in danger. There is no point in discussing whether nuclear weapons can protect us from cyber warfare, because clearly they cannot.

However, as with the threat of terrorism, the threat of cyber warfare raises additional concerns about the safety of having nuclear weapons around. Nuclear weapons and everything to do with launching and targeting of nuclear weapons is heavily dependent on computer software. There have already been cyber attacks on nuclear facilities, including an attack which actually destroyed equipment at a nuclear reactor site in Iran, believed to be the work of Israeli government hackers. Three nuclear power stations in the US have been shut down in recent years by computer bugs and viruses[4] getting into the system, illustrating the potential danger to civil nuclear facilities.

A US Department of Defence study which looked into the vulnerabilities of vital IT infrastructure found that nuclear weapon facilities could be vulnerable to cyber attack.[5] The report warned that the US and its allies could not be confident that their defence systems would be able to survive a concerted cyber attack from a sophisticated opponent like Russia or China. A former White House spokesperson claimed that the report was not correct because nuclear weapons software was a closed system not accessible from the outside.[6]

Other computer experts, however, have countered this by saying that 'the reality is that *any* defence facility, or national public or private infrastructure service, could be hacked.' They warn that the techniques of cyber warfare are advancing all the time and there are many ways of accessing a closed system using smartphones, memory sticks and other electrical components, as was the case with the cyber attack in Iran mentioned above.[7] However unlikely it may be, nuclear weapons, like all other modern weapons systems, are heavily dependent on computer software, making them potentially vulnerable to cyber attack. So instead of helping to fight cyber warfare, once again nuclear weapons actually make the countries which have them more vulnerable.

However, the existence of nuclear weapons on board several of the British ships which sailed into the South Atlantic warzone posed a serious threat to those ships themselves. After years of denial, the UK Ministry of Defence finally admitted in 2003 that nuclear weapons were indeed on board those ships. There followed a parliamentary review of how and why that could have happened and the risks it posed to the British military.

What about Russia?

During the Cold War, the West faced what it believed to be an 'existential threat' from the Soviet Union (and vice versa). These were two power blocs with opposing ideologies whose success depended upon the elimination of the other.

Under these circumstances, there were those in the West whose motto was 'better dead than red'. In other words, even nuclear war seemed preferable to some than to succumb to Soviet rule.

Today, there are some in the West who think we are entering another Cold War with Russia:

'Russia has become more aggressive, authoritarian and nationalist,' says the UK government. 'We cannot rule out the possibility that it may feel tempted to act aggressively against NATO allies.'[8] We need to first of all look at what is going on with regard to Russia and NATO, and then secondly look at what, if any, impact nuclear weapons may have on this.

Ukraine and the Crimea

Ukraine has been sharply divided politically since its independence in 1991 between those in the more prosperous and westward looking parts of the country and those in the poorer decaying industrial areas of eastern Ukraine. This conflict goes back centuries and mirrors to some extent what happened in Yugoslavia, where the more prosperous western parts (Croatia and Slovenia) were looking westward to the EU as their model while the more traditional Russian-facing parts to the east (Serbia) were looking eastward to Russia. Electoral maps showing voting patterns in Ukraine since independence highlight this sharp east-west divide in Ukraine very clearly.[9]

The 'Euromaidan' revolution of 2014 and the months and years leading up to it have all been about this political divide over the future of Ukraine, with western Ukrainians wanting Ukraine to join the EU and NATO while eastern Ukrainians wanted closer ties to Russia. It is likely that Russia has been providing support to the eastern rebels fighting the present Ukrainian government just as it is likely that the US was providing support to the Euromaidan rebels before the removal of President Yanukovych.[10] But this conflict is not about Russia or other outside parties; it is about the internal politics of Ukraine.

What Russia would find very difficult to accept would be for Ukraine to join NATO and take control of the key Russian naval base in the Crimea. The Crimea has always been of strategic importance to Russia/the Soviet Union because it is home to Russia's only year-round fully ice-free port, Sevastopol. The Russian Black Sea Fleet is based there, along with 15,000 Russian sailors. The naval base itself was leased to Russia when Ukraine got its independence in 1991.

Under the terms of independence, the Crimea was declared an 'autonomous republic' within Ukraine. Crimea has always been predominantly Russian-speaking with only a small Ukrainian minority. After centuries of rule by various other empires, including Greeks, Roman, Byzantines, Mongols and Ottomans, the Crimea was incorporated into the Russian empire in 1783. It was 'gifted' to Ukraine in 1954, at a time when Ukraine was still fully part of the Soviet Union. It was thus not a real transfer of 'sovereignty' as such.

Ukraine and nuclear weapons

It is sometimes suggested that if only Ukraine had kept its arsenal of nuclear weapons inherited from the Soviet Union, it could have deterred Russia from annexing Crimea or from intervening in support of rebels in eastern Ukraine. Since these were actually Russian missiles under Russian control, the idea that they could have been used by Ukraine against Russia is rather absurd. What *is* likely is that had Ukraine still possessed nuclear weapons at the time of the 'Euromaidan' revolution and subsequent war in the east, the risk of nuclear weapons falling into the hands of some rebel group or other would have raised alarm bells across the world. Who can imagine anything more dangerous than a country with nuclear weapons in the midst of a civil war, with military units changing sides and a government that is not fully in control of the military or of all parts of the country?

And where do nuclear weapons fit into this picture? What if Ukraine had already been a member of NATO at the time of the Euromaidan revolution? Would the US have come to the rescue of a NATO ally and threatened Russia with its nuclear weapons if they tried to annex any part of Ukraine? How might that have played out in the event of a referendum taking place and Russian troops seizing control of key facilities in Crimea? Would the US then have launched nuclear weapons at Russia as a result? It is difficult to imagine how nuclear weapons could play any kind of role at all in real-life situations like this, let alone a positive or constructive role.

North Korea

Kim Jong-un became 'supreme leader' of North Korea after the death of his father, Kim Jong-il, in 2011. He rules a very secretive and repressive state, and is considered by many in the West to be the most dangerous man in the world to have his finger on the nuclear button.[11]

It is claimed by many Western diplomats and commentators that Kim Jong-un is acquiring nuclear weapons and long-range missiles in order to be able to launch a pre-emptive nuclear attack on the United States. These people argue that it is only a matter of time until he achieves this capability and must be stopped before he does.

A similar argument was being made until recently with respect to Iran. In that case, it was believed that it would only be a matter of time before Iran acquired the capability to fire a nuclear weapon at Israel, and that as soon as Iran acquired that capability, that is exactly what it would do.

These arguments may have some truth to them, but are frankly implausible if only for the reasons given in chapter 4 with regard to the concept of Mutually Assured Destruction. Even if Iran were intent on destroying the state of Israel with a nuclear weapon, to do so would almost certainly result in the utter destruction of Iran (by the USA if not by Israel). The same applies to North Korea.

If North Korea were to launch a nuclear attack on the United States there can be little doubt that the total destruction of North Korea would follow. Is it really likely that even someone like Kim Jong-un does not know that or would be prepared to take the risk anyway? Even in a world of hotheads, megalomaniacs and head-in-the-sand skeptics, it does not make sense that political leaders responsible for an entire country would purposely set out to destroy their own country.

What is a more likely explanation for why Kim Jong-un, and his father before him, would be so determined to acquire a nuclear weapons capability for North Korea?

The contrast between North and South Korea in terms of economic development and prosperity could not be greater. South Korea is a hugely advanced, highly industrialised and thriving 'Asian Tiger', trading with the rest of the world and closely tied to Japan, Australia, the USA and even China. North Korea, on the other hand, is poor, isolated, technologically backward and highly repressive.

During the 1990s, North Korea went through some very difficult times, including a famine which killed hundreds of thousands, if not millions, of its people. Floods and drought knocked out 85 per cent of its electricity generation, and with the collapse of the Soviet Union around that time, North Korea was left with China as its only ally and benefactor. Today, even China is tiring of the situation in North Korea, as UN sanctions bite even further into an already bleak and desperate situation there.

Kim Jong-un, however irrational he may be, has one overriding priority, and that is the survival of his country.[12] He believes, for reasons which are only too clear to anyone reading this book, that nuclear weapons are the key to his survival. It would be surprising for him not to be convinced, by all the claims that the US and other countries continue to make on a regular basis, that the possession of nuclear weapons is an effective 'deterrent' against any country intending to attack or invade North Korea.

It would also be surprising for him not to be convinced, by all the claims that the US and other countries continue to make on a regular basis, that the possession of nuclear weapons gives the people of his country a certain status which he is unable to give them in any other way. No doubt they would prefer food and electricity and consumer goods, but when those are in short supply, showing off a nuclear weapon or two might just be enough to keep them happy.

The real threat in relation to North Korea is the likelihood of a pre-emptive strike against their nuclear weapon facilities by the United States. Not only could this provoke a full-scale war on the Korean peninsula, but the belief that a pre-emptive strike was coming could itself be sufficient to convince Kim Jong-un to launch whatever nuclear weapons he has before he loses them.

'Use them or lose them' is the most dangerous aspect of the nuclear deterrence game. Both the US and Russia already risk losing their most threatening ICBMs before they can be launched if the other side strikes first – unless they launch their missiles before they are hit, in a 'launch on warning' scenario that leaves no time for double-checking whether an attack really is underway. This is the situation facing North Korea right now, and it could lead them into a very rash and dangerous mistake.

Summary

Since the end of the Cold War nearly 25 years ago, politicians and military figures in the NWSS have insisted that we still need nuclear weapons 'now more than ever before'. If nuclear weapons are keeping us safe today, what are they keeping us safe *from*?

The UK's National Security strategy lists six 'tier one' security risks facing the UK (and other Western countries) over the next five years: terrorism, cyber warfare, international military conflict, instability overseas, public health, and major natural hazards.

No one is suggesting that nuclear weapons have any role to play in protecting public health or combatting major natural disasters. Instability overseas is in no small measure a direct result of international military conflict, as are terrorism and the threat of cyber-attacks. It is difficult to see how nuclear weapons contribute to any of these security risks facing the world today. If anything, nuclear weapons make us all more vulnerable to both terrorism and to cyber-attack, because of the risk of someone hacking into, damaging or stealing a nuclear weapon.

Nuclear weapons are utterly useless in terms of deterring a terrorist attack or responding to a terrorist attack if one occurs. Terrorists have no obvious military or political headquarters to attack with nuclear weapons, so the threatening to attack them is meaningless. Terrorism as a military strategy is aimed at provoking a heavy-handed response that will strengthen support for the terrorists among their own population. All military responses to terrorism are counterproductive because they play directly into the terrorist's strategy. A nuclear response would be counter-productive to a correspondingly massive degree.

Since the end of the Cold War, Russia has remained the principal target of the West's nuclear weapons, despite posing no direct threat to them. Russia's military involvement in Georgia and then more recently in the Ukraine are seen as signs that Russia has become more 'aggressive' and a potential threat to NATO allies. Some have even suggested that if Ukraine had retained its Cold War nuclear weapons and/or joined NATO, it could have successfully deterred recent interferences from Russia.

Like all conflicts, the situation in Ukraine is complex and nuanced. Adding nuclear weapons into an already complex and volatile situation is hardly likely to have improved matters. Would the US have threatened to launch nuclear weapons at Russia if it tried to annex Crimea? What would have been the response from Russia had the US made such a threat? And what would the US have done if Russia had annexed Crimea anyway?

CHAPTER 8

Do Nuclear Weapons Protect Us From Future Risks?

AS WE HAVE seen in previous chapters, there is little evidence for the claims that nuclear weapons forced Japan to surrender in WWII, or that they deterred the Soviets from attacking western Europe during the Cold War or that they have played a role in deterring any other threat since. They cannot be considered 'essential' for the defence of the US or its allies because we face no clear or present threat. What about the future, though? Surely, we need nuclear weapons as the 'ultimate insurance policy' against unknown threats in the future?

No one can predict the future. We live in a rapidly changing world with many state and non-state actors making decisions that can affect us and our future security. Surely some sort of insurance policy against the possibility of future threats is reasonable and prudent under the circumstances.

Using the insurance analogy

It sounds intuitively logical to compare nuclear weapons to an insurance policy. It makes them sound like a sensible investment in the future, a protection for the years ahead, something that will be well worth the cost if and when we come to need them one day, and terribly short-sighted to try to do without.

In most cases, governments are careful to argue that nuclear weapons are needed now *as well as* being an insurance policy for the future, but logically speaking you cannot have it both ways. By using the insurance metaphor, governments are implicitly undermining the argument that nuclear weapons are also needed now, because if they are needed now, it makes no sense to be talking about insurance.

Insurance is by definition something you invest in so as to give you what you might need at some point in the future. If you need something in the present, you're too late to take out insurance. No insurance company will insure you against something you already need at this moment, precisely because it negates the whole concept of insurance to do that. If you miss your flight home, you don't take out travel insurance, you take the next flight. The only time you *can* take out travel insurance is when you don't need it, ie before you travel. The same applies to every other kind of insurance, including, of course, life insurance.

Insurance is also something that normally pays out to 'remedy' a misfortune such as sickness, accident, fire, missed flight, death... In the case of death, the 'remedy' is to provide ongoing support to a bereft spouse or children, while in other cases it is the person who takes out the insurance who benefits from whatever the 'remedy' may be. It is a strange form of insurance indeed which pays out by raining down even more death and destruction as a 'remedy' for being invaded. That is a bit like having fire insurance which burns down your neighbour's house rather than repairs the fire damage on your own house.

But let's continue with the analogy and try to imagine that there is some scenario in the future for which it makes sense to take out nuclear insurance now as a precaution, bearing in mind that insurance is, as we have seen, a misleading analogy. What might such a scenario look like?

Facing down another Hitler

The most common fear driving people to support nuclear weapons as an insurance policy for the future is the fear that another Hitler might arise and try to take over Europe and/or the world. We might call this the '1940 argument' because it harks back to the days when Britain stood alone against Hitler and there was no one to come to its defence. We need not argue here about how likely such an event might be, only whether having nuclear weapons would somehow protect us in those hypothetical circumstances.

As we saw in Chapter 6, one of the arguments against the theory that British, French and US nuclear weapons prevented the Soviets from attacking and invading western Europe during the Cold War is that had those weapons been used against the Soviets, they almost certainly would have provoked a counter-strike with nuclear weapons at least as ferocious as anything that might have been launched against them. What would have been the net result of such an exchange? Perhaps the Soviet Union would have been unable to invade Western Europe, but by that point there would have hardly been anything left of Western Europe for them to invade.

Possession of nuclear weapons cannot *prevent* a nuclear attack unless those weapons are used in a pre-emptive first strike with a near 100 per cent success rate in destroying all the incoming nuclear weapons of the opposing side.

We will look in later chapters at the whole question of NATO and the US nuclear 'umbrella'. But for now, we need only focus on what nuclear weapons would contribute to preventing, deterring or protecting the world from an all-out attack by a resurgent power bent on world domination.

The honest and difficult truth is that no country that was hell-bent on taking over the world with nuclear weapons could be stopped with nuclear weapons. It simply does not work like that. However much destruction nuclear weapons could cause in retaliation for an all-out attack, those nuclear weapons would be unlikely to stop a leader who was determined to take over the world, come what may.

And the even more troublesome truth is that nuclear weapons would almost certainly never be used at that point. Why? Because it would mean certain suicide for the whole country, as we have seen in Chapter 4. By launching a nuclear attack against a more powerful and presumably nuclear-armed adversary, we would be inviting a response in kind which could have far more devastating consequences even than the initial attack.

In the real world, the only response to the threat of a nuclear-armed Hitler is not to arm ourselves to the teeth with nuclear weapons ourselves, but to build the international structures and systems that will collectively prevent such a thing from ever happening. Many of these are already in place, through institutions like the UN and the growing body of international law which protects human rights and limits the sovereignty of dictators to do as they please. Rather than putting our faith in nuclear weapons to protect us from future threats, we would be better placed to put our faith in the UN and these other institutions.

Nuclear blackmail

Another possible future threat against which nuclear weapons could be claimed to protect us is nuclear blackmail, or the idea that some country might threaten us with nuclear weapons unless we agreed to do their bidding. It is hard to understand the difference between the theory of nuclear deterrence and the concept of nuclear blackmail, other than the fact that when we use our own nuclear weapons as a threat, that is called deterrence, whereas when another country uses their nuclear weapons to threaten *us*, it is called nuclear blackmail.

Let us try to imagine a scenario that could be conceivably defined as nuclear blackmail. Let us say there is another Falklands War, only this time the UK has given up its nuclear weapons while in the meantime Argentina has acquired them. Let us further imagine that Argentina has acquired a lot of other sophisticated military hardware and used these to launch another successful invasion of the Falklands/Malvinas. Once again, a British task force sets sail from the UK to fight a war in the South Atlantic, only this time Argentina announces that it will bomb the British task force with nuclear weapons and effectively wipe out the Royal Navy unless it turns round and sails back to the UK.

From the Argentine viewpoint, they are using their nuclear weapons as a deterrent in exactly the way foreseen by nuclear deterrence theory – as a threat against another country which they hope will not need to be carried out because the other country would see it as inflicting unacceptable damage and decide to desist from their planned course of action. From the UK point of view, this would look like nuclear blackmail, since it is a threat using nuclear weapons to try to prevent the UK from doing what it believes to be its right and duty, namely the defence of British territory from external invasion.

What might happen next is anyone's guess. However, what *should* happen according to international law is quite clear. First, the matter should be taken to the UN Security Council as a breach of international peace and security. The Security Council should then call on the UK and Argentina to negotiate a peaceful solution to the problem, offering to mediate if necessary. They might ask the International Court of Justice for a ruling on who legitimately 'owns' the disputed islands. They might call for an arbitrated settlement or set up a UN trusteeship to put the islands under neutral international control. They might call for a referendum by the islanders to decide their future.

If none of these peaceful means to resolve the dispute were successful, the Security Council would then be authorised to rule who is at fault and to impose sanctions on either or both parties unless they follow the instructions of the Security Council. Even if the Security Council were to rule in favour of the UK being the rightful owner of the islands and victim of an illegal invasion by Argentina, they might still order the British task force back to port until the crisis is resolved.

If all else failed, the Security Council might then authorise the use of force under Chapter VII (see Chapter 12) to remove the Argentine occupying forces. This would not be a British force but an international force, possibly not even including the UK but perhaps including the US and other South American countries, for instance. Would Argentina threaten the US and other neighbouring countries with nuclear weapons, or would it have deferred to the international community long before it reached that point?

Incitement to proliferation

All of the arguments used by existing NWSs to justify having their own nuclear weapons could be just as equally applied to every other country in the world.

But no other argument in favour of nuclear weapons is as much an incitement to nuclear proliferation as the argument that we need them as a 'general insurance against an uncertain future' or that they 'might play a decisive future role'. This lowers the bar pretty much to the floor in terms of an argument for 'needing' nuclear weapons since, as we have suggested above, this kind of language implies that they are *not* needed now but only *might* be in the future.

Iran is virtually surrounded by the nuclear weapons of potentially hostile states: Pakistan to the east, Russia not that far to the north, Israel not that far to the west and a US nuclear fleet in the Persian Gulf to the south. On what basis can a country like the UK, which by its own admission does not face a serious military threat from any other country, say that Iran should not have its own nuclear weapons when the UK insists on needing them for an 'uncertain future'? On what grounds can the US insist that North Korea has no right to its own nuclear weapons when the US itself reserves the right to attack North Korea for having those weapons? Or for that matter, what leverage does the US or the UK have to argue that India or Pakistan should not have nuclear weapons, when all those countries have done is to follow the lead of more powerful countries like the US and the UK?

The risks of relying on outdated technology

It is impossible to predict what the international political environment will look like in 10, 20 or 30 years from now. We can confidently assume, however, that technology will continue to advance in the decades to come, especially in the military sphere.

Already, cyber warfare technologies are outpacing the security technologies designed to provide protection against cyber attacks. Underwater drones and advances in sonar technology are making invulnerable submarines suddenly appear much more vulnerable to tracking and monitoring even in the depths of the open sea.[1] Anti-ballistic missile defences are also advancing, making ballistic missiles increasingly vulnerable to the possibility of being destroyed in mid-air before reaching their target.

With greater targeting accuracy also comes new ways to protect targets from attack, for instance burying nuclear missile silos and command bunkers ever deeper under tonnes of earth and concrete or spreading them out over vast distances which would require many more times the number of missiles in order to 'take them out'.

The nature of warfare throughout human history has been one of advances in offensive capabilities that are followed by advances in defensive capabilities and vice versa. Whatever advantage may have been gained by one side through the latest technological development is very soon offset by technological developments on the other side. Despite the unprecedented destructive power of nuclear weapons, the basic dynamics of warfare remain the same. Today's nuclear weapons will assuredly be as obsolete in 20 or 30 years time as the bayonet or the cavalry charge is today.

Summary

We live in an unpredictable and rapidly changing world. The claim is that nuclear weapons are an insurance policy that protects us from those unknown future risks.

What kind of world will these weapons be operating in by the 2050s or 2060s, and what kind of threats would they be protecting us from? Some commentators suggest we could face a re-emergence of the 'Russian threat', a newly emerging nuclear threat from, for instance, Iran, or the threat of biological terrorism from an unspecified but state-sponsored source.

It is not clear how nuclear weapons might play a decisive role in any of these scenarios. In the case of Russia, it is hard to see how the threat or use of nuclear weapons against Russia at any time in the future could achieve anything except a catastrophic counter-attack as described in chapter 4.

In terms of Iran or another emerging nuclear power, it is again hard to see how nuclear weapons would be more successful at reducing the potential threat than, for instance, international negotiations such as those recently concluded. Terrorism, whether with biological weapons or any other kind of weapons, cannot be deterred or successfully responded to by nuclear weapons, as we already saw in the last chapter.

In the long term, there are only two conceivable scenarios that can emerge. One is a world that is safe from nuclear weapons because all countries have agreed to get rid of them, or a world that is awash with nuclear weapons because more and more countries decide they need them as an 'insurance policy' against future risks. By arguing that we need nuclear weapons as an insurance policy, we are encouraging other countries to follow our logic and our example. A world full of nuclear weapons is a far more dangerous world than the one we live in right now. The insurance argument therefore makes the world less safe, not safer.

PART THREE

We Need Nuclear Weapons to Maintain Our Place in the World

CHAPTER 9

Do Nuclear Weapons Guarantee a Seat at the Top Table?

IN THE UK GOVERNMENT'S official report proposing renewal of Trident in 2016, it specifically rules out 'status' as one of the reasons for retaining nuclear weapons. However, this is one of the most common reasons given when the issue of Trident was being debated up and down the country prior to the renewal decision. Prime Minister John Major claimed on Radio 4, for instance, that scrapping Trident would lose Britain its place on the UN Security Council:

> If we lost Trident... our role in NATO would be reduced. Our relations consequently with the US would be damaged. The United Kingdom would be weaker in every international body it attends. It would certainly be weaker in the EU in the forthcoming negotiations. We would lose our seat at the top table in the UN.
> John Major, on the Today programme, BBC Radio 4, 9 Sept 2014

In his memoirs published in 2010 Tony Blair claims that, having looked at the pros and cons of renewing Trident from a military point of view, 'in the final analysis I thought giving it up too big a downgrading of our status as a nation...'[1]

So do nuclear weapons give a nation status, and if so, how?

UN *Security Council*

The structure of the UN, including the Security Council and who would sit on it as permanent members (the 'P5'), was agreed by the allied powers at the Dumbarton Oaks conference in 1944 and ratified by the founding members of the UN in June 1945.

This was all before any country had nuclear weapons and before WWII was even over (in the Pacific). The decision as to who would sit as permanent members on the UN security council was based on the assumption that the allies would win the war and that the major parties in that war, barring the defeated Axis powers, would be the key players in the post-war world order.

From 1945 to 1949, the US was the only P5 member with nuclear weapons, and from 1949 to 1952, only the US and the Soviet Union had nuclear weapons. In 1952 the UK was added to the nuclear club and in 1960 France was added. Until 1971 the Chinese seat on the security council was held by Taiwan, which did not (and still does not) have nuclear weapons. So only from 1971 have all P5 members had nuclear weapons.

But by 1974, India had tested its first nuclear weapon. Pakistan then joined the nuclear club in 1998 and North Korea in 2006. Therefore it was only between 1971 and 1974 that all the P5 countries had nuclear weapons and that only these countries had them (although even during this period it is believed that Israel was already in possession of nuclear weapons). There is, of course, nothing in the UN charter referring to nuclear weapons, since, as we have established, the UN charter predates the invention of nuclear weapons.

There have been many proposals over the years for reform of the structure and voting system of the Security Council, and these have included removing or restricting the veto power of the P5, giving the EU a permanent seat and then giving the seats of UK and France, who would be represented by the EU, to other emerging powers like India or Brazil, or radically changing the whole structure of the Security Council to better reflect the different regions and power dynamics in the world today.

None of the proposals so far mooted or discussed among UN members has ever included the suggestion that only countries with nuclear weapons should have permanent seats on the Security Council. In fact, such a suggestion would go against so many fundamental principles of the international system that it would be laughed out of court if ever proposed.

For starters, such an idea would encourage countries to develop their own nuclear weapons and reward them for doing so, in utter contradiction to everything the Non-Proliferation Treaty stands for (see Chapter 12). It would also mean that existing pariah states like North Korea would be catapulted into positions of enormous power and influence on the world stage, which probably not a single other country at the UN would support. Israel is likewise a very controversial UN member for having ignored, violated or broken more UN resolutions than any other country by far, including at least 32 binding Security Council resolutions.[2]

Simply put, Israel would never be allowed a permanent seat on the Security Council without a huge row that could split the UN apart as an institution. So the suggestion that P5 membership be linked in any way to possession of nuclear weapons is a non-starter.

Being accorded status as a nuclear weapon state

Officially, the Non-Proliferation Treaty, or NPT, defines the five countries which had nuclear weapons as of 1967 as 'nuclear weapons states' or NWS. All other state signatories to the treaty are defined as 'non-nuclear weapons states' or NNWS.

Some have tried to suggest that this means the recognised NWS cannot legally change their status from being a NWS to being a NNWS without re-negotiating the treaty. This, however, contradicts the intention of the treaty, which is aimed not only at preventing the proliferation of nuclear weapons but at achieving their total elimination.[3]

Unfortunately, it has become the practice to refer to the five nuclear weapon states acknowledged by the NPT as the 'P5', since as we have seen above, they happen to be the five permanent members of the Security Council at the moment. Strictly speaking, they should be called the 'NPT5' or the 'NWS5' or just the 'N5' to distinguish them politically from the P5, even if at the moment they are one and the same countries.[4]

Other international forums

Other international forums in which the different NWSs play a significant part include the G8, the G20 and the OECD.[5] The G8 includes the US, UK, France and Russia, so four of the 'N5', but also includes Germany, Italy, Japan and Canada as four other large and 'important' world economies. Is there any reason to suppose that any of the four NWSs would be expelled from this club for giving up their nuclear weapons when only half the club currently has them and the other half does not?

The G20 is a larger grouping of 20 industrialised countries, as is the OECD, which includes 34 industrialised or industrialising countries. These larger groupings include many more states which do not possess nuclear weapons, so once again it is hard to argue that a state would be penalised in some way if it were to renounce its status as a nuclear weapons state.

The NWSs play an important, and often leading, role in many other international forums, including NATO, the OSCE, the Commonwealth, the IMF, the World Bank, UNESCO and many others. None of these organisations, apart from NATO, have any interest at all in whether a state possesses nuclear weapons or not. The majority of countries in these organisations do not have nuclear weapons, and it does not enhance anyone's status thereby to have them.

Summary

National status is not something that is easily quantified or even put into words. When politicians talk about national status being enhanced by having nuclear weapons, they most often mean status with the US government above all else. But even this changes with a change of US President, a change of mood, a change of public opinion. The US is a very big country with a wide diversity of views, including many who are opposed to nuclear weapons or who see no point at all in other countries having their own nuclear weapons.

When it comes to Japan or Germany or other major countries in Europe and around the world, what is it that enhances or diminishes their national status? This is more influenced by the way they behave in international affairs than by their possession or not of nuclear weapons.

What are some of the things that have actually enhanced the UK's status in the world for instance? Playing a constructive role in the treaty to eliminate landmines gave the UK some kudos in terms of its standing in the world, as did its constructive role in creating the International Criminal Court, playing a positive role in promoting and standing up for human rights around the world, constructive work in the Millennium Development Goals and the subsequent Sustainable Development Goals and perhaps most of all, its generous ongoing contribution to international development through the work in many developing countries funded by the Department for International Development (DFID) and the government's commitment to meet the OECD target of 0.7% GDP spent on overseas development aid.

These kinds of contributions to a better, fairer and more peaceful world are what give a nation-state like the UK 'status', not the number of missiles it can launch from submarines or the numbers of people it can kill and cities it can annihilate with those missiles.

CHAPTER 10

Being a 'Responsible' Nuclear Weapon State

THERE IS NO hard evidence to indicate that nuclear weapons have ever protected any country from external threats and there is little reason to believe they would do so in the future. Possession of nuclear weapons is also no guarantee of a seat at the 'top table' of world affairs. But do the countries who already sit at that top table have a responsibility to protect other countries, even if that puts themselves at greater risk? This is how the argument is sometimes framed.

> The truth is that, in the world as we have it, the upholding of international order and the rescue of the innocent from mass atrocity sometimes require the naked use of armed force... We need some states to be ready to exercise it... Hard power is morally necessary [by] those powers able and willing to use it, not least because so many [other countries] are barely able and seldom willing.
>
> Nigel Biggar, Regius Professor of Moral and Pastoral Theology at the University of Oxford

Britain supposedly went to war to defend Belgium in WWI, and to defend Poland in WWII. The logic now is that Britain – or another NWS – should be ready and willing to go to war to defend Estonia or Latvia, or any other NATO member, should they be attacked. To be a responsible world power and to play one's part in protecting democracy and freedom against tyranny and aggression means sharing the burden of responsibility – and cost – of defending smaller and more vulnerable countries that may be on the 'frontline' in ways that they themselves are not.

Politicians in Britain who consider nuclear weapons to be part of the 'noblesse oblige' of being a world power are similar to politicians in the US who consider that country to be the 'world's policeman'. In both cases, it is the duty, even the *moral* duty of a world power to have nuclear weapons in order to protect the rest of the world (see chapter 19 for moral considerations of this).

Of course, it must be recognised that countries like the US and the UK are part of a global community and have a role to play in that community, perhaps a rather big one at that. So let us acknowledge that these countries *do* have responsibilities beyond their borders, that they can and should play their part in world affairs and that there is no 'retreat' from being complicit in those affairs.

There is a contradiction here, however, between the recognition that the security of one country is intimately bound up with the security of other countries and the claim that certain countries need their own nuclear weapons to protect themselves. These cannot both be true. Either we live in a world where each country is out for themselves and must defend themselves against any and all possible threats, or we live in a world where all countries are responsible for ensuring that no one country threatens another. The UN was established to make the latter a reality. The possession of nuclear weapons is only consistent with the former reality.

We have already looked at the difference between deterrence and defence. We have also looked at the reality of mutually assured destruction when it comes to nuclear weapons being targeted at each other. No country can emerge 'victorious', in any meaningful sense of the word, from a nuclear conflict. So in what circumstance can it possibly make sense to act alone against a serious nuclear-armed threat, even if you are the most powerful nuclear-armed country in the world?

All countries in today's world are, like it or not, dependent on each other for their defence. It cannot be any other way in the world of the 21st century, where any nation-state or even a non-state armed actor, could attack, if they chose to do so, with enormous ferocity and speed from thousands of miles away. There is literally nothing any one state, by itself, can do to prevent that from happening, except by working closely with other countries to ensure the whole world is safe from such a scenario.

CHAPTER 11

The Special Case of NATO

DURING THE COLD WAR, NATO and the Warsaw Pact were two military blocs, locked in an arms race with each other that involved not only nuclear weapons but also more and more sophisticated and deadly conventional armaments arrayed against each other as well. While many believe that the nuclear deterrent is what kept these two great blocs from going to war against each other, no one disagrees that it was a highly dangerous situation for Europe.

Then the Berlin Wall came down in 1989, Germany was unified, the Soviet Union was broken up into 15 different countries and the Warsaw Pact was dissolved. NATO, however, expanded to include increasing numbers of the former Warsaw Pact countries and then countries of the former Soviet Union itself. If the ultimate ambition were to include even the Russian Federation within NATO, that would have been quite interesting. However the reality is that NATO continues to exist in order to be a military counter-weight *to* Russia.

It is beyond the scope of this book to look more deeply into the wisdom of encircling Russia with NATO forces and using a new version of the 1950s 'containment' policy to try to keep Russia from expanding its influence beyond its borders. But is it fair to ask whether this kind of approach is making Europe and the world safer or less safe?

Collective security and the UN

If Russia presents an existential threat against the members of NATO (a rather big 'if' as we saw in Chapter 6), perhaps it makes sense for those countries to band together for their collective defence against Russia. However, in a world which is no longer split into two incompatible ideological camps but instead is more nuanced and more complex than that, collective security is not just about ganging up to protect ourselves from one country or group of countries.

Collective security is the underlying basis of the UN itself, and is sometimes distinguished from collective 'defence' as in the case of a military alliance like NATO. Collective security means that all participating countries treat an attack or an act of aggression against one of their members as an attack against all, and undertake to prevent that happening and if it does happen, to defeat it collectively.

Chapter VI of the UN Charter spells out what the UN and member states must do in order to prevent an act of international aggression and Chapter VII spells out the arrangements for responding collectively to any aggression that does occur. Chapter VII includes provisions for a UN military staff committee and other procedures for pooling of military assets which have never been put into practice. However the principles and procedures for a collective response to international aggression are all there in Chapter VII and have been used, for instance, in UN Security Council Resolution 678, which authorised the first Gulf War in 1991 to evict Iraq from Kuwait.

Chapter VIII of the UN Charter also authorises 'regional arrangements' which may be used to prevent and respond to breaches of the peace without involving the whole international community. These regional arrangements must, however, be in line with the principles of the United Nations and recognised as such by the UN Security Council. NATO is explicitly excluded as a recognised regional arrangement because it was set up as an instrument of 'collective self-defence' under Article 51 of the UN Charter rather than as a regional arrangement under Chapter VIII.[1]

The Organisation for Security and Cooperation in Europe

The Organisation for Security and Cooperation in Europe (OSCE) is, however, the UN-recognised regional arrangement for the collective security of the European continent. Every country in Europe, including Russia and each of the other states of the former Soviet Union, is a member of the OSCE. The OSCE grew out of the Helsinki process which finally 'ended' WWII with a set of treaties and agreements in 1975.

The OSCE has played a hugely important yet relatively unknown role in resolving disputes, protecting civilians, preventing conflict and negotiating peace agreements all over Europe, from the Baltic states to the Balkans to the Caucasus, as well as dealing with disputes, human rights issues and elections as far away as Kyrgyzstan and Mongolia.

Could the OSCE fill the role that NATO now fills in terms of providing military protection for Western Europe? Since the OSCE is not a military alliance, let alone a nuclear alliance, it certainly cannot fill a role that *looks* like the role NATO fills. However it could be argued that the OSCE has already done more to protect Western Europe from war than NATO has ever done.

It is the OSCE, not NATO, which currently has monitors in Eastern Ukraine and has so far successfully kept that conflict from escalating further than it has done. It was the OSCE, not NATO, which brokered agreements in the Baltic states to protect Russian minorities and prevent violent conflict that almost certainly would have involved Russian troops in the immediate aftermath of the break-up of the Soviet Union. It was the OSCE, not NATO, which was successfully monitoring the return of Albanians to their homes in Kosovo prior to the Kosovo War, which pitted NATO against Russia and led to a situation where even today Kosovo is not a recognised member of the UN because of the animosities which remain.

The future of NATO

In the US and in the UK, specifically, the public is told that we must have nuclear weapons in order to contribute to the defence of other NATO allies. France, of course, has nuclear weapons and is also a member of NATO. Although France was a founding member of NATO, it withdrew from the integrated military structure in 1959 and has never put its nuclear weapons under NATO command. NATO members Denmark, Norway and Iceland prohibit NATO nuclear weapons from being stationed on their territory in peacetime and do not allow NATO's nuclear-capable ships to visit their ports. NATO members Spain and Lithuania also have legislation prohibiting NATO nuclear weapons on their territories.[2]

Greece and Canada both used to host NATO nuclear weapons, but they have ceased to do so. At the present time, the only NATO countries allowing nuclear weapons on their soil as part of NATO nuclear-sharing arrangements are Germany, Italy, Turkey, Belgium and the Netherlands. In 2005, the Belgium senate voted to negotiate the eventual removal of US nuclear weapons and in 2015 the Flemish parliament voted to have them removed.[3] There have also been calls for US nuclear weapons to be removed from Germany but in September 2015 the US began preparations for deploying a new generation of B61-12 nuclear bombs at its airbase in Buchel, Germany.[4]

What if?

What would NATO look like without nuclear weapons? Would it look any different to most NATO countries or to the citizens of those countries? Norway, a NATO member, hosted a conference on the 'humanitarian impacts of nuclear weapons' in Oslo in 2013. This led directly to what has now become the nuclear ban treaty (see Chapter 12), that makes possession of nuclear weapons illegal under international law. Although Norway is not currently a signatory to this treaty, there is nothing in the NATO charter that prevents its members from deciding to be an alliance without nuclear weapons if it so chose.

What would Europe look like without NATO? If NATO had disbanded in 1991 along with the Warsaw Pact, would any tears have been shed? A military alliance that was set up to protect Western Europe from the Soviet Union could have gone down in history as an unqualified success story once the Soviet Union had come to an abrupt and unexpected end. Subsequent NATO missions in Bosnia, Afghanistan and elsewhere could just as easily have been conducted by ad hoc coalitions of countries if they had wanted to provide a collective military presence. More importantly, these missions might have been handled by the UN or through the UN structures such as the OSCE if NATO had not existed.

Summary

NATO came into existence as a defensive military alliance of Western countries, against a perceived threat from the Soviet Union. When the Soviet Union collapsed, NATO, instead of disbanding as the Warsaw Pact did, continued to expand, taking in not just former Warsaw Pact countries, but countries formerly part of the Soviet Union itself.

NATO military power now dwarfs that of present day Russia and its reach extends deep into the former Soviet Union. NATO war games, including the simulated use of nuclear weapons, take place right on the border of Russia in the Baltic States, Poland, and on the Balkan Peninsula.

NATO's nuclear policies are subject to continual review by NATO member countries. Although France has its own nuclear weapons, these are not assigned to NATO and France does not take part in NATO nuclear policy. Denmark, Norway, and Iceland explicitly prohibit NATO nuclear weapons on their soil. Spain and Lithuania also refuse to allow nuclear weapons. Greece and Canada used to host NATO nuclear weapons but have since withdrawn from that arrangement.

Out of 28 NATO member states, only five allow nuclear weapons to be stationed on their territories. Three of these, Belgium, Netherlands, and Germany have large popular movements opposed to this arrangement. While NATO remains a 'nuclear alliance' at present, there is no requirement that it will continue as one.

PART FOUR

Nuclear Weapons are Legal, Safe, Affordable

CHAPTER 12

Are Nuclear Weapons Legal?

IN 1996, the World Court (officially the International Court of Justice, or ICJ) gave an 'advisory opinion' on the legality of nuclear weapons. One of their conclusions was that a decision could not be reached on whether use of nuclear weapons would be legal or not 'in the extreme case of self-defence when the very survival of the state is at stake'. This language has been used ever since by countries like the UK to define the only circumstances under which they would ever use nuclear weapons, implying that their use of nuclear weapons under those circumstances would be legal.

However, the international judges of the ICJ did not rule that the use of nuclear weapons was *legal* in the extreme case of self-defence, merely that they could not decide whether it was legal or not. This is an important distinction.

According to Justice Bedjaoui, who was presiding judge of the ICJ at the time, the advisory opinion has been widely misunderstood and misused on this point. What the ICJ clearly *did* say was that nuclear weapons are illegal in all other circumstances. What it also clearly said was that the use or threat of use of nuclear weapons can *only* be legal if it is in conformity with all other existing international law. We shall look at what constitutes existing international law relating to war and weapons of war below. First, we need to clarify what is meant by 'self-defence'.

The right of self-defence

The inherent right of self-defence, when it comes to countries, was enshrined in the UN Charter as Article 51. This article supersedes all previous legal definitions of self-defence and has, once again, been constantly misunderstood, misinterpreted and misquoted more times than not.[1] Article 51 of the UN charter does not provide for an unlimited and unconditional right of self-defence, no matter what the circumstances or however a state may wish to define their actions as 'self-defence'. Instead, it places the right of self-defence within the overall framework of the United Nations as the only body which is now legally authorised to use force. It reads in full:

> Article 51: Nothing in the present Charter shall impair the inherent right of individual or collective self-defence if an armed attack occurs against a Member of the United Nations, until the Security Council has taken measures necessary to maintain international peace and security. Measures taken by Members in the exercise of this right of self-defence shall be immediately reported to the Security Council and shall not in any way affect the authority and responsibility of the Security Council under the present Charter to take at any time such action as it deems necessary in order to maintain or restore international peace and security.

If it *were* a genuine situation of self-defence where a country was under attack (ie not 'imminently' facing attack or 'possibly' under attack, but *actually* under attack, as stated in Article 51) and before the UN Security Council could act, it might be considered legal to use nuclear weapons against the attacking forces *provided* that all other legal requirements had been met.

The ICJ opinion states very clearly that the use of nuclear weapons would be illegal under all circumstances other then the extreme case of self-defence when the very survival of the state is at stake. But it also says that even in that extreme case of self-defence, it would only be legal to use nuclear weapons if all other legal requirements could be met under international humanitarian law and the laws of war as laid down in numerous treaties, conventions and protocols.

The laws of war which apply to nuclear weapons

What are these other legal requirements? The laws of war have developed over many centuries but are mainly codified in the Hague and Geneva Conventions of 1899, 1907, 1922, 1948 and 1977.

These conventions and protocols set down the conditions under which weapons of war can be legitimately used. The ICJ Advisory Opinion of 1996 sums up what it calls the 'cardinal principles' of international humanitarian law coming out of the various Conventions and Protocols listed above:

> The cardinal principles contained in the texts constituting the fabric of humanitarian law are the following. The first is aimed at the protection of the civilian population and civilian objects and

establishes the distinction between combatants and non-combatants; States must never make civilians the object of attack and must consequently never use weapons that are incapable of distinguishing between civilian and military targets. According to the second principle, it is prohibited to cause unnecessary suffering to combatants: it is accordingly prohibited to use weapons causing them such harm or uselessly aggravating their suffering. In application of that second principle, States do not have unlimited freedom of choice of means in the weapons they use...[2]

In other words, when it comes to nuclear weapons,

> The methods and means of warfare which would preclude any distinction between civilian and military targets, or which would result in unnecessary suffering to combatants, are prohibited. In view of the unique characteristics of nuclear weapons, to which the Court has referred above, the use of such weapons in fact seems scarcely reconcilable with respect for such requirements.[3]

The ICJ additionally refers to the 'Martens Clause', which was first included in the Hague Convention of 1899 and continues to be referred to in subsequent conventions, including for instance the Geneva Additional Protocol 1 of 1977. This extends the protection of both combatants and non-combatants under international humanitarian law to new forms of warfare that may not already be foreseen, by specifically stating that:

> In cases not covered by this Protocol or by other international agreements, civilians and combatants remain under the protection and authority of the principles of international law derived from established custom, from the principles of humanity and from the dictates of public conscience.

Protocol I of the Geneva Conventions, which the US has signed but not yet ratified, includes specific and detailed language prohibiting indiscriminate attacks on civilian populations. Article 51, paragraph 2, for instance, outlaws the bombing of cities:

> 2. The civilian population as such, as well as individual civilians, shall not be the object of attack. Acts or threats of violence the primary purpose of which is to spread terror among the civilian population are prohibited.

According to the ICJ, the principles of international humanitarian law are so fundamental and 'intransgressible' that they form a body of customary international law, that applies to all countries, whether they have signed up to the various treaties and conventions or not.[4]

In addition to the two basic principles of protecting civilians and avoiding unnecessary suffering to combatants, a number of other specific protections are defined in international law. The most important of these for the purposes of nuclear weapons is the inviolable right to neutrality, which includes not only the right of neutral countries not to be attacked or invaded but also not to be adversely affected by warfare that may be going on in neighbouring countries.

Finally, there are specific treaties and commitments to which most nuclear weapons states are bound. These include all the treaties establishing nuclear-weapon-free zones in, for instance, Latin America, the Pacific region, Africa and some parts of Asia. Except where a country has signed a specific protocol giving it the right to abrogate those treaties under certain circumstances, it is obligated not to use or threaten countries in those regions with nuclear weapons.

At the NPT Review Conference of 1995, all five of the 'recognised' NWS furthermore gave a written undertaking to all NNWS signatories to the NPT that they would not use or threaten any of them with nuclear weapons 'except in case of invasion or attack on them or their allies'.

When would use of nuclear weapons be legal?

There is really only one conceivable circumstance in which any country could have theoretically used nuclear weapons 'legally' up to now, and that would have been in the case of a nuclear weapon state launching an invasion by sea and the invading warships being attacked while on the high seas with a low yield nuclear weapon. Such a case might have been deemed legal so long as it involved comparatively few civilian casualties, no radioactive fallout landing on neutral countries and no unnecessary or prolonged suffering to the combatants on board the ships.

How such conditions could apply to any other conceivable use of nuclear weapons is difficult to imagine. The deliberate targeting of cities or civilians, as is still the implication of a purely 'deterrent' strategy is clearly illegal under international law. The targeting of government buildings is similarly illegal, since these are by definition occupied by civilians rather than by military personnel. Even the targeting of 'legitimate' military targets within or near to a large city like Moscow would be illegal because a nuclear weapon would not be able to distinguish combatants from non-combatants and the human suffering would be out of all proportion to the military targets chosen.

As we have seen in Chapter 2, the use of nuclear weapons to attack hardened military targets away from population centres, such as Russian missile silos, would require groundburst detonations to be effective. This would result in much more serious radioactive fallout and depending on wind direction and speed is more likely to affect civilian populations at some distance from the intended target, including potentially neutral third countries. It might furthermore result in high altitude fallout traversing the globe before coming down and therefore affecting many more civilians in many more parts of the world. All of this would render such an attack illegal under international law.

The use of nuclear weapons against an attacking ground force crossing Europe or some other large land mass would similarly affect civilians, whether airburst or groundburst detonations were used. Even if it were possible to target only military personnel in such a situation, it is hard to imagine that they would not be subject to unnecessary and aggravated suffering due to the effects of radiation.

Any use of nuclear weapons not directly related to the immediate self-defence of a country whose very survival as a state was at stake would, of course, likewise be illegal according to the ICJ ruling. This includes all 'sub-strategic' roles that might involve protecting trade routes or other 'vital interests', engaging in military interventions to contain or prevent the spread of terrorist organisations or any other role short of the immediate defence of a country from attack that threatens 'the very survival of the state'.

Use and threat of use

The ICJ ruling refers to the 'use and the threat of use' of nuclear weapons. In legal parlance, there is no distinction between use and threat. If committing some act is illegal, like murder, to threaten to commit that act is also illegal. In England and Wales, for instance, the maximum penalty for threatening to kill someone is life imprisonment, just as it is for actual murder.[5] The ICJ made it clear that in the case of the legality of nuclear weapons, any situation in which the use of nuclear weapons would be illegal under existing international law, the threat to use nuclear weapons in that situation would also be illegal.[6]

That means that in all of the cases just mentioned, where the use of nuclear weapons would be illegal, the threat to use nuclear weapons in those cases is also illegal. The ICJ did not rule on the concept or practice of nuclear deterrence as such. However, as we have seen in Chapter 3, deterrence is nothing other than a threat, and to be credible it must involve a willingness or 'intent' to follow through on the threat if the deterrence 'fails'.

Thus it has been illegal up to this point not only to use nuclear weapons in any case other than the remote example of a ship on the high seas clearly in the process of attacking and destroying another state, but also to *threaten* to use nuclear weapons under any other circumstance. This actually negates the whole concept of nuclear deterrence, since having the capacity to destroy a few ships on the high seas under very limited conditions is not very credible or even particularly threatening to a potential aggressor of any description.

There are also critical implications here for the targeting of nuclear weapons, the yield of the warheads, the fusing options (see Chapter 1) and other technical details that determine how a nuclear weapon might be used and whether such use would be legal. If the whole nuclear weapons system is configured so as to destroy half of Moscow rather than a ship on the high seas, it follows that such a configuration is inherently illegal.

The legal obligation to disarm

Before we leave the issue of legality, we must also address the legal obligation to disarm as defined in Article VI of the Non-Proliferation Treaty (NPT). The ICJ advisory opinion referred to this obligation as 'without any doubt an objective of vital importance to the whole of the international community today'.[7]

The NPT was signed in 1967, and came into force in 1970. It was the result of a 'grand bargain' between the countries which at that time had nuclear weapons and the rest which did not. In order to convince those countries without nuclear weapons never to obtain them, the countries *with* nuclear weapons were agreeing to get rid of theirs.[8] This would mean that eventually no country would have nuclear weapons rather than ending up with all countries having them.

This legal commitment of the NWS to eliminate their nuclear arsenals is enshrined in Article VI of the Treaty:

> Each of the Parties to the Treaty undertakes to pursue negotiations in good faith on effective measures relating to cessation of the nuclear arms race at an early date and to nuclear disarmament, and on a treaty on general and complete disarmament under strict and effective international control.[9]

As with all treaties and conventions, the wording is open to interpretation and has been claimed to mean different things by different people. During the NPT negotiations back in 1968, however, the UK ambassador to the UN made very clear what the NWSS were committing themselves to in Article VI:

As I have made clear in previous speeches, my government accepts the obligation to participate fully in negotiations required by [NPT] Article VI and it is our desire that these negotiations should begin as soon as possible and should produce speedy and successful results. There is no excuse now for allowing a long delay to follow the signing of this treaty.[10]

The NPT agreement was that NWSs would negotiate nuclear disarmament 'in good faith' and 'at an early date'. That was a commitment made in 1967 and yet 50 years later these governments have still not fulfilled that commitment.

The ICJ clarified in their 1996 opinion that Article VI of the NPT gives the NWSs an obligation not merely to 'negotiate' nuclear disarmament – which could go on indefinitely, and so far has done – but to negotiate 'and bring to a conclusion' an agreement for the total elimination of their nuclear weapons.[11]

At the 1995 NPT Review Conference, the nuclear weapons states gave an 'unequivocal undertaking' to seriously meet their obligations under Article VI and to work towards the complete elimination of their nuclear arsenals.

This legal obligation overrides all the pro-nuclear weapons arguments given in Chapters 5–11 of this book, since there really can be no justification for maintaining nuclear weapons if the NWSs are legally committed to getting rid of all their nuclear weapons. To argue that nuclear weapons are necessary for national security, even in the remote example of being able to destroy a ship on the high seas, contradicts the legal obligation to disarm. To argue that nuclear weapons are necessary for maintaining the NWSs place in the world is even less of a justification if they are already legally committed to getting rid of them. The claim that the NWSs somehow have a 'right' to maintain nuclear weapons because they are democratic countries capable of looking after nuclear weapons safely and responsibly is in direct contradiction with this international obligation to disarm.

The 2017 Treaty on the Prohibition of Nuclear Weapons

In December 2014 the Austrian government, at the third international conference on the humanitarian impacts of nuclear weapons issued a pledge to 'fill the legal gap' with respect to nuclear weapons and invited other countries to join them.

By the end of 2014, just a few weeks after the close of the Vienna conference, more than 30 countries had signed up to the pledge. By spring 2015 this number had reached 70 and by summer 2015 it had exceeded 100. In September 2015 the number of countries signed onto the Austria Pledge stood at 121, just one shy of the number of countries who initiated negotiations leading to the landmines treaty in 1997.

At the UN General Assembly in December 2015, 139 countries voted in favour of resolution A/C.1/70/L.38, which was based on the Austrian Pledge and called for negotiations to fill the legal gap on nuclear weapons. A UN working group was set up to consider how to move this forward. The Open-Ended Working Group (OEWG) met several times in 2016 and recommended to the UN General Assembly in September 2016 that negotiations should begin on a new international treaty to ban all nuclear weapons.

Negotiations for the new treaty began at the UN during the last week of March 2017. A total of 135 countries took part in the negotiations, which concluded on 7 July 2017. The US and most of its nuclear allies boycotted the negotiations, but could not prevent them from taking place.

There is now an international treaty banning nuclear weapons, and a majority of UN Member States are in favour of it. (See Appendix III: Final Text of a Treaty to Ban Nuclear Weapons).

There are three generally accepted categories of 'Weapon of Mass Destruction' (WMD): nuclear, chemical and biological. Biological weapons were banned by international treaty in 1972. Chemical weapons were banned by international treaty in 1993. And nuclear weapons have now been banned as of 2017.

Anti-personnel mines and cluster munitions were banned by international treaties in 1997 and 2008, respectively, because of their disproportionate and indiscriminate effects on non-combatants. Dum-dum bullets and exploding bullets were banned by international treaties back in the 19th century because of the unnecessary and disproportionate suffering caused to combatants themselves. Nuclear weapons are weapons of mass destruction. They also cause disproportionate and indiscriminate suffering to combatants as well as to non-combatants. They invariably violate the neutrality of third countries. They disproportionately endanger the environment and other species.

The fact that nuclear weapons are now banned by international treaty has yet to fully sink in for most people. As of 2018, only a few countries have so far ratified the treaty, and it does not come into effect until 50 countries have done so. Nevertheless, even if the nuclear weapon states and many of their nuclear allies do not sign it, this treaty will have an impact on them.

Technically, the treaty only applies to the countries who sign it. However, as this treaty forms part of the body of international law governing the conduct of armed conflict, even countries like the United States will find themselves in a difficult position if they choose to ignore it – particularly once some of their NATO and other allies sign it. As we have already outlined in this chapter, the use and threat of use of nuclear weapons is *already* illegal in all but the most hypothetical of situations. The new treaty, therefore, merely codifies and consolidates, from a legal standpoint, what is already the case.

Summary

By signing the NPT, the NWSs agreed to pursue negotiations for the elimination of their nuclear weapons 'in good faith' and 'at an early date'. That was 50 years ago.

While these countries cling on to their nuclear weapons, they do so claiming that it is legal to use them as a last resort 'in the extreme case of self-defence when the very survival of the state is at stake'. This is a reference to the ICJ opinion in 1996 that it could not rule 'whether it would be legal or not' to use nuclear weapons in that extreme case.

However, saying they could not rule whether or not it was legal is not the same thing as ruling that it would be legal in that case. The ICJ made very clear in their 1996 opinion that use of nuclear weapons would only be legal, even in the extreme case of self-defence, if all other international laws of war could be met.

The cardinal principles of international law as they relate to warfare and weaponry are that to be legal, warfare must never be waged against civilians nor cause unnecessary suffering to combatants. Weapons which by their very nature cause unnecessary suffering or are unable to distinguish between combatants and non-combatants are therefore illegal under international law.

The sole case given to the ICJ as a possible legal use of nuclear weapons was the case of a low-yield nuclear weapon being used against an invading armada on the high seas.

On top of this, the ICJ opinion of 1996 made clear that if a particular use of nuclear weapons cannot be legal, then the threat to use nuclear weapons in that particular case is also not legal.

The policy of deterrence amounts to a threat to use nuclear weapons not against ships on the high seas, but against the population centres and government buildings in Moscow and elsewhere. This threat is therefore illegal under the terms defined by the ICJ in 1996.

The new Treaty on the Prohibition of Nuclear Weapons, adopted by 122 countries at the UN in 2017, makes it crystal clear that the international community considers any use or threat of use of nuclear weapons to be illegal. The full legal significance of this Treaty is yet to be revealed.

CHAPTER 13

Are Nuclear Weapons Safe?

The Naval Service operates its submarine fleet under the most stringent safety regime, which is subject to independent scrutiny. The Naval Service does not put a submarine to sea unless it is safe to do so, and there are appropriate procedures in place to deal with any issues that may arise during its deployment. There are robust regulatory mechanisms, both within the Ministry of Defence (MOD) but independent of the Royal Navy and, externally with the Office of Nuclear Regulation, to ensure this.[1]

Secretary of State for Defence Michael Fallon, 28 May 2015

THE NWSS pride themselves in having the highest standards of safety and security for their nuclear weapons and nuclear facilities. Safety measures relating to nuclear materials include multiple layers of redundancy so that if one system fails, other measures will kick in to prevent errors or accidents. But does this mean the risk is zero? As we saw in Chapter 4, the risk of any kind of deterrence failing at some point cannot be zero, which means in the long term the risk of it failing is actually quite high. Does the same apply to the safety and security of nuclear weapons, even if they are never used?

Thankfully, in 70 years there has never been an accidental detonation of a nuclear weapon by any of the nuclear weapons states. That is an important statistic in itself although, as we shall see below, the number of times a nuclear weapon *could have* detonated by accident during that period is alarmingly high.

The risk of an accidental release of nuclear material is one area of concern. The risks associated with miscalculation and errors of judgment is another. Ultimately, however, it is the risk of theft or sabotage of nuclear materials by terrorist groups that gets the most attention. Any country which possesses nuclear weapons makes itself not only a target for nuclear attack by potential enemies but also a target for terrorist attack by those who want to get hold of nuclear materials for their own purposes.

US record on nuclear weapons safety

The US has had nuclear weapons over a longer period than any other country and has thus had more opportunity to face a range of safety challenges with regard to the mere possession of this type of weapon. The US relies on multiple safety mechanisms that would all need to fail simultaneously for there to be a serious accident or mishap. Yet history shows that multiple simultaneous failures have indeed happened on several occasions.

Eric Schlosser, in his 2014 book *Command and Control*, recounts some chilling moments when some of the largest and most powerful ICBMs ever produced, carrying multiple nuclear warheads each a thousand times more powerful than the Hiroshima bomb, have suffered multiple simultaneous malfunctions and come dangerously close to exploding. Simple human errors like dropping a spanner into a missile silo coupled with a malfunctioning valve that had been reported but not yet fixed, inexperienced operators on duty pressing the wrong buttons, etc have led to uncontrollable fires inside a missile silo, accidental but luckily aborted launch of a missile, release of fatal amounts of radioactivity without actual detonation of a nuclear warhead and other very serious accidents.[2]

In 2013, 17 serving airforce personnel responsible for guarding America's ICBM nuclear missiles were stripped of their duties because of 'a pattern of weapons safety rule violations, possible code compromises and other failings' over an extended period.[3] This followed a number of incidents where personnel responsible for nuclear weapons were caught sleeping, drunk on duty, working whilst under the influence of drugs or unable to pass basic tests about their job. In 2003, half of the Air Force units responsible for nuclear weapons in the US failed their safety inspections despite being given a three-day warning that the inspections were coming.[4]

The most serious accidents involving nuclear weapons took place in the 1950s and '60s, when US bombers were routinely flying around the world with nuclear weapons on board. In 1961, a B-52 bomber on routine patrol crashed after running out of fuel because of a leaky fuel tank. Two massive 3 MT bombs were on board and landed in fields outside Goldsboro, North Carolina. On one of the bombs, five out of six arming mechanisms had been activated but the sixth prevented it from exploding.[5] The other bomb plunged into muddy ground at 700 mph and broke up without detonating. Parts of the second bomb were recovered, but the rest of it, including most of its radioactive fuel, is still 180 feet underneath a field in North Carolina.[6]

In 1966, another B-52 collided in mid-air with a fuel tanker over Palomares, Spain. Four hydrogen bombs were released on that occasion; one fell into the sea and was later recovered, one landed intact with no explosion and two exploded but only with the outer conventional explosives and a release of radioactive materials inside. Fortunately a full nuclear explosion did not take place. In 1968, a B-52 crashed in Thule, Greenland, after some foam cushions caught fire in the navigator's compartment. Four hydrogen bombs were released but again, the final arming mechanisms prevented them from detonating, although large amounts of radiation were apparently released, requiring a major clean-up operation. Parts of at least one of the bombs were never recovered.[7]

Other accidents have involved nuclear weapons lost and never found again. In 1959, a US Navy aircraft dropped a nuclear depth bomb by mistake off Puget Sound, Washington. The bomb sank to the bottom of the sea and was never recovered.

The US has also had a number of nuclear accidents involving submarines. In 1963, the USS *Thresher*, a nuclear-powered submarine of the US Navy (but one not carrying nuclear weapons) broke up in deep water and sank to the ocean floor with all 129 crew on board off the coast of Cape Cod, Massachusetts. In 1968, the USS *Scorpion* sank in mid-Atlantic and was never recovered. This was another nuclear-powered submarine but had nuclear-tipped torpedoes on board. Altogether, as many as 50 nuclear warheads have been lost at sea and never recovered.[8]

Nuclear safety record of other countries

The worst accident involving a nuclear missile submarine took place on 12 August 2000 when the Russian submarine, *The Kursk*, suffered an explosion on exercise off Norway, probably due to leaking torpedo propellant. The ensuing fire then caused seven other torpedoes to detonate in a massive explosion detected as far away as Alaska and measuring 4.2 on the Richter scale.

The Kursk was one of the most advanced submarines in the Russian navy at the time, with two nuclear reactors for propulsion instead of a single reactor, 24 cruise missile tubes capable of being fitted with 500 KT nuclear warheads, plus an array of torpedoes and other sophisticated equipment designed to target and destroy a US aircraft carrier and associated ships. Russia claimed at the time that no nuclear weapons were on board, but this has since been disputed.[9] The wreckage of the *Kursk* was eventually recovered after an enormous salvage operation at a cost of US$65 million, but none of the men on board survived.

In October 1986, the Soviet submarine K-219 sank in mid-Atlantic following an explosion in one of the missile tubes, probably caused by a leaky seal that let salt water mix with the missile fuel, creating an explosive chemical reaction. The K-219 apparently had 15 nuclear missiles on board, each of which probably contained two or three 200 KT warheads. All were lost at sea.[10]

The UK's most serious accident involving a nuclear missile submarine is minor in comparison to those described above, but it illustrates that the UK is not immune to naval accidents even when nuclear weapons are on board. The Trident submarine HMS *Vanguard* was on routine 'CASD' patrol in February 2009 when it collided with the French nuclear missile submarine *Le Triomphant* in the North Atlantic, also on its routine patrol. Both subs were submerged and travelling at 'very low speeds'. They each had a full complement of up to 48 nuclear warheads.

The French sub apparently suffered extensive damage to its sonar system, while reportedly HMS *Vanguard* experienced only 'scrapes and dents'. There were a total of 14 accidents involving British nuclear-powered (as opposed to nuclear missile) submarines between 1988 and 2008. These include nine cases of grounded subs, one collision with an iceberg, two snagging of fishing vessels and one collision with a yacht.[11] Between 1987 and 2008, there were 213 'small' fires on board British nuclear-powered submarines, mostly related to electrical faults, 21 'medium-scale' fires requiring 'significant on board resources' to extinguish, and three fires requiring external resources to be extinguished, which luckily all took place while the subs were docked at port.[12]

Nuclear design flaws?

Bob Peurifoy is a former director of weapon development at Sandia Labs in the US. He worked on nuclear weapons designs and especially on safety features of US nuclear weapons systems for more than 30 years and is an acknowledged expert in the field. He told Eric Schlosser, when being interviewed for Schlosser's book, *Command and Control*, that he felt confident about the safety features of all the nuclear weapons currently in the US stockpile, except for two: the W76 and W88. These are the two warheads used in the US Trident submarines and they sit atop the Trident D5 missile. The Trident D5 is also the same missile used in UK Trident submarines.

Bob Peurifoy's concern, which has apparently been discussed for more than 20 years in the US, is that in order to save space on the submarine and increase the range of the missiles, the US Navy insisted on using conventional explosives in the warhead and locating the warhead inside the third stage of the missile rocket motor, surrounded by high-energy rocket propellant. This combination makes the W76 warhead on top of a D5 missile more susceptible to accident than other US warheads, and if one were to happen it would be more likely to result in serious consequences. According to Peurifoy:

> An accident with one missile could detonate the third-stage propellant, set off the high explosives of the warheads and spread a good deal of plutonium around...[13]

There are also known generic defects in the nuclear reactors that run some of the Trident submarines. Cracks in the cooling system were discovered on HMS *Warspite* in 1989 and similar cracks have subsequently been found on other submarines with the same nuclear reactor design.[14] As of December 2015, HMS *Vanguard* has been taken out of service for a second 'deep maintenance period'. This is to include a complete replacement of the reactor core at an additional cost of £120 million. This is because of generic problems in the reactor core identified in 2012 and not dissimilar from those found on previous nuclear subs.[15]

The revelations of Able Seaman William McNeilly

In May 2015, a young submariner training to be a missile technician on board the UK Trident submarine, HMS *Victorious*, wrote an 18-page report of what he considered to be the 'shockingly extreme conditions that our nuclear weapons system is in right now'.[16] He sent his report to a number of journalists and peace activists and it eventually made its way into the news, prompting the official response quoted at the opening of this chapter and sparking a heated debate in parliament about the safety and security of Britain's nuclear weapons.

McNeilly describes fires being started because toilet paper was being stored in the wrong place, flooding onto electrical equipment caused by blocked toilets not being cleaned, electrical faults due to people throwing wet towels on machinery, people not following the correct operating procedures, lax security arrangements, leaky valves, alarms that don't work or are ignored because they go off too often and other safety and security concerns. Following McNeilly's allegations and media attention they received, the UK MOD conducted their own investigation into the safety and security breaches being described. They concluded that:
- The claims were factually incorrect or result of misunderstanding or misinterpretation.
- Much of what he claimed was based on historic events or hear-say about things he did not witness.
- There is no evidence McNeilly had raised any of his concerns

through the chain of command as he claimed, or even privately voiced his concerns to other crew members.
- Concerns about base security were confined to one part of Faslane and did not take into account the complex layers of security around the whole site.
- Ministers, the MOD and the RN is satisfied that the deterrent is viable, safe and secure but are not complacent and will continue to test and develop procedures.
- Not all the claims made can be refuted in public as they are too sensitive from a security point of view.[17]

Despite these denials, the safety and security concerns raised by McNeilly sound all too plausible given what we know about other naval accidents and especially about the lack of due care and attention found among personnel responsible for nuclear weapons in the US (see above). Lack of due care and attention is perhaps the most serious of all the problems relating to the safety of nuclear weapons. All mechanical systems eventually break. It requires competent and alert human beings to notice when things are not working and to take corrective action before worse things happen.

Reports from nuclear regulatory bodies have consistently raised concerns that the level of experienced personnel is not sufficient for safe handling of nuclear weapons. The British Navy cannot find enough recruits to fill specialised places needed to run nuclear equipment.

Miscommunication, misunderstandings, misperceptions and miscalculation

So far, we have looked at the safety of nuclear weapons in terms of the risk of accidents and mechanical failures. These are exacerbated by lack of experienced personnel handling those weapons and the systems needed to keep them safe. But there is also another element of the human dimension to take into account; the people at the tops of the chains of command, decision-makers, politicians, generals, policy advisors and so on, can also make fatal mistakes of judgement.

The 2014 Chatham House report, *Too Close for Comfort: Cases of Near Nuclear Use and Options for Policy*, focuses on this aspect of nuclear risk.[18] The report examines 13 incidents between 1962 and 2002 when the world came close to all-out nuclear war. All of these cases illustrate the same kind of simple human errors that are compounded by multiple failings into a dangerous scenario that can quickly spiral out of control. In these cases, however, we are not talking about the possible accidental detonation of a single nuclear warhead somewhere, but the deliberate, calculated launch of all-out nuclear war involving thousands of nuclear weapons and the certain destruction of modern civilisation as we know it.

We have already looked at the Cuban Missile Crisis in Chapter 3, so let us leave that one aside for the moment. Whereas that crisis brought the world to the brink of nuclear war in a very public way which most people even today have heard about, almost no one has heard of the 12 other times that human civilisation almost ended in a nuclear conflagration.

For instance, in January 1995 a research rocket was launched in Norway and mistaken on Russian radar screens for an incoming nuclear missile aimed at the Kola Peninsula where Russia's nuclear submarines are based. The radar operators immediately informed the commander of Russian Radar Forces, who immediately informed President Yeltsin. Yeltsin was handed the nuclear 'briefcase' and was on the phone with another general to decide the response when it was calculated that the rocket would land outside Russian airspace and therefore not pose a threat. In this case, the Norwegians had officially informed the Russian government about a research rocket launch, but the message had not been passed on to the appropriate people by the time the launch took place.[19]

In November 1983, a large NATO exercise called 'Able Archer' took place in central Europe. It involved a simulated NATO attack on the Soviet Union with nuclear as well as conventional forces. This was a period of heightened tensions between the Soviets and the west. A Korean airliner had been shot down after straying over Soviet territory, the first nuclear cruise missiles had arrived at Greenham Common in England and US President Reagan had recently made his famous quip about the Soviet Union being an 'evil empire'. The Soviets were especially nervous about a possible 'first strike' by NATO against the Soviet Union.[20]

What was not known by NATO planners at the time was that because of the heightened tensions and specific nervousness of the Soviets, they had deployed an intelligence gathering ring to NATO capitals with specific warning signs to look out for and report back immediately if seen. These warning signs would indicate to the Soviets that this was more than just an exercise but actually a cover for a surprise first-strike attack against the Soviet Union.

Two of the signs the Soviets were looking for were the raising of the alert status of NATO bases and the use of new communication channels not previously used. Both of these took place during Able Archer. New 'nuclear weapons release procedures' were also in use, which would have raised the level of Soviet concern. In the end, a Soviet double-agent in London warned NATO commanders to tone down the exercise before it led to a nuclear war.

Some Soviet forces had meanwhile been raised to high alert, other military operations suspended and the Chief of Soviet General Staff was reputedly already based in a wartime command bunker ready to issue instructions.[21]

A UK Trident submarine commander is duty bound to launch nuclear missiles only on the direct instruction of the UK Prime Minister. But what if the submarine loses radio contact with London? In that case, the submarine commander is apparently instructed to tune into the BBC. If the BBC is no longer broadcasting, that is supposed to be the definitive signal that a nuclear war has begun and therefore the commander must open and read the 'last orders' of the Prime Minister stored in a sealed envelope in the ship's safe. But what if there is a fault with the radio signal *and* the BBC signal goes down for some entirely different reason at the same time? It may then be down to the judgment of a submarine commander as to whether Moscow and London are reduced to radioactive cinders…

Summary

The 'doomsday clock' on the cover of the *Bulletin of Atomic Scientists* indicates how close its editors think the world is to a nuclear war. It currently stands at two and a half minutes to midnight. It was moved forward by 30 seconds in January 2018 and now stands at the closest it has been to midnight since the 1950s. How, 25 years after the end of the Cold War and with more than 75 per cent of the total nuclear stockpiles at the height of the Cold War now dismantled, is it possible that we can be *more* at risk of nuclear war than we were when the US still had nuclear bombers flying around the clock and Nikita Khrushchev was saying 'we will bury you'?

> Unchecked climate change, global nuclear weapons modernizations, and outsized nuclear weapons arsenals pose extraordinary and undeniable threats to the continued existence of humanity, and world leaders have failed to act with the speed or on the scale required to protect citizens from potential catastrophe. These failures of political leadership endanger every person on Earth.

This is what the atomic scientists are saying.[22]

In 1975, the Nuclear Regulatory Commission in the US produced a detailed study of the probability of a major accident at one of the 100 civil nuclear power stations in the US. On the basis of detailed calculations of the stress factors of different materials used, the likelihood of different parts malfunctioning, the redundancy built into the system to ensure that if one part failed another part would kick in to the rescue and so on, they came up with a figure. The report concluded that the probability of a major nuclear accident occurring in the United States in any given year, with 100 nuclear power stations operating at once, was one in five billion.[23] Four years later, the worst nuclear accident in US history happened at the Three Mile Island nuclear plant in the USA (and since then there has been Chernobyl in Ukraine and Fukushima in Japan).

The chance of an accidental nuclear detonation in any given year may likewise be one in five billion or some other wildly large number. But that does not mean it can't happen. In fact, if the chances are greater than zero, then sooner or later it *will* happen.

Risk is normally defined in terms of likelihood and consequences. If the likelihood is very, very low (not zero) but the consequences are catastrophic, the overall risk is high because a non-zero probability means that something that is potentially catastrophic is going to happen sooner or later. This is the case with nuclear weapons.

No matter what precautions are taken and no matter how many failsafe systems are in place to prevent a catastrophe, no government can guarantee that sooner or later a catastrophe will not happen.

CHAPTER 14

Are Nuclear Weapons Affordable?

IN THE UK, considerable controversy surrounds the expected cost of Trident renewal and what impact that might have on other government spending. For those who believe nuclear weapons are essential for national security, the cost is more or less irrelevant. For those who feel nuclear weapons are important more for maintaining that country's place in the world, cost is more of an issue. And for those who see nuclear weapons more as something that will eventually be negotiated away, paying a large amount of money for them to last another 50 years puts the whole issue into stark relief.

> To those who say we cannot afford a nuclear deterrent, I say that the security of our nation is worth the price.
> David Cameron, *Daily Telegraph*, 2 April 2013

When the renewal of the UK's Trident system was first floated in 2006, the cost of replacing four submarines was estimated to be £11–14 billion at 2006 prices. This price tag had risen to £15–20 billion (in 'outturn', or actual figures) by 2010 and to £31 billion (in actual figures), with a further £10 billion as 'contingency' by 2015. These are just the estimated costs for replacing the submarines.

In addition to the costs of the submarines as such, the UK government has invested hugely in the Barrow shipyard to enable it to undertake the construction. Other investment to extend the facilities at Faslane has also begun. The biggest investment programme by far, and apparently not included in these figures, is the ongoing development of Aldermaston and Burghfield, where the Trident warheads are designed, developed and manufactured.

The Trident D5 missiles have already been upgraded to the D5LE. However, these upgraded missiles will also need replacing before the expected lifespan of the new submarines is completed, and that could add a further £2 billion to the cost.[1]

Although the warheads themselves are not expected to be upgraded for another ten years or more, research and development work at AWE Aldermaston has already begun. Altogether, total capital costs at Aldermaston could come to as much as £16.7 billion between 2012 and 2062, based on current investment plans.² This means that altogether the *capital* costs of renewing Trident could be as much as £50.6 billion at outturn prices.³

Officially, the UK government has stated that the running costs of Trident come to approximately 5–6 per cent of the MOD budget and it is expected that will remain the case throughout the lifespan of the Successor programme. This amounts to somewhere between £1.7 and 2.3 billion, but by how much this is likely to rise over the coming decades is anyone's guess. This puts the total cost of the UK's Trident programme, including capital and running costs for the next 30 years, at well over £200 billion.

France, on the other hand, does not have a deal with the USA that gives them cut-price bargain basement costs for such things as the D5 missile, which technically the UK merely 'rents' from the US. Where the UK spends 5–6 per cent of its ongoing military budget on the day-to-day possession of nuclear weapons, France spends nearly double that, at roughly 10–11 per cent of its military budget.

With a military budget of roughly $55.7 billion in 2016, France is now spending roughly $6 billion a year on its nuclear weapons, almost double what it was spending ten years ago. This is to cover their own modernisation programme akin to the British upgrading of Trident (see chapter 16).

These are not inconsequential amounts of money for governments facing a tight squeeze on public finances, austerity budgets and political battles over spending on conventional defences. These figures pale into insignificance, however, in comparison with the spending on nuclear weapons in the United States.

US spending on nuclear weapons has averaged around $20 billion per year over the last ten years. Since the total cost is spread over the Department of Defence, the Department of Energy and other government departments, it is not always easy to find the real costs of the US nuclear weapons programme. However, as calculated by the Congressional Budget Office (CBO), total spending on nuclear weapons is expected to be over $26 billion in 2017, rising to over $40 billion per year by 2026.

In fact, budgets agreed during the last year of the Obama administration would have the Pentagon spending over $350 billion over the next ten years on a massive nuclear modernisation programme that could add up to over $1.2 trillion over the next 30 years (see chapter 16).

This level of spending is out of all proportion to what any other country spends on nuclear weapons – or indeed on the whole of their military. Yet there are many who argue that the collapse of the Soviet Union was caused more by the cost of trying to keep up with the US in the nuclear arms race than by any other factor.

For the 11 countries who gave up their nuclear programmes and the 37 other countries who have the capacity to develop nuclear weapons if they wanted to, cost has certainly been one of the main factors. Obtaining the necessary fissile material, as we saw in chapter 1, is already highly complex and massively expensive.

Designing and building nuclear warheads, longe-range missiles for them to go on, nuclear submarines, etc add enormously to the total cost. And the costs of ongoing maintenance, upkeep, security and all the rest that goes along with having the most dangerous weapons on earth continue to mount up.

Decommissioning and other costs

The one cost that is not often considered, and which could end up being the biggest cost of all for nuclear weapons, is the cost of getting rid of them. All nuclear-powered and nuclear missile submarines, together with all other nuclear-related facilities (including civilian nuclear power stations) must be fully decommissioned at the end of their useful life, to safely remove and dispose of all irradiated materials that pose a threat to human health. The UK has a budget line for 'nuclear liabilities' that cover the anticipated costs – over the next 100 years or so – of decommissioning all existing nuclear-related facilities.

In 2006, these nuclear liabilities were estimated at nearly £10 billion. This included £3 billion for research and development at Aldermaston and Burghfield, £1 billion for eventual 'deep waste' disposal, plus £500 million for the berthing of 27 submarines still awaiting decommissioning and £330 million for eventual berthing of the four Vanguard subs (plus eventual decontamination of other naval sites).[4]

However, these figures do *not* include the full costs of 'deep disposal' which no one has yet figured out how to achieve. The total cost of dealing with nuclear waste just from the UK has been estimated at nearly £70 billion over the next 100 years or so.

The so-called permanent solution to nuclear waste, which must be kept safe from humans and out of the environment, not just for the next 100 years but for the next 100,000 years, is expected to be in place by the 2040s. The International Atomic Energy Agency (IAEA) calculated in 2004 that the total cost of decommissioning nuclear power reactors worldwide would come to around US$187 billion; fuel cycle facilities US$71 billion; research reactors US$7 billion; and all military reactors for the production of weapons-grade plutonium, research fuel facilities, nuclear reprocessing facilities, etc. US$640 billion. In other words, the total cost to decommission the nuclear industry, military as well as commercial, could be over US$ 1 trillion to the year 2050. Even this calculation takes no account of the possible costs over the subsequent millennia...

The full costs of maintaining – and eventually disposing of – nuclear weapons must be weighed against other demands on a country's defence budget as well as in other government departments. Most Western economies are still dominated by the 'austerity' narrative, involving deep cuts in many government programmes.

All government expenditure is a matter of political choice. The total pie is determined by how much governments are willing to raise in tax and other revenues, and how the pie is divided up is on the whole determined by governmental priorities, with some exceptions over which they have little or no control.

Money not spent on nuclear weapons would not automatically mean more money available, either for other defence expenditure or for the budgets of other departments. However, governments are making a clear choice when they opt to spend large sums of money on nuclear weapons as opposed to spending it on other programmes.

The world today faces enormous challenges. Chief among these are climate change, growing inequalities, conflict and mass migrations as a result of these and many other factors. Tackling these challenges requires money, and funds which are spent on nuclear weapons are funds which are not being put towards these other needs. Addressing climate change alone will cost trillions of dollars. These are choices which are being made.

As President Eisenhower expressed so eloquently back in 1953:

> Every gun that is made, every warship launched, every rocket fired signifies, in the final sense, a theft from those who hunger and are not fed, those who are cold and are not clothed. This world in arms is not spending money alone. It is spending the sweat of its laborers, the genius of its scientists, the hopes of its children. The cost of one modern heavy bomber is this: a modern brick school in more than 30 cities. It is two electric power plants, each serving a town of 60,000 population. It is two fine, fully equipped hospitals. It is some 50 miles of concrete pavement. We pay for a single fighter with a half-million bushels of wheat. We pay for a single destroyer with new homes that could have housed more than 8,000 people...
> Speech to the American Society of Newspaper Editors, Washington, DC, 16 April, 1953

Summary

The total cost of renewing Trident in the UK and maintaining 'continuous at-sea' patrols for an additional 30 years or more is likely to be more than £200 billion. France is spending a similar amount upgrading and maintaining its own nuclear forces well into the second half of this century.

The US meanwhile is upgrading every aspect of its nuclear programme at a cost of up to $1.2 trillion over the next 30 years. While these countries appear able and willing to spend these amounts of money on nuclear weapons, the opportunity costs are considerable, in terms of pressing world problems, like climate change, which are still not being sufficiently addressed.

PART FIVE

We are Doing All We Can to Disarm

CHAPTER 15

Is there a Commitment to 'Multilateral' Disarmament?

WHEN PRESSED, ALMOST every politician who supports nuclear weapons will say that of course they are in favour of nuclear disarmament, who isn't? They too want to see a world that is eventually free of nuclear weapons. As we have seen in Chapter 12, this is not just an aspiration but a legal obligation. But getting rid of our own nuclear weapons 'unilaterally' is not, they say, the way to achieve this. Rather, what they will invariably say is that they are for 'multilateral' nuclear disarmament and that they have always been fully committed to this approach.

> As a responsible Nuclear Weapons State we are committed to the long-term goal of a world without nuclear weapons and we recognise our obligations under all three of the pillars of the NPT. We will work with our international partners to tackle proliferation and to make progress on multilateral disarmament... We will continue to press for key steps towards multilateral disarmament, including the entry into force of the Comprehensive Nuclear Test Ban Treaty and successful negotiations on a Fissile Material Cut-Off Treaty in the Conference on Disarmament.[1]

Sir Jeremy Greenstock was UK ambassador to the United Nations from 1998–2003, during which time he was in the unenviable position of trying to secure UN Security Council support for the invasion of Iraq. His book about the Iraq War was subsequently blocked from publication by the UK Foreign Office. While his views on the Iraq War are still somewhat controversial, his position on nuclear weapons is quite clear. In his defence of the government's 'step-by-step' approach to nuclear disarmament, Sir Jeremy insists that the UK has done all it can – and more than other nuclear weapon states – to steer the process of multilateral disarmament towards the eventual elimination of nuclear weapons as obligated by the Non-Proliferation Treaty.[2]

Disarmament and Arms Control

It is certainly the case that the NWSS have taken part in negotiations concerning nuclear weapons. But what is their actual record on multilateral disarmament? And just how serious are they about achieving nuclear disarmament through multilateral negotiations?

First of all, we need to distinguish between what is known as 'disarmament' and what is euphemistically called, 'arms control'. Disarmament involves the destruction of weapons leading to an overall reduction in weapons and eventually their elimination. Examples of disarmament treaties in the nuclear field include the INF Treaty of 1987, which got rid of a whole class of nuclear weapons in Europe, and the START and New START treaties, which reduced the numbers of strategic nuclear weapons held by the two superpowers by up to 50 per cent in each case.

The Landmines Treaty, the Biological Weapons Convention and other such treaties have also led to the near complete elimination of certain types of weapons. These are therefore disarmament treaties.

By contrast, arms control treaties have curtailed certain activities or even put a lid on certain activities but without leading directly or indirectly to a reduction in the numbers of weapons involved. Examples of this are the Non-Proliferation Treaty, which seeks to prevent other states from obtaining nuclear weapons but did not curtail existing nuclear weapons states from continuing to increase their nuclear stockpiles. Another example is the Partial Test Ban Treaty, which prohibited nuclear testing in the atmosphere but did not stop testing altogether (which continued underground). Nor did it stop the nuclear weapons states from continuing to increase their nuclear stockpiles.

In terms of nuclear disarmament, as opposed to arms control, the *only* multilateral treaties that have led to actual disarmament, that is, a decrease in the numbers of nuclear weapons, have been between the US and the Soviet Union/Russia. None have involved any of the other NWSS and as we shall see in the next chapter, all the reductions in the nuclear arsenals of NWSS other than the US and Russia have been the result of unilateral action on the part of those governments, not as a result of multilateral negotiations.

In support of its claim that the UK, for instance, is working to 'make progress on multilateral disarmament', the UK government likes to point to 1) its work with Norway on verification; 2) its work to bring into force the CBTB; 3) its work towards a Fissile Material Cut-Off Treaty. These are all useful and important multilateral developments but none of them involve disarmament as such but are instead all examples of arms control.

Progress on disarmament verification

The UK, together with Norway, has been working to advance verification technologies that can monitor compliance with disarmament and arms control treaties and obligations. Verification of nuclear testing is comparatively straightforward, since seismological equipment for monitoring earthquakes is now installed in key locations around the globe and these sites are linked up to each other in an effort to provide better warning of earthquakes and tsunamis. Nuclear tests, even underground and underwater ones, are large enough to register as small 'earthquakes' on seismological equipment and therefore it is virtually impossible for any country to conduct a nuclear test without it being picked up by such equipment.

Satellite imagery, including infrared photography which picks up signs of intense heat, is also able now to effectively monitor above ground nuclear explosions taking place anywhere in the world. Satellite monitoring has also been used to demonstrate that disarmament agreements have been kept, for instance allowing the Soviets to see for themselves the destroyed, chopped up US long-range bombers spread out on the ground in compliance with the START treaty.

The UK–Norway Initiative is a collaboration between experts from Norway and the UK to investigate technical and procedural challenges associated with verification of nuclear warhead dismantling.[3] Already there are many well-established procedures in place for weapons inspectors to verify that nuclear materials from nuclear power stations are not being diverted to weapons use, for instance. Further steps in building confidence that verification of nuclear disarmament measures is possible and practically feasible are important. But these are only a small part of an actual disarmament process and do not constitute disarmament itself.

A Comprehensive Test Ban Treaty (CTBT)

The Soviet Union unilaterally stopped their nuclear testing, underground as well as in the atmosphere, in 1991. The US followed suit in 1992 and France and China in 1996. Since UK underground testing was dependent on US facilities for nuclear testing in Nevada, this also stopped when US testing stopped.

The Comprehensive Test Ban Treaty was designed to consolidate these unilateral decisions into a legally binding treaty that would also prevent other countries from conducting nuclear tests. Negotiations on the CTBT began in 1993 and were concluded in 1996. At the time of publication, 183 countries have signed the CTBT, but it has not entered into force because three countries with nuclear weapons have not yet signed it (India, Pakistan and North Korea) and are continuing with their nuclear tests. Three other countries with nuclear weapons have signed but not ratified the CTBT: the US, China and Israel. As long as the US and China do not ratify the Treaty, it cannot enter into force according to the terms of the treaty.

There has not been any progress on this front in the last 20 years, since the US and China are still refusing to ratify.

The Fissile Material Cut-Off Treaty (FMCT)

The Fissile Material Cut-Off Treaty (FMCT) is a treaty that would prohibit any further production of nuclear weapons-grade fissile material (enriched uranium and plutonium) and thus make it less likely that countries which do not already have weapons-grade fissile material would be able to build nuclear weapons.

But as the name suggests, it is a 'cut-off' treaty, stopping production of fissile material where it is at the moment. Thus it is an arms control rather than a disarmament measure as defined above. Countries which already have large stockpiles of weapons-grade fissile material, like the US, Russia, China, France and the UK, would not be required under this treaty to reduce or eliminate their existing stocks.

Like the Partial Test Ban Treaty and the Comprehensive Test Ban Treaty, the FMCT would help to reduce the future production of nuclear weapons from those countries which do not have any. But in fact, the five declared nuclear weapons states (N5) have more than enough fissile material to meet their requirements for a very long time. As the NWS decommission and dismantle old, unstable warheads from the 1950s, they merely recycle their fissile material into newer warheads. Even then they have more fissile material left over than they need. So a FMCT in fact does nothing at all to reduce or even to incentivise the N5 to reduce their nuclear stockpiles still further. Indeed, the UK alone has a stockpile of 140 tonnes of Plutonium, enough to make 20,000 Nagasaki sized bombs.[4]

The FMCT, like the CTBT, are examples of arms control initiatives that favour the N5 and allow them to continue modernising and upgrading their nuclear weapons while making it seem as if they are working towards disarmament.

Conference on Disarmament

The NWS' preferred 'chamber' for multilateral negotiations on nuclear disarmament is the UN Conference on Disarmament.[5] This is a forum that was established by the international community in 1979 for multilateral negotiations on disarmament issues. The Chemical Weapons Convention, signed in 1993, was successfully negotiated in this forum and other negotiations have been initiated in this forum, including the FMCT and the CTBT. Currently the conference is made up of 65 countries, and it operates on the basis of consensus, meaning that any one of the 65 countries can veto a decision.

Since 1997, the CD has been deadlocked with vetoes used not just to prevent a programme of work being agreed but even to prevent agendas from being set, meaning for much of that time, the Conference on Disarmament has not even been able to agree on what they are going to talk about, let alone on any matters of substance. This stalemate has made the CD the laughing stock of the international community. Sixty-five countries have been sitting around a table in Geneva, week after week, year after year, giving speeches to each other but accomplishing absolutely nothing.[6] And this is the forum through which the NWSS claim they are working towards multilateral nuclear disarmament.

There are other multilateral forums available for discussing nuclear disarmament, including the UN First Committee, which deals with disarmament affairs, the UN General Assembly, which votes every year on a raft of resolutions from the First Committee, and the UN Security Council, which also has its share of discussions and resolutions relating to matters of nuclear disarmament.

Where do the NWSS stand in relation to these multilateral discussions?

Voting record of NWSS in the UN General Assembly

It is difficult to conclude that the NWSS have taken multilateral disarmament seriously when they have voted against nearly every initiative or proposal put forward for multilateral disarmament in the United Nations General Assembly. This voting behaviour goes back not just years, but decades. Sometimes it has been only the US and the UK who have voted against disarmament measures put forward by other countries. Sometimes they have been joined by most or all of the other nuclear weapons states, and sometimes by other NATO allies and/or other countries which for whatever reason have opposed particular proposals.

As an example of the collective position of the recognised NWSS on multilateral nuclear disarmament at the UN, the following statement was issued on behalf of the N5 in response to the recent vote in December 2015 on 'taking forward multilateral nuclear disarmament' in the UN General Assembly, which all five nuclear weapons states voted against:

This resolution attempts to promote nuclear disarmament whilst ignoring security considerations. We do not believe that such an approach can effectively lead to concrete progress. Our five States, like many others present here, are concerned with this divisive approach, which in no way brings the international community closer to nuclear disarmament.[7]

The Open Ended Working Group and Oslo Process

In an effort to break the deadlock in the Conference on Disarmament and to address the lack of progress on promises made in the NPT, the UN agreed in 2012 to set up an 'Open Ended Working Group on Taking Forward Multilateral Nuclear Disarmament Negotiations' (OEWG). The N5 voted against the setting up of this group and did not take part in any of its deliberations.

A joint statement by the UK, US and France made clear that they were not only opposed to the establishment of the OEWG, but to 'any outcome it may produce.'[8] This seems a rather extraordinary position for countries claiming to be working for multilateral disarmament.

In 2013, an international conference was held in Oslo on the 'humanitarian impacts of nuclear weapons'. Again the N5 countries refused to take part.

The N5 continued their opposition to what became the 'humanitarian initiative' coming out of the Oslo conference, boycotting a follow-up conference in Nayarit, Mexico, in 2014. The US and the UK did attend the third and final international conference on humanitarian impacts, held in Vienna in December 2014.

However, the statement issued by the UK delegate to the conference reiterated the UK's position on nuclear disarmament, stating that the UK would retain its nuclear weapons 'for as long as it is necessary', and declaring that a treaty banning all nuclear weapons would 'jeopardise strategic stability.'[9] The UN General Assembly agreed in December 2015 to set up another Open Ended Working Group, which again the N5 NWSS voted against and did not participate in.

2015 NPT Review Conference

The NPT comes up for 'review' every five years. Intense deliberations take place over a period of three or four weeks and normally there is a final report outlining any areas of progress made and steps to be taken over the next five years. This must be agreed by consensus of all 189 countries who are parties to the treaty, so if just one country is not in agreement with the text, it cannot be adopted. In 2015, the final outcome document was rejected by three countries, meaning that the whole four weeks of negotiations among 189 countries came to nothing.

The three countries who threw out the final text of the 2015 NPT Review Conference were the US, Canada and the UK. Why did they do that? It was a last minute intervention by Israel, which is not a party to the NPT, which convinced the three countries to veto the final outcome. This was because the final text included a commitment to hold a conference in 2016 on the setting up of a nuclear-free zone for the Middle East.[10]

Setting up a nuclear-free zone for the Middle East was actually a commitment which all members of the NPT agreed to 20 years ago in 1995. Successive UK governments have insisted that this was one of their primary objectives to achieve on the nuclear non-proliferation front. While Israel has always declared itself opposed to setting up such a zone, the 1995 'indefinite extension' of the NPT would not have been possible without this commitment on behalf of the N5.[11]

Nevertheless, despite its commitments to a NFZ for the Middle East as agreed in 1995, despite its claim in successive reports to parliament that it was pursuing this aim, and despite all the effort that went into the 2015 NPT review conference, including many other positive steps that will not now be implemented, the UK government chose to block the final report along with the US and Canada in order to protect Israel from a commitment to hold this conference.

Nuclear Ban Treaty

As a result of the growing pressure from civil society and a large majority of the non-nuclear weapons states at the UN to find a way to break the deadlock on nuclear disarmament, the historic decision was made by the UN General Assembly in December 2016 to start negotiations for a new international treaty to ban nuclear weapons. On this occasion, China broke ranks with its N5 partners and abstained on the vote, along with India and Pakistan. Somewhat bizarrely, North Korea voted in favour.

Cracks also began to appear among NATO and other US nuclear allies in Asia, with Japan voting against the negotiations but promising to take part. NATO members Netherlands, Albania, Italy and Estonia all voted in favour of the negotiations, but then the latter three said they had 'made a mistake' and asked for their vote to be changed.

As the negotiations for a nuclear ban treaty got underway at the UN in New York on 27 March 2017, the US held a protest outside the conference hall. Flanked by the UK Ambassador and other officials from France and 17 other NATO countries, the US Ambassador to the UN, Nikki Haley, accused the countries inside negotiating of not 'looking out for their people' or 'understanding the threats' they face. Ambassador Rycroft of the UK went on to claim that the negotiations 'cannot and will not work' or 'lead to effective progress on global nuclear disarmament'.

It remains to be seen whether any of the NWSS will sign this treaty. In the meantime, however, it seems to be business as usual for the NWSS – saying they want a world free of nuclear weapons but voting against, blocking or boycotting every initiative being put forward to achieve it.

Summary

The NWSS have insisted that their preferred route to nuclear disarmament is through 'multilateral' negotiations rather than through 'unilateral' action. Their record in the many multilateral platforms that have sought to achieve nuclear disarmament is nevertheless worse than disappointing.

These governments have shown not only by their determination to press ahead with major upgrades and modernisation of their nuclear weapons but also by their behaviour at the UN, that they have no real commitment to multilateral nuclear disarmament at all. Instead, they press ahead with nuclear weapons as if they will be with us forever and do only the barest minimum to deflect criticism of this 'nuclear weapons forever' position.

Even the initiatives which these governments choose to highlight as evidence of their serious commitment to multilateral disarmament belie their real intentions. The three programmes normally highlighted in this context are the UK's involvement with Norway in disarmament verification, efforts to bring the Comprehensive Test Ban Treaty (CTBT) into force and progress towards a Fissile Material Cut-Off Treaty.

All three of these initiatives are 'arms control' rather than 'disarmament' initiatives. Unlike the INF treaty, START or the New START Treaty, these initiatives do not involve destruction or disarmament of a single nuclear warhead. What's more, all three are targeted specifically at other states, rather than at the reducing the stockpiles of existing NWS.

The CTBT prohibits all nuclear testing that involves actual nuclear explosions, underground as well as above ground. Without such tests it is virtually impossible to design and develop new types of nuclear weapon. However, with the aid of sophisticated computer-simulated tests which do not involve an actual nuclear explosion, the US has been able to design and develop new types of nuclear weapons without violating the CTBT. So far, only the US has mastered this technology (and given the UK access to it), giving these two countries an unfair advantage over other NWS.

The FMCT would stop countries from producing any more fissile material.

But existing NWSS already have more than enough fissile material to make as many nuclear weapons as they could possibly want in the coming decades. So, again, this is aimed at countries which do not already have the stocks of fissile material which the older nuclear powers already have.

The N5 have collectively voted against, blocked or boycotted virtually every other multilateral nuclear disarmament initiative – and there have been many. At the 2015 NPT Review Conference, three countries shamefully blocked the entire outcome of four week's work by 189 countries to make progress on a whole range of nuclear weapons issues.

CHAPTER 16

Haven't We Already Disarmed to the Minimum?

AS WAS POINTED out in Chapter 1, at the peak of the Cold War in the mid-'80s, there were as many as 70,000 nuclear warheads deployed worldwide. Today, there are estimated to be just under 15,000, and this number will continue to decrease as older weapons continue to come out of service. All of the reductions in nuclear stockpiles of the smaller NWSS have been as a result of unilateral withdrawals by those countries. Only the US and Russia have signed agreements reducing their respective stockpiles by agreed amounts.

The Intermediate Nuclear Forces (INF) Treaty between the US and the Soviet Union in 1987 was the first multilateral agreement that actually removed an entire class of nuclear weapons from the inventories of those two countries. A total of 2,692 intermediate range nuclear missiles were withdrawn from service and destroyed as a result of that treaty.

While the SALT I and SALT II treaties of the 1970s were meant to 'limit' the nuclear weapons of both sides, in fact the numbers kept on increasing after both of those treaties. By contrast, the START process, which began in 1990 before the fall of the Soviet Union, saw major reductions in nuclear weaponry of both sides, which have continued to this day.

START I, signed in 1991, resulted in over 8,000 nuclear warheads being dismantled on both sides over the next few years. START II would have led to further cuts but was never ratified by the US Senate.

The SORT Treaty, signed in 2002, cut warhead numbers on both sides by another 8,000 and the NewSTART Treaty, signed in 2010 by President Obama and President Medvedev of Russia, commits them to destroying another 1,752 warheads in total by 2018.

In addition to cuts brought about by these treaties, both sides decided unilaterally in the aftermath of the INF Treaty to begin withdrawing not just their intermediate nuclear missiles as required by the treaty, but *all* their battlefield nuclear weapons then stationed in Europe. This led to the largest reduction by far in the arsenals of all NWSS since the Cold War peak.

By the early 1990s, all of the so-called 'battlefield' nuclear weapons were withdrawn from both sides in central Europe, including those owned by the US but operated by other countries, such as the British Army of the Rhine (BAOR) in (West) Germany as well as those operated by Germany itself, Greece, Italy, Netherlands and Belgium.

Battlefield nuclear weapons

What were the battlefield nuclear weapons that were withdrawn from service at the end of the Cold War? One of these was the WE-177A, a nuclear depth charge designed to be dropped by Sea King helicopters flying over Soviet nuclear submarines. Former Royal Navy Commander Rob Green, who was responsible for a Sea King helicopter crew training to drop the WE-177A, described it as a 'suicide mission', since the nuclear explosion below the sea would assuredly destroy the helicopter above it before the crew would be able to get out of range.[1]

Another was the W48, a 155mm nuclear-tipped artillery shell, designed to be fired by NATO troops in the heat of battle. Three thousand of these shells were scattered across Europe in heavily guarded ammunition dumps.

The W54 warhead, or Special Atomic Demolition Munition (SADM) was designed to be strapped on the back of a soldier and carried or parachuted into battle, where it could be set up at the desired location and detonated (hopefully from a distance).

At 6 KT, this size of weapon could nonetheless explode with nearly half the destructive power of the Hiroshima bomb. Less powerful versions were also available and some of these deployed on jeeps or on portable gun tripods.

As many as 20,000 of these and other battlefield nuclear weapons were withdrawn by the US alone in the late '80s and early '90s.

It is of course to be lauded that these weapons were withdrawn from service. However, these weapons were withdrawn from service primarily because they were dangerous to have lying around and no longer seen as useful or appropriate by the military themselves. The real question is how they could ever have been considered useful or appropriate in the first place.

From Polaris and Poseidon to Trident

The US replacement of its entire fleet of Poseidon submarines with more advanced and powerful Trident submarines in the 1990s involved an overall reduction in the total number of warheads by the US. The UK replacement of its Polaris fleet by the new Trident submarines also involved an apparent reduction in total warheads for the UK. However total warhead numbers are misleading in this case, since a qualitative increase in the capabilities of the new warheads more than made up for the smaller numbers.

The older Poseidon and Polaris missiles had a range of 2,500 nautical miles (4,630 km), which meant that to reach Moscow, for instance, these submarines had to stay within a certain portion of the North Atlantic to be within range. That in turn made them more vulnerable to detection and possible attack by the Soviets. Trident missiles, on the other hand, have a potential range of more than 7,400 km (depending on payload), or nearly double the range of the Polaris missiles, giving them much greater freedom to roam the seas further away from the US or UK and further away from Soviet submarine detection vessels. Trident submarines can also travel faster, at greater depths, and much more quietly than their Polaris equivalents, making them much more difficult to track down and destroy.

An important measure in the development of nuclear weapon technology is what is called 'circular error probable', or CEP. This measures the distance within which the warhead is likely to reach its intended target. Trident missiles, with a reputed CEP of only 300 feet,[2] were the first class of nuclear weapon which were powerful enough and accurate enough, even after being launched from a random location at sea, to be able to destroy a 'hardened' target like an underground command bunker or an ICBM missile silo, both likely to be buried under many feet of reinforced concrete.

Polaris missiles had a CEP of 1,800 feet, which was not sufficient for this level of precision targeting. Thus the switch from Polaris to Trident, seemingly involving a unilateral reduction of warheads as well as of warhead destructive power, actually involved a significant increase in terms of nuclear weapons technology.

This is also the case when it comes to some of the other reductions in nuclear arsenals that have taken place under the START and SORT agreements. Much older and less reliable missiles and warheads were taken out of service and replaced with fewer, smaller but in many ways more deadly and dangerous missiles and warheads.

The Titan ICBMs, for instance, with their massive 9 MT warheads, had been deployed across the US since the 1950s. Replacing these with much smaller Minuteman III missiles was not a 'sacrifice' in terms of nuclear capacity, since the newer missiles are far more accurate, far more reliable and far more sophisticated.

Minimum needed for deterrence

One of the claims made especially by the smaller NWSs, like the UK and France, is that they now have only the 'minimum' number of nuclear weapons needed for deterrence – the 'minimum credible deterrent' needed to keep them safe from nuclear attack. But how many nuclear weapons is that, exactly? In 1988, British Prime Minister Margaret Thatcher said the minimum credible deterrent for the UK was 512 nuclear weapons, at sea and ready to fire at a moment's notice. In 1995, that number was reduced to 300. In 1998 it was reduced still further to 200 and in 2006 it was reduced to 160. In 2015, it was announced that the minimum deterrence needed to protect the UK was 120 nuclear warheads on continuous at-sea patrol.³

France currently has approximately 300 nuclear weapons, and considers *that* to be the 'minimum credible deterrent' needed to protect France from a nuclear attack. When France had 500 nuclear weapons, no doubt they claimed that was the number needed.

The truth is there is no way to define what constitutes a 'minimum' deterrent and no calculation that will provide us with one. The UK at one time considered their contribution to NATO to be able to destroy 40 per cent of the people and infrastructure of Moscow, the so-called 'Moscow criterion'. To do that would theoretically require one megatonne of nuclear power, but there is no reason to think that 40 per cent destruction is any more of a deterrent than 30 per cent or indeed 20 per cent.⁴

The US and Russia both had, at the height of the Cold War, astronomical numbers of nuclear weapons, and they apparently thought they needed every one. As the numbers have come down since then, they continue to make the case that every remaining warhead is somehow necessary 'as a minimum'.

Since, as we have discussed in chapter 3, the whole concept of nuclear deterrence must be questioned, the idea that there can be a 'minimum' number of nuclear weapons that meet this imaginary criteria begins to look quite fanciful.

Replacing or upgrading

The US Nuclear Posture Review of 2010 states that the nuclear modernisation programme underway in the US 'cannot support new military missions or provide for new military capabilities.' Tony Blair gave a similar commitment with regard to Trident renewal in 2007 promising that this would not involve any 'upgrade or expansion' of the current Trident system.⁵ All nine NWSS are currently undertaking modernisation programmes to upgrade their nuclear weapons. And yet there is a widespread belief that nuclear weapons are being 'downgraded' rather than upgraded as the Cold War continues to recede into the fog of history.

As we have just seen, the replacement of Polaris and Poseidon submarine systems with the current Trident system involved a considerable increase in terms of technical advancement.

Further upgrading of the Trident missiles has involved changes to the Arming, Fusing and Firing (AF&F) mechanism which enables Trident missiles to more reliably detonate as a 'groundburst' explosion (see Chapter 2). This increases the ability of Trident to be used as a first strike weapon against Russian hardened missile silos and underground command bunkers. This kind of technical improvement increases the risk of launch-on-warning and therefore must count as an escalation in the nuclear arms race.[6]

The new *Dreadnought* class of submarines now being built for Trident are bigger, better, faster, quieter and more deadly than their Ohio-class and Vanguard-class predecessors. The same goes for more or less every other aspect of the US nuclear arsenal. Enhancements underway to the Minuteman III missiles include more sophisticated targeting systems, new re-entry vehicles, better propellant, and a new guidance system. All these features increase the chances of a missile hitting its target, and thus provoke counter-measures by the Russians to compensate for this.

Russian nuclear modernisation therefore includes more warheads on existing missiles, more sophisticated mobile launch platforms, new generation of cruise missiles, new bomber force and so on. In every NWS, these new technological advancements raise the stakes in terms of the threat posed to each other by nuclear weapons and thus require counter-measures to compensate. This is an arms race not of numbers but of technology.

Summary

The NWSs have reduced their total stockpile of nuclear weapons from a peak of around 70,000 in the mid-1980s to the present number of around 15,000 in total. Most of the warheads that have been withdrawn from service were obsolete, unusable weapons designed for use on the battlefield. It is good that these weapons have been withdrawn, but does it signal an intention on the part of the NWSs to continue reducing their nuclear stockpiles until they reach zero?

The reduction of warheads and of warhead yield does not necessarily represent a real reduction in nuclear firepower but can instead involve a substantial *increase* in the capability of nuclear weaponry to attack and destroy military targets on the other side. Governments talk of having reduced the nuclear stockpile to the 'minimum' needed for deterrence, but there is no way to determine what that minimum actually is.

CHAPTER 17

Would Disarmament by any of the NWSS Have Any Effect?

IT IS THE OLDEST argument in the book: 'If I didn't do it, someone else would be doing it.' And conversely: 'If everyone else is doing it, then there can be no harm in me doing it...'. These arguments can be used to justify pretty much anything, from selling drugs or weapons to cheating on your taxes to falsifying your exhaust emission results.

> We have to have nuclear weapons because 'they' have them. And us getting rid of ours is not going to make a blind bit of difference. So don't expect us to disarm any faster than we have been doing.

Of course, there are national variations on this theme. In the case of the UK, France and China, their line of reasoning is that as long as Russia and the US hold between them 99 per cent of the world's nuclear weapons stockpile, there is no point in talking to *us* about nuclear disarmament. Talk to them! Once they have got their arsenals down to the size of ours, only then can we start discussing how to get rid of our own weapons.

In the case of the US and Russia, it is more of a reciprocal argument: we only have *our* nuclear weapons to protect ourselves from *their* nuclear weapons. We cannot discuss giving up ours until they have agreed to give up theirs... And between India and Pakistan it is the same story.

But there is another aspect to this argument, which is the assumption that any one of the NWSS deciding to give up their nuclear weapons would make no difference at all – even to the other NWSS. This is a slippery argument which makes no sense at all if you think about it.

As discussed in Chapter 2, nuclear deterrence is all about *perceptions*. It is therefore at least as much about what other countries think as it is about what one's own country actually does. Deterrence theory is primarily about what potential adversaries think, but in the case of NATO, it is also intricately tied into what the US and other NATO countries think and do.

For instance, if the US suddenly decided to give up its nuclear weapons, where would that leave the UK? Even if France decided to give up its nuclear weapons at this stage, it would have profound implications on the 'credibility' of UK deterrence theory, since it would imply that France had calculated that nuclear weapons were no longer needed and/or no longer functioning as a 'deterrent'. How could the UK pretend that its own nuclear weapons were still needed and acting 'every minute of every day' as a deterrent if its closest neighbour had decided otherwise? The same applies in reverse.

The fact is that if any one of the existing nuclear weapon states took the decision to give up its nuclear weapons at this stage, the impact would be significant – not least on the other nuclear weapon states, whose rationale for continuing to maintain their own nuclear arsenal would be put into question.

What influence does one country have?

We looked in Chapter 9 at the question of whether possession of nuclear weapons gives a country a 'seat at the top table' that it would not otherwise have. There is a contradiction between thinking that such a country would lose its influence in the world if it gave up nuclear weapons and thinking that giving up its nuclear weapons would have no influence on any other country.

All the NWSs, and especially the N5, have considerable influence in the world. But as NWSs, they have even more influence on each other.

Despite differences of opinion on many other matters, the interests of these five states coincide perfectly when it comes to nuclear weapons. It seems to be in their collective self-interest to manage the expectations of other countries so as to keep the hope of nuclear disarmament alive while at the same time dampen any sense that this will happen any time soon. The 'N5' meet regularly to review the commitments they have made to successive NPT review meetings, and these meetings are always described as 'cordial', despite all the hard talk about Ukraine and the imposition of sanctions against Russia by US, UK and France.

The N5 regularly vote together at the UN when it comes to voting *against* nuclear disarmament proposals. They often issue joint statements in support of their position as the official nuclear weapons states, as we have seen in Chapter 15. The key stumbling block preventing further progress in multilateral nuclear disarmament is the belief, or the claim, that the security conditions 'are not right' for disarmament at the moment. Another is the claim that 'only a step by step approach' can ensure there is sufficient trust among the NWS for disarmament to take place.

The most pernicious of reasons for the lack of progress is that further disarmament will 'destabilise' international relations and be bad for world. In other words, the NWS want to carry on maintaining their monopoly of nuclear weapons and have no real intention of giving them up.

What are the possible implications of disarming?

So what would happen internationally if any one of the NWSs decided to eliminate its arsenal of nuclear weapons? We cannot know the future, of course, but we can postulate what might be some of the reactions from the other N5 NWS, from the other non-N5 NWS (especially India, Pakistan and Israel), from the non-nuclear states who nonetheless come under the nuclear 'umbrella' of NATO and from the other non-nuclear weapon states.

The N5, as the world's premier nuclear 'club', would be devastated to have one of their number break ranks and renounce their nuclear weapons. Officially they would undoubtedly say that they 'fully accept the sovereign will of the people' and might even try to downplay its implications, saying that, 'of course, they have a right to do this in order to save money at a time of austerity', and that this 'in no way reduces the resolve of the other four NWS to continue their efforts to maintain international peace and security through nuclear deterrence' and so on.

Privately, the other NWS would almost certainly be worried what impact this might have on their own public opinions and elected assemblies. After all, if one country has decided it no longer 'needs' nuclear weapons, why should any other country 'need' them? Public opinion in the US would be particularly affected by a decision like this, for all the reasons mentioned above. No doubt some in Congress would call for the US to increase its nuclear weapons arsenal to make up the difference for the loss and some would no doubt be calling for sanctions against the disarming country 'abandoning' its commitments to the US and to NATO, leaving NATO 'exposed', shifting even more of the nuclear 'burden' on to US taxpayers...

There might even be calls in the US Congress for the US to pull out of Europe and leave them to their 'fate' if they are not willing to pull their weight in NATO. We have heard all of this before during crucial periods of the Cold War and even as recently as 2015 when President Obama castigated Europeans for not spending enough on defence. This kind of talk could also, however, lead to calls for a further *reduction* in the US arsenal and a cutting of the huge expenditure currently being used to upgrade every aspect of the US nuclear arsenal. If one of the NWSs is pulling out of the nuclear business, why should the US continue carrying such a heavy burden for the NATO nuclear 'umbrella'?

Once one country decides to give up its nuclear weapons and people notice that it is not suddenly invaded by the Russians as a result, all kinds of questions might start to surface as to why other NWS need to hold on to theirs. The spell would be broken. This could lead to renewed calls for the US and the Russians to go back to the negotiating table and make some progress in further reducing their arsenals. China in particular, which has a much smaller nuclear arsenal than the US or Russia, might be tempted to renounce its nuclear weapons. There is no guarantee that this would happen, of course, but China has consistently been the one member of the N5 club with the least vested interest in the status quo and thus most likely to 'break out' of the club.

India and Pakistan, as former British colonies and members of the British Commonwealth, both have hugely important ties with the UK, not least because there are nearly 2.5 million people of Indian or Pakistani origin living in the UK. The UK has had very little leverage on the governments of India and Pakistan when it comes to nuclear weapons precisely because the UK has always insisted on its own right to have them. On what grounds could the UK tell India or Pakistan that they should not have them as well?

Renouncing nuclear weapons in the UK, however, while in and of itself might not have that big an impact on countries like India and Pakistan, if coupled with a newly energised zeal for promoting a nuclear-free world and encouraging other countries to also disarm, could have a much larger effect.

One of the stumbling blocks to a more comprehensive peace in the Middle East has been that Israel maintains nuclear weapons and continues to block any progress towards a nuclear-weapons-free zone for the Middle East. How might this be affected by a country like the UK renouncing its nuclear weapons?

We looked at the NATO question in more detail in Chapter 11, but here it is worth noting that NATO is already hugely divided internally on the issue of nuclear weapons. Were any NWS to renounce its nuclear weapons, this would be likely to bring the issue out into the open and almost certainly encourage further questioning of NATO's reliance on nuclear weapons. Public opinion in countries like Belgium, Germany and the Netherlands is already very divided on nuclear weapons. This could easily push the governments of those three countries to review their continued deployment of the B-61 nuclear bombs as part of their NATO nuclear-sharing arrangements, for example.

By far the biggest impact of any decision to end dependency on nuclear weapons would be felt in the 150 or more non-nuclear, non-NATO countries which have been demanding for years that the NWS disarm. It is hard to imagine the scale of the shock, disbelief and then utter jubilation that might follow such a decision. It could be as significant as South Africa giving up apartheid or the Berlin Wall coming down in terms of global impact.

Even if the impact on the US and other NWS was minimal and muted, the impact on the rest of the world would be such that the US and other NWS could hardly be unaffected by it. There is already a large global movement calling for the total elimination of nuclear weapons. This boost to their campaign would send shock-waves through the capitals of the NWS and enormously boost the indigenous anti-nuclear movements in countries like the US.

Sooner or later, one of the nuclear weapons states has to be the first to go non-nuclear. It could be the UK, it could be China – it could even be the US. The rationale for maintaining nuclear weapons grows weaker and weaker every day, while the threat they pose and the risk that one will go off by accident or by design grows stronger. With more than 50 countries already signed on to the Nuclear Ban Treaty, as many as 146 countries willing to sign it, and 115 countries already inside nuclear-free zones, the time will soon come when the pressure to disarm is no longer possible to contain.

Summary

What might be the impact internationally, if a single NWS announced it would give up its nuclear weapons?? Would it be 'dangerous and destabilising' or would it have no effect at all? While it is impossible to know for certain, it is likely that the impact would be significant and mostly positive.

The US might well react negatively and even lash out with some kind of punitive response were the UK or France to exit the nuclear club. This is because such an exit would immediately put the US under new and powerful pressure to do likewise. It would undermine their existing rationale for needing nuclear weapons themselves.

Other NATO countries would almost certainly welcome such an exit and it could well create a new momentum for a radical renewal of NATO's nuclear posture. It would likely lead to renewed calls in Belgium, Netherlands and Germany for an end to deployment of US nuclear weapons in those countries. Some would no doubt interpret this as 'de-stabilising' to the NATO alliance. For others it would be a welcome step forward.

In the rest of the world, a decision to renounce nuclear weapons by any one of the existing NWSs would almost certainly be received with nothing short of jubilation. While it may matter more to some politicians what the US government thinks than what assorted third world governments think, there can be little doubt that a country's stature among the vast majority of the world's countries would soar in the event of a break out from the nuclear club.

For more than 50 years, the 'big five' nuclear weapons states have maintained an iron grip on their nuclear status and refused to let go of it. For any of the NWS, to take the first step towards total elimination of its nuclear weapons would be electrifying and create a whole new international environment for further steps toward nuclear disarmament.

PART SIX

The Bomb is Here to Stay

CHAPTER 18

'But You Can't Uninvent the Bomb'

SINCE WE CANNOT 'uninvent' nuclear weapons – put the genie back in the bottle, so to speak – they are with us forever. The best we can hope for is to manage them safely and responsibly and hope they are never used. This is the final argument of those who grow impatient with the whole issue of disarmament and creating a nuclear-free world. 'It's simply not possible,' they insist.

It is undeniably true that nuclear weapons cannot be 'uninvented'. The knowledge of how to make them is not only out there, it is in the public domain and freely available on the internet. Even if all nuclear weapons were dismantled and the world was declared nuclear-free, what's to stop any country at any time from building new ones?

Here is where we must get practical as well as philosophical. Yes, it will always remain possible for someone to build a nuclear weapon no matter what steps are taken to achieve global nuclear disarmament. But, first of all, is that an argument to continue indefinitely holding on to nuclear weapons? As we have seen in Chapter 3, having nuclear weapons may or may not 'deter' someone else from attacking that country. If an aggressor is determined to attack or destroy another country, having nuclear weapons cannot stop them. And if the world abolished nuclear weapons and some regime somewhere was determined to defy the international community and build them anyway, how likely is it that such a regime would be deterred from using them?

The possession of nuclear weapons does not prevent another country from obtaining their own nuclear weapons, nor is it likely to deter them from using them if that is what they intend to do. Either way, the fact that you can't uninvent nuclear weapons or prevent other countries from obtaining them is not in itself an argument to hold on to nuclear weapons. Surely it is in fact *less* likely that a rogue regime would want to have their own nuclear weapons *or* want to target them at a country if that country itself did not have any?

The case of poison gas

You cannot uninvent poison gas, or other chemical or biological weapons, either. It is far easier for any country to make their own chemical weapons than it is for them to make their own nuclear weapons, as we shall see below. Yet poison gas was not used in WWII, even though both sides had vast stockpiles of it. All chemical weapons have now been banned by international treaty and although they were allegedly being used in Syria, those weapons have now largely been removed under the terms of the Chemical Weapons Convention. Countries like the UK once maintained stockpiles of chemical weapons and continued to develop new ones right up to the time of the Convention, but they have now destroyed their stockpiles and ceased to develop chemical weapons (as far as we know).

The truth is that even if something has been invented and cannot be uninvented, that does not mean we have to live with it. Even in the nuclear weapons field, many different types of weapon and delivery system have been tried and even deployed in the field before being withdrawn as unworkable, too dangerous, outmoded or just plain crazy. As we saw in chapter 16, these have included deployment of nuclear warheads to be fired from the back of a jeep, nuclear 'demolitions' bombs strapped onto the back of a soldier to be hand-placed in the battlefield and nuclear depth-bombs dropped from ships and helicopters. The biggest H-bombs of the Cold War era have all been dismantled by now for the same reasons.

Ward Wilson, in his book *Five Myths about Nuclear Weapons*, describes all sorts of weapons systems and other technologies which have become obsolete and long-since abandoned.[1] Why should nuclear weapons not share the same fate as these?

Most countries do not have nuclear weapons

Out of 193 member states of the United Nations at present, only nine are known to have nuclear weapons. That means 184 countries do not. Twenty-nine of those countries come under the NATO or other nuclear 'umbrella' relationships with the US, but still they do not have nuclear weapons of their own. Many of those 29 are among the 37 who, according to the IAEA have the *capacity* to build nuclear weapons at the present time. Eleven countries have started nuclear weapons programmes and then abandoned them. South Africa built several nuclear weapons before dismantling them and abandoning their nuclear weapons programme. Thirty-one countries have civil nuclear power stations from which they could, if they wished, obtain weapons-grade plutonium. Another 46 countries have uranium deposits from which they could, theoretically, obtain weapons-grade uranium.

So what are the reasons that so few countries in fact have chosen to build and possess nuclear weapons? One reason is the expense. As we have seen in chapter 14, nuclear weapons are hugely expense to build and maintain. The NWSS are currently investing $billions in modernising their weapons systems.

Even these costs do not take into account the years of research and development that have gone into nuclear weapons technology up to now and the enormous costs involved with that. Not many countries have that kind of money to spend on nuclear weapons, or if they did, might choose to spend it on other priorities. Some historians have argued that it was the cost of keeping up with the US in the nuclear arms race that 'broke' the Soviet bank account and caused the collapse of the Soviet Union.[2]

There are many other reasons why the vast majority of countries have chosen not to develop their own nuclear weapons capacity, including all the reasons covered in other chapters of this book – legal, moral, practical, utilitarian and security reasons. Most of all, there is a large and growing consensus throughout the world that nuclear weapons make the world less safe and not more so. Why would anyone choose to develop a weapon that is going to make them less safe?

Tony Blair, in his memoirs, said that if Britain didn't already have nuclear weapons, he wouldn't choose now to acquire them. But then he went on to say that since we *do* have them, we don't want to now get rid of them.[3] For all the reasons we have been looking at in this book, most countries by now realise that the tide has turned on nuclear weapons. They are a weapon of the past, not of the future. But if progress on disarmament is not achieved, will countries such as South Korea, Japan, Egypt and others remain so convinced?

Verifying disarmament

Fortunately for those who want to see a global ban on nuclear weapons, the process for ensuring that countries comply with such a ban is far more straightforward than for, say, chemical weapons or landmines. Because nuclear explosions are so massive, they are very hard to hide. While it is conceivable to produce nuclear weapons without ever testing one, and Israel may have managed to do that, although they probably tested their first weapon jointly with South Africa, most countries that would want to produce a nuclear weapon would want to test it out, not only to see if it works but also to show to the world that they have one.

There is no place left on earth, under the earth or even under the sea, where a nuclear explosion would not be detected by infrared satellite imaging and/or by seismic equipment used for detected earthquakes. So it is literally impossible for a country to test a nuclear weapon without it being known. This is not something that can be said for any other type of weapon system.

To produce a working nuclear weapon also requires a delivery system of some kind – airplane, missile, mobile bomb launcher, whatever. While there may be some rather crude delivery systems available for detonating a nuclear device *in situ* wherever that may be, in most cases delivering a nuclear weapon requires very sophisticated missile technology, which even the UK itself does not have (UK warheads are put on Trident missiles made by the US). Heavy bomber aircraft for delivering nuclear weapons also require a level of sophistication which most countries do not have. Once again, testing of medium or long-range missiles or aircraft is very hard to do in the modern world without detection.

By far the biggest challenge of building a nuclear weapon is not the design, which can be obtained from the internet, but obtaining the raw materials for making the bomb: either highly-enriched uranium or plutonium. The enrichment of uranium is a vastly expensive and complicated process which requires sophisticated and high precision equipment.

Plutonium can be created (it does not exist naturally) in certain designs of nuclear power station, but since civil nuclear power stations can be monitored by the IAEA it is difficult to produce plutonium undetected without withdrawing from the IAEA and sounding a warning bell to the international community as was the case with Iran.

The recent deal reached between Iran and a group of countries trying to prevent it from building a nuclear weapon is a good example of how difficult it is for any country to produce nuclear weapons without being noticed. Of course any country can choose to go ahead anyway, but there may be global consequences for doing so.

In the 1980s, following the INF Treaty which abolished all intermediate-range nuclear weapons in Europe, Russian inspectors were invited onto US bases to verify withdrawal and dismantling of nuclear weapons systems and US inspectors were invited onto Soviet bases to verify the same thing on the other side. In the case of the START Treaty which required destruction of a certain number of existing long-range nuclear bombers on both sides, the US and Russia both chopped up planes into pieces and left them spread out on the ground until satellite reconnaissance from the other side could verify that they had been destroyed.

Summary

While it is not possible to 'uninvent' anything, it is certainly possible to get rid of things we no longer want or need, including obsolete weapons systems. All that is needed is the political will and ways can be found to verify disarmament moves and to monitor compliance.

The reality is that most countries do not have nuclear weapons. Some have the capability to produce nuclear weapons and have chosen not to. Others have developed them or begun developing them and then decided to abandon their nuclear programmes.

Because nuclear weapons are so massive in their destructive power and require such sophisticated and expensive facilities to manufacture, their elimination is much easier than any other weapon to monitor and verify.

There will always be the possibility that an advanced industrialised country could at some point in the future manufacture nuclear weapons if they chose to. Current monitoring and verification technologies mean that it will be much more difficult for them to do so without the rest of the world finding out about it. And in a world in which nuclear weapons have become unacceptable under any circumstances, the norm will be established in which it is less likely that any country will choose to manufacture them once they have been eliminated.

CHAPTER 19

Can Nuclear Weapons be Morally Acceptable?

SIR MICHAEL QUINLAN was a key architect of Britain's nuclear deterrence policy and also a devout member of the Roman Catholic Church. He claimed no contradiction between his work and his Christian faith. Quinlan defended nuclear deterrence on moral grounds, insisting that nuclear weapons, nuclear deterrence and indeed nuclear war could be justified according to the 'just war' criteria of the Roman Catholic Church. The Church of England's General Synod, in February, 1983, appeared to agree with Quinlan when they took the position that nuclear weapons were necessary to the defence of the realm:

> It is the duty of Her Majesty's Government and her allies to maintain adequate forces to guard against nuclear blackmail and deter nuclear and non-nuclear aggressors.

Lesser of two evils

During the Cold War period, public support for nuclear weapons was based largely on the presumption that these weapons were all that was saving the West from being overrun by an evil, 'totalitarian' regime considered by many to be as bad, if not worse, than Hitler's Nazism. That belief was supplemented, especially among Christians, with the threat which 'godless communism' posed to Christianity. 'Better dead than red' was the battle cry for those who rejected the moral arguments for doing away with nuclear weapons.

Even for those who fear or despise Putin and claim we are in a new Cold War with Russia now, the same arguments about godless communism no longer apply. What then, are the moral and/or theological arguments in favour of retaining nuclear weapons in an age where the threat of Communism is no longer relevant and where Russia's prosperity depends on trading relationships with the international community? There are, of course, those moral crusaders who have transferred their fear and loathing from communism to Islamist extremism and describe the world today as a battle for the soul of humanity between Christianity and Islam.

That argument is not relevant with respect to Russia, but could perhaps be used in relation to a possible nuclear threat from Iran, Pakistan or some new form of nuclear-armed Islamic extremist threat to the West. However, even during the crusades against Islam in the 11th century, Christians were expected to follow the rules of just war and to be bound by them.

Just War Theory

In order for a war to be 'just', according to St Augustine of Hippo in the fourth century AD, certain conditions must be met, and these fell into two categories: first, the conditions for *going* to war ('jus ad bellum') and second, the conditions for *waging* war ('jus in bello'). Thomas Aquinas further elaborated on these in the 13th century and they have continued to be refined ever since. While the complete list of just war criteria can vary according to who is compiling it, the most common criteria include the following:

Jus ad bellum:
- Just cause – the reason for going to war must itself be just.
- Competent authority – only a properly constituted authority (ie government) can wage war justly.
- Probability of success – there must be a reasonable chance of winning the war.
- Last resort – all other means short of war must have been tried first.
- Proportionality – the benefits of winning the war must outweigh the expected costs of waging it.

Jus in bello:
- Distinction – acts of war must be targeted at all times at combatants and not at non-combatants.
- Proportionality – any harm to civilians must be proportionate to the military advantage to be gained.
- Military necessity – war must be conducted, and targets of attack chosen, solely to achieve victory.
- Fair treatment of prisoners of war – no torture or mistreatment.
- No means *malum in se* – no inherently 'evil' or inhumane weapons to be used.

Sir Michael Quinlan believed that these criteria could be met, even in the case of a nuclear war.[1] However, few theologians today would agree with him. In 1982, a Working Party of the Church of England, under the chair of John Baker, Bishop of Salisbury, produced a detailed and comprehensive examination of Britain's nuclear weapons policy as seen from a moral perspective. This was entitled *The Church and the Bomb: Nuclear weapons and Christian conscience*[2] and it was a significant contribution to the debate at that time. The report called for the UK's renunciation of its 'independent nuclear deterrent', cancellation of (the original) nuclear weapons and a phased withdrawal of all nuclear weapons.[3]

> It is in our view proven beyond reasonable doubt that the Just War theory, as this has developed in Western civilisation and within the Christian Church, rules out the use of nuclear weapons...[4]

As we have already seen in Chapter 12, the legal requirements for waging war are based largely on the distinction between combatants and non-combatants, the latter being protected under a whole raft of international conventions and protocols from the indiscriminate and disproportionate effects of warfare.

When it comes to nuclear war, these distinctions become quite difficult to sustain, since even the smallest nuclear weapons are extremely powerful. Even if these are targeted at a purely military target, it is hard to imagine that civilian populations would not be severely affected. This is especially the case because of the uniquely harmful properties of ionising radiation and the fact that radioactive fallout can travel considerable distances before coming down to contaminate people who have nothing to do with the fighting or may even be in a neutral third country which has specifically chosen to stay out of the fight.

The reality is that the vast majority of nuclear weapons in the world today are *not* minimum yield, 'small' nuclear weapons but in fact weapons many times more powerful than those dropped on Hiroshima and Nagasaki.

To what extent can weapons capable of destroying a medium to large size city be considered 'proportionate' or 'discriminate'?

Retaliation

In terms of the actual use of nuclear weapons, we described in Chapter 1 the two situations in which they might conceivably be used:

1. In a first strike against a nuclear weapon state, either threatening to invade or in the process of invading.
2. In a second, or retaliatory, strike after being hit by one or more nuclear weapons.

In the second of these two situations, where the 'deterrent' has failed and a country has already been hit by nuclear weapons, would it be morally right to retaliate?

We live in a society which uses punishment to change behaviour. We punish children for doing something wrong and we punish criminals for doing something wrong. Surely, we also punish a country for launching weapons of mass destruction against us.

There are, however, legal as well as moral restrictions on the forms of punishment we use. It is no longer legal in most countries to inflict corporal punishment on children, nor to inflict capital punishment on convicted criminals. Punishment, like war, is required to be proportionate and discriminating. In particular, 'collective punishment' of a whole community for the sins of one or a few of them, as condoned in the days of the Old Testament, is now considered illegal and immoral, since it does not discriminate between those who are perpetrators and those who are innocent.

It is children, elderly, sick and disabled people who often suffer the most from collective forms of punishment. These are probably the least culpable for whatever the punishment is in response to. Dropping nuclear weapons on another country as an act of retaliation is therefore a disproportionate and indiscriminate form of collective punishment at best. At worst, it is nothing other than an act of revenge – a lashing out in anger against someone (or in this case a very large number of people) to compensate for a loss or tragedy for which those particular people may not even be directly responsible. Can that ever be morally acceptable?

First strike

When it comes to a first strike with nuclear weapons, under what conditions might this be considered morally acceptable? Let us make the assumption that this is genuinely in the interests of self-defence. A country is being invaded and in order to stop the invading army from gaining a foothold they are bombed.

Let us make the further assumption that in this scenario all diplomatic efforts have failed, that every precaution has been made to target the invading army in such a way as to minimise civilian casualties, that the yield is 'small' and will mostly kill troops and destroy their tanks and other vehicles or ships. Are the conditions of just war sufficiently met to allow for a moral justification for the use of nuclear weapons, at least under these very limited circumstances and within the boundaries of just war theory?

To be the first to use a nuclear weapon in a world which has so far avoided any use of nuclear weapons since the first bombs were dropped in 1945 would be a big step. It is hard to imagine that it would be met with anything other than horror and opprobrium from every corner of the world. It is also hard to imagine the scenario above matching any kind of real life situation, since an invading army would by definition be very near, or already on, the territory of the country being invaded. Thus bombing them with nuclear weapons would mean, in effect, dropping nuclear bombs on the country being invaded rather than on the country doing the invading. The use of a 'small' nuclear weapon which would be able to minimize destruction beyond the military target itself is likely to be ineffectual. Such a scenario would then lead to more such bombs being dropped, moving us all into a full-scale nuclear war and far beyond the limits of just war theory.

Inhumane weapons

In any conceivable scenario in which we might be tempted to claim that it could fit within the criteria for a just war, we must finally look at the last of these criteria, the injunction against use of weapons that are in themselves inherently evil or inhumane. Weapons which 'unnecessarily aggravate the sufferings of disabled men, or render their death inevitable' fall under this category. That was the basis on which the exploding bullet was outlawed in 1868,[5] the dum-dum bullet in 1899[6] and asphyxiating, poisonous and other gases in 1925.[7]

Nuclear weapons, as we have seen, have the unique property of releasing large quantities of highly dangerous radiation, not only into the immediate surroundings but also high up into the atmosphere where it can be carried for thousands of miles. The effects of radiation also vary, but even at relatively low levels can cause sterility, long-terms cancers and leukaemia as well as birth defects in subsequent generations. At higher levels it destroys cells and internal organs, damages blood and bone marrow and causes other debilitating diseases that lead to death over a matter of days, weeks or months.

It is hard to see how a weapon like this can be considered 'humane' even when used only on combatants, since it would inevitably cause unnecessary and prolonged suffering not only to the soldiers themselves but to their progeny as well.

Just war revisited

Just as some lawyers will continue to argue that the use of nuclear weapons can be legal under international law, some Christian theologians will continue to argue that the use of nuclear weapons can be morally justified in terms of just war theory. The reality, however, is that the nature of nuclear weapons makes a mockery of both these arguments.

In a statement to the Vienna Conference on the Humanitarian Impacts of Nuclear Weapons, Pope Francis declared that

> the provisional justification [the church] once gave for possession of nuclear weapons for the sake of 'deterrence' during the Cold War is no longer valid... Now is the time to affirm not only the immorality of the use of nuclear weapons, but the immorality of their possession, thereby clearing the road to nuclear abolition.[8]

Other faiths

Other religions too have spoken out on the morality of nuclear weapons. They all contain injunctions against killing and especially against the indiscriminate killing of women, children or other unarmed non-combatants.

In the Quran, for instance, it is clear that there are 'limits' to fighting and killing, even in the case of jihad: 'Fight in the cause of God those who fight you, but do not transgress limits; for God loveth not transgressors.'[9] These limits, according to Islamic scholars, include protecting the innocent: 'Do not kill women, children, the old, or the infirm; do not cut down fruit-bearing trees; do not destroy any town...'[10] The limits also forbid aggression and suggest that violence is only acceptable when it is in response to violence: 'Fight in the way of God against those who fight against you, but begin not hostilities. Lo! God loveth not aggressors.'[11] and 'if the enemies incline towards peace, do you also incline towards peace.'[12]

In Judaism, war is only permitted in self-defence and only after every effort has been made to make peace. There are many rabbinic and other traditions in Judaism which severely restrict what is allowed to take place in war, including an unusual requirement in the Talmud explicitly prohibiting the waging of war that involves killing more than one-sixth of the population in the process.[13] The protection of non-combatants and prisoners is also of paramount concern:

> The soldier shall make use of his weaponry and power only for the fulfilment of the mission and solely to the extent required; he will maintain his humanity even in combat. The soldier shall not employ his weaponry and power in order to harm non-combatants or prisoners of war, and shall do all he can to avoid harming their lives, body, honour and property.[14]

In Eastern religions,[15] there is a much stronger emphasis on nonviolence and non-killing in general. Interestingly, there are some ancient texts which expressly forbid the use of weapons of mass destruction. For example, in the Ramayana (Hindu scripture) Lakshmana tells Rama that he has a weapon of war that could destroy the entire race of the enemy, including non-combatants. Rama advises Lakshmana that destruction en masse is forbidden by the ancient laws of war, even if the enemy is unrighteous.[16]

From a humanist, or 'non-theist' perspective, the dignity and worth of every human life is also central to any consideration of morality. A weapon that is so shocking in its ability to kill, maim and genetically damage future generations and the environment cannot meet the test of being morally acceptable.

Ethics of deterrence

If the use of nuclear weapons cannot be justified on moral grounds, what about the concept of nuclear deterrence? We have already seen that nuclear deterrence is nothing other than a threat to use them, and for that threat to be 'credible' the government must be ready and willing to actually use them. Moreover there must be, in effect, a declared intention to use them after deterrence has failed. We have also seen in Chapter 12 that in legal terms, a threat or conspiracy or intention to commit an illegal act such as murder is legally equivalent to having committed it and in many cases leads to an equivalent prison sentence.

Sir Michael Quinlan was himself the first to admit that nuclear deterrence rests solely on the willingness to actually use nuclear weapons. If it cannot be morally justified to use these weapons, it cannot be morally justified to threaten to use them, nor to possess them for possible future use nor to base a defence policy around the threat to use them. 'Security policies based around the threat of the use of nuclear weapons are immoral and ultimately self-defeating...' says the UK Multi-Faith Statement on Nuclear Weapons.[17]

But there is in fact a further moral argument against nuclear deterrence itself as a concept. For the whole concept of nuclear deterrence, as we have seen in Chapter 3, rests on the idea that at the very moment of intense crisis, when the very survival of the state is at stake, political leaders on both sides of a potential nuclear conflagration will be able to rationally weigh up the costs and benefits of different options for nuclear escalation and de-escalation and make the correct calculations that the theory of deterrence tells them they should make.

In a series of letters between Michael Quinlan and the theologian, Walter Stein, Stein makes the charge that this kind of thinking is 'deliberately irresponsible' because it assumes that rational decision-making will take place in a situation where there has been 'catastrophic loss of control', 'unparalleled pressures of time, shock and uncertainty,' resulting in 'critical vulnerabilities of command and control systems'. Stein calls this 'not just a mere occasion of sin, but a consent to the evils built into the strategy that are inescapable consequences of that strategy'.[18]

In other words, as we know in fact from the Cuban Missile Crisis, the concept of nuclear deterrence inevitably puts people in situations where they cannot be expected to make perfectly rational decisions and yet the survival of the human race depends precisely upon them making perfectly rational decisions under those very circumstances. That in itself is not only irrational but irresponsible, as Stein puts it, because we are simply setting ourselves up for a disaster, in this case the ultimate disaster.

Summary

All of world's major religions include in some form or other the basic principle, 'thou shalt not kill'. In Eastern religions, this has tended to be taken more literally than in the West, where philosophers and theologians have tried for centuries to define and codify the exceptions to this rule.

According to the various formulations of 'just war' theory, killing can only ever be justified, even in warfare, if certain conditions are met. Principle among these are the requirements to target only combatants and legitimate military targets, to limit the killing to that which is absolutely necessary for victory and not even to initiate hostilities unless there is a strong likelihood of success and other means short of war have been tried and failed.

Many of the just war criteria are already enshrined in the various conventions and protocols that form the laws of war in a strictly legal sense. But the moral criteria go beyond this, by challenging the very notion of a war which by definition no one can 'win.' Can the potential unleashing of all-out nuclear war, threatening the very survival of life itself ever be morally justified?

Can anyone, with any degree of confidence, claim that the use of a single nuclear weapon will not unleash a chain of events leading to an all-out nuclear war? Even the hypothetical case of a potentially 'legal' use of low-yield nuclear weapon to destroy invading ships while still on the high seas cannot meet this moral standard, since it is first of all unlikely in this day and age that such an attack would be 'successful' in and of itself. And secondly, it is impossible to predict what might follow as a result of such an attack.

Comparatively 'low-yield' nuclear weapons were removed from the European continent and eliminated from the arsenals of both sides because it was realised that these made all-out nuclear war more likely rather than less likely. Low-yield nuclear weapons lower the threshold for using any nuclear weapons and once nuclear weapons are used, no one can predict where it will stop.

The use of low-yield nuclear weapons risks escalating a small-scale conflict into all-out nuclear war. The use of high yield nuclear weapons risks endangering all life on Earth. An 'airburst' nuclear attack against cities would result in the mass slaughter of innocent civilians whilst a 'groundburst' nuclear attack on purely military targets risks radioactive fallout killing, injuring, and causing genetic damage to people in faraway neutral countries and even in the country that fires the weapon.

Launching a nuclear weapon against a country which does not itself have nuclear weapons would be an act of aggression that should attract global condemnation, while launching nuclear weapons against another country with nuclear weapons could result in nuclear retaliation.

Launching nuclear weapons in a 'first strike' means being willing to accept both the global condemnation and nuclear retaliation, while launching them in retaliation after being attacked is not only pointless but is also an act of pure revenge for which there can be no moral justification.

In seeking to justify the possession of nuclear weapons, as opposed to the actual use of nuclear weapons, the argument is often made that possession prevents use. Indeed, it was Sir Michael Quinlan's belief that by preventing war, nuclear weapons were actually a moral 'good'. But as he himself pointed out, 'weapons deter by the possibility of their use, and by no other route'.[19]

Possession of nuclear weapons, in and of itself, is not a moral issue if there is no possibility to ever use them. However, the concept of nuclear deterrence depends not only on the 'possibility' of their use but on the *willingness* to use them, and indeed on the *intention* to use them if and when the circumstances are deemed appropriate. Otherwise it would be utterly pointless to have them and 'deterrence' would be meaningless.

Possessing nuclear weapons with the intention to use them, even if only in the extreme circumstance where the very survival of the state is at stake, is a moral issue of immense proportions. It means that the state stands ready to destroy not only an 'enemy' population but also its *own* population in the belief that by doing so it would somehow 'protect' itself as a state. What moral code, anywhere, gives a state that kind of absolute supremacy over its own citizens?

Morality, surely, is not about laws or commandments or even moral codes. It is about the dignity and respect which we afford to each other as human beings. Nuclear weapons and all the language that goes with them are about as far removed from the universe of human morality as it is possible to be.

CHAPTER 20

Do Nuclear Weapons Fit the World of Today?

THOSE OPPOSING nuclear weapons are sometimes labelled 'starry-eyed idealists' living in 'La-La Land', with no idea of what the real world is actually like. The real world is assumed to be one in which nuclear weapons play a necessary and important role in the affairs of state, and that it is therefore unrealistic to imagine a situation in which nuclear weapons would no longer be present. Much of this thinking goes back, not just to the Cold War, but the dark days of 1940, when the world was being overrun by Fascist and Nazi regimes that seemed bent on global domination.

> A British Prime Minister would never give up Britain's place as a nuclear weapon state as long as the memory of 1940, standing alone and the Battle of Britain, remained fresh...
> Sir Frank Cooper, former permanent secretary of the MOD[1]

The world of 1940 and the world of today

In 1940, the United States was not a major player on the world stage. It was busy re-building after a devastating depression, and was trying to stay out of the wars raging in both Europe and Asia. Britain, on the other hand, was an empire with over 50 colonial 'possessions' all over the world, including the whole of the Indian sub-continent, huge swathes of Africa and the Middle East and a large part of the Caribbean. It was still a period of history when countries went around claiming 'colonies', invading and occupying each other and fighting wars to increase their territorial possessions or to gain access to land and raw materials.

In 1940 there was no NATO, no OSCE, no EU and no UN. There was no World Court, no Geneva Convention, no Universal Declaration of Human Rights, no Amnesty International, no Oxfam, no Christian Aid. There was no body of knowledge known as peace research or peace studies, little understanding of mediation or conflict resolution or of the processes of interpersonal communication and negotiation.

Very few people had their own telephone in 1940. Most people had not ever been on an aeroplane. Immigration from former European colonies in Asia, Africa and the Caribbean had not yet begun, so Britain, and most of Europe, was overwhelming white and Christian.

That world is part of history. We now live in a shrinking world that is increasingly interconnected, with instantaneous communications, internet, mobile phones and television in every home. People see the world on their smartphones and TV screens. They travel the world with ease.

The community of nations

The world of the 21st century is not just one in which we are all more closely connected with each other at a personal level. The problems facing any one country such as climate change, terrorism and even housing or the rise of income inequalities, are not problems that can be solved by that country alone. The global economy links countries intimately to what is happening economically in other countries, just as the climate of one country is directly affected by the carbon produced by other countries.

When it comes to international disputes and crises, it is no longer the case that one country is left on its own to deal with them. The United Nations system, comprising not only the General Assembly and the Security Council, but another 33 specialised agencies, programmes and international bodies, monitors and supports the daily needs of billions of people around the world. For all its faults and shortcomings, the UN system and the body of international law it has created, make the world a far safer place for far more of the world's population than ever before in human history. We live in a world populated by over 40,000 non-governmental organisations. They work in every country of the world and help to hold governments accountable, to monitor press freedoms, to protect human rights, to respond to international emergencies, to support families and communities in need and to build a fairer and safer world for all.

What does this mean in terms of the reliance on nuclear weapons? Undoubtedly, the world remains an unstable and uncertain place. Wars continue to happen, along with terrorism, genocide and other forms of oppression, tyranny and violence. But is it up to any one country to respond to any of these unilaterally (or in sole bilateral partnership with the US only)?

The reality is that we are all part of a global community of around 200 independent states that need to work together to solve global problems and resolve disputes when they arise. These states are legally committed to the principles and procedures laid down in the UN charter for achieving this. This is the 'real world' of the 21st century. There is no place in this world for nuclear weapons and most countries have accepted that: 115 out of 193 countries in the world already live in nuclear-free zones which outlaw the presence of nuclear weapons. One hundred and thirty-five countries took part in the UN negotiations that created the 2017 Treaty on the Prohibition of Nuclear Weapons; and 37 countries have the capacity to develop nuclear weapons but have chosen not to.

> Nuclear weapons are held by a handful of states, which insist that these weapons provide unique security benefits and yet reserve uniquely to themselves the right to own them. The situation is highly discriminatory and thus unstable; it cannot be sustained.[2]
> Canberra Commission

The emerging global norm

A very small number of countries are fighting to retain nuclear weapons in the face of persistent and growing calls for their total elimination. These calls come from the vast majority of other states, but also from eminent and respected world leaders who have put their names to a growing list of commissions, reports, statements and initiatives demanding the total elimination of all nuclear weapons. The Canberra Commission, for instance, consisted of the sitting Australian Prime Minister at the time, Paul Keating, former President of France Michel Rocard, former US Secretary of Defence and architect of deterrence theory Robert McNamara, former UK Chief of Defence Staff Field Marshall Lord Carver and others of that professional standing.

Other mainstream, 'realpolitik' figures who have in recent years put their name to the goal of eliminating all nuclear weapons include former US Secretary of State Henry Kissinger, former Commander of US Strategic Air Command General Lee Butler, and former US Secretary of State George Schultz.

In the UK, senior military officers like Lord Carver, Lord Mountbatten, Commander Robert Green and Sir Hugh Beach have long signalled their opposition to nuclear weapons. More recently, however, former Chief of the Defence Staff Field Marshal Lord Bramall, General Lord Ramsbotham and Major-General Patrick Cordingley, erstwhile Commander of the 7th Armoured Brigade, among others, have added their names to the growing list of military professionals opposed to nuclear weapons.[3]

These are not starry-eyed pacifists or people with their heads in the clouds. These are people who have worked with nuclear weapons and engaged with nuclear deterrence, who now think better of it. While it is perhaps regrettable that most of these people made their views known about nuclear weapons after retiring from public life, nonetheless it is important that these voices are heard, especially by those who still support nuclear weapons and the theory of nuclear deterrence.

Summary

The final insult thrown at those who believe that a nuclear-free world is possible is that they are living in 'La-La Land'. The 'real world', as we are told all too often, consists of states, the dynamics of state power, competition between states, and war, deterrence and nuclear weapons. But which of these is the 'real world'?

We live on a small, increasingly interconnected and interdependent planet with high-speed travel and trade that bring people from every corner of the globe together like never before. A community of nearly 200 independent states interact with each other on the basis of commonly agreed principles and practices that are laid down in a huge and growing body of treaties and international law.

None of this existed in 1940, when Britain stood alone against Hitler and developed the mindset for having its own nuclear 'deterrent'. The world was an utterly different place. In 1940, people still thought it was acceptable to have 'colonies' and for the British Empire to lord itself over a fifth of the world's population without their consent or participation. In 1940, people still accepted the idea that countries had a right to invade and occupy other countries purely to increase their own territory or gain access to raw materials.

But that is not the 'real world' of the 21st century and there is no going back to such a world. While there are still wars and conflicts and new forms of terrorism to contend with, these are vastly outnumbered by the number of peace treaties being signed, the number of military dictatorships which have been transformed into democracies, and the number of dialogues, discussions and negotiations which have averted wars and ended bloodshed across the globe.

Nuclear weapons are no more of the 'real world' of today than colonialism, slavery or apartheid. In fact, politicians and civil servants in the nuclear weapons states are living inside a 'bubble', where talk of 'needing' nuclear weapons for our security appears normal and talk of nuclear disarmament is scandalous.

The multilateral nuclear disarmament initiatives that have been repeatedly boycotted or voted against by the NWSS have had overwhelming support from the vast majority of other countries. A growing number of statesmen and women, including high ranking generals and others who have worked with and been responsible for nuclear weapons, have come out saying that nuclear weapons must go.

Pursuing nuclear disarmament is not 'La-La Land'. It is the real world of the 21st century.

PART SEVEN
Wrapping it all up

CHAPTER 21

The Truth About Nuclear Weapons

SO WHAT IS the truth about nuclear weapons? The truth is that we live in a world that is not as it was in 1939–40, when Britain stood alone against Nazi Germany and prevented an invasion by a combination of wits, luck, geography, will power, enormous self-sacrifice and the skill of some RAF fighter pilots. The idea that nuclear weapons would protect any country in a similar situation is not only outmoded but dangerous, since it assumes that country can act independently and to its own ends in a world that is increasingly interdependent and interconnected.

Nuclear weapons are weapons of mass destruction. Most nuclear warheads are many times more powerful than the bomb dropped on Hiroshima. One UK nuclear weapons submarine alone contains more destructive power than was dropped on Germany and Japan throughout the whole of WWII, *including* the bombs dropped on Hiroshima and Nagasaki. If any country were ever to use one of these weapons, even against purely military targets, it would cause millions of deaths and millions more injuries. The radioactive fallout would cause deaths and injuries, not only where the weapon was used but around the world. Climate change affecting global food supplies could not be ruled out as another possible result.

The theory of nuclear deterrence rests on the threat to use these weapons if an aggressor were ever to threaten or attack. That threat is only credible if there is the political and military will to actually use these weapons under those circumstances. No deterrent can be 100 per cent effective and the longer we play the deterrence game, the greater the chances of a nuclear weapon being used, by accident or by design.

We know from WWII that mass destruction of cities does not in itself win wars or even dent the war-fighting capability of a determined adversary. There is therefore little reason to suppose that the threat of mass destruction of cities by nuclear weapons, any more than by conventional weapons, is an effective deterrent. Although Japan surrendered shortly after the atom bombs were dropped on Hiroshima and Nagasaki, there is strong evidence to suggest that these were not the deciding factor in ending the war.

Even during the darkest days of the Cold War, had an overwhelmingly larger and more powerful adversary like the Soviet Union *chosen* to invade and occupy Western Europe, nuclear weapons would probably not have stopped them.

The Cold War is now over, and yes, the world is a dangerous and uncertain place – made especially so by the existence of nearly 15,000 nuclear weapons. Do these 15,000 nuclear weapons make the world safer? Or is it closer to the truth to say that on balance, the continued possession of nuclear weapons actually makes the world *less* safe?

Security in today's world does not come from military might, or from threatening other countries with nuclear destruction. It comes from working effectively with others through multilateral institutions such as the UN to ensure that *all* countries are secure from threats like fascism, genocide, megalomaniacal attempts at global domination and other ideologies that potentially threaten all of us.

Only by working incessantly to ensure that *no* country has nuclear weapons can we be protected from the threat of nuclear weapons ourselves. By insisting that any country has an inalienable right to possess nuclear weapons for their own security, they are merely encouraging other countries to follow their example. A world in which every country possesses nuclear weapons for their own security is an infinitely more dangerous place than a world in which there are no nuclear weapons.

Does a nuclear-free world sound utopian? Perhaps if it does, it is worth pondering for a moment on the alternative. The longer the nuclear weapon states go on claiming that they need these weapons for their security, the greater the likelihood becomes of one of these weapons being used. This is not just because of the mind games involved in convincing oneself that these weapons are still 'credible' as a deterrent. It is a simple matter of statistics. The chances of an accident or miscalculation are always going to increase the longer a system this risky is kept in place.

If the detonation of a single nuclear warhead somewhere in the world triggers a 'launch on warning' retaliatory strike because it is assumed to have been an act of war by Russia or the US, even if launched by another country, then we are all finished as a human species. All-out nuclear war spells the end of human civilisation as we know it.

If, on the other hand, a nuclear detonation goes off somewhere and yet does *not* trigger all-out nuclear war, perhaps hundreds of thousands of people will be dead, depending on where it goes off. Millions more will be homeless, facing various forms of radiation sickness and other diseases. The world's humanitarian response agencies will be totally overwhelmed by the unprecedented scale of such a disaster. If the disaster happens in London, or Glasgow, or New York or New Delhi or Moscow or Tel Aviv or Beijing, the repercussions will be immense, not only on the immediate victims but on the surrounding infrastructure that a whole country may be dependent upon.

What is likely to be the overwhelming response of the world community to such an unprecedented disaster resulting from a single nuclear explosion somewhere in the world? With one voice the world will be crying out, 'Get rid of these weapons NOW before that can ever happen again!' Why wait for a catastrophe of unparalleled proportions before deciding to do what is already the obvious thing and get rid of these weapons once and for all? Either we do the right thing now or we wait until disaster strikes and we do it then. That is the choice before us.

In fact, the NWSS are already morally and legally obligated to eliminate their nuclear weapons. In signing the Non-Proliferation Treaty in 1967, these states committed themselves to negotiating nuclear disarmament 'in good faith' and 'at an early date'. In 1995, the NWSS reiterated their commitment to this goal with an 'unequivocal undertaking' to fulfil their obligation to disarm.

All of the arguments covered in the first half of this book are in fact irrelevant if it is accepted that the NWSS must disarm in accordance with their legal commitments. To argue that a country 'needs' nuclear weapons when it has already agreed to get rid of them is nonsensical. The only question that should be on the table is how nuclear disarmament can best be achieved. Unfortunately, the NWSS continue to vote against multilateral disarmament initiatives, to boycott multilateral nuclear disarmament negotiations currently taking place and to obstruct the efforts of the vast majority of other countries to achieve a global ban on nuclear weapons. These actions do not indicate a commitment to acting 'in good faith' to achieve nuclear disarmament 'at an early date'.

The deeper truth about nuclear weapons is that by retaining them, seemingly for an indefinite future, the NWSS are signalling their defiance to the rest of the world and to the commitments made to them. They are saying to the world, 'we remain willing, indefinitely, to threaten the very survival of the planet in order to somehow 'defend' ourselves from unknown future threats'. What kind of partner does that make them in the community of nations? What message does it send, not just to other countries, but to our own communities and our own children? Can we retain nuclear weapons and still retain our dignity as human beings and our respect for other human beings on this small and precious planet of ours?

30 'Truths' About Nuclear Weapons

1. An all-out nuclear war between the US and Russia would have such catastrophic consequences that we cannot rule out the possibility that it would extinguish all life on earth.

2. A more 'limited' regional nuclear war, for instance between India and Pakistan, North and South Korea, or Israel and Iran, would still cause such devastation and climactic changes that there is the possibility of up to two billion people dying from starvation alone.

3. Launching the warheads from a single UK Trident submarine could result in the deaths of more than five million people even if aimed at purely 'military' targets in Russia, for example.

4. Just one nuclear weapon going off, by accident or by design, anywhere in the world, would be sufficient to cause a humanitarian catastrophe of unparalleled proportions.

5. The theory that nuclear weapons are in and of themselves purely a 'deterrent' is unproven and riddled with contradictions.

6. A deterrent can fail, and is increasingly likely to be used in order to remain 'credible' as a deterrent.

7. Deterrence depends on the leaders of another country being sufficiently sane and rational to make a calculated decision that attacking a country with nuclear weapons would have more costs than benefits, while at the same time assuming that our own leaders under the same circumstances will be insane and irrational enough to follow through with a nuclear attack if the attacker called the bluff.

8. Use of nuclear weapons against another nuclear weapon state would almost certainly result in a devastating nuclear attack in retaliation since many nuclear weapons may be at sea or on mobile launchers, ready to strike back.

9. Nuclear weapons were probably not the main cause of Japan's surrender in WWII and in general, the bombing of cities, whether with conventional bombs or nuclear weapons, is not what wins wars.

10. If bombing of cities does not win wars, then the threat of bombing cities, as in nuclear deterrence, is unlike to deter a potential aggressor from attacking.

11. Nuclear weapons are probably not the cause of relative 'peace' between the major powers since 1945 or the reason the Soviet Union never attacked the West. There are many other more plausible reasons.

12 The longer countries with nuclear weapons continue to maintain that they are 'necessary' for national defence, the more likely other countries will seek to obtain their own.

13 A world awash with nuclear weapons is an infinitely more dangerous one than a world with no nuclear weapons at all.

14 Nuclear weapons make a country more of a target, for nuclear attack as well as for terrorism.

15 Nuclear weapons do not guarantee a country a seat at the top table. These countries play a leading role in the world because they are major industrial nations with a long history.

16 To use a nuclear weapon would be illegal under international law as it would cause disproportionate and indiscriminate harm to civilians, long-term damage to neutral countries, unnecessary and prolonged suffering to combatants and genetic damage to future generations. To threaten an illegal act is legally tantamount to the same thing.

17 It is absurd to think that countries can continue to develop, build and deploy nuclear weapons indefinitely without them ever being used.

18 Nuclear accidents, mishaps and errors of judgment are occurring all the time and it is only luck that has prevented a major catastrophe so far. The longer we maintain these weapons the greater the chance of an accident becomes.

19 The full cost of maintaining a nuclear arsenal is out of all proportion to other military and social expenditure.

20 The P5's voting record at the UN and in other multilateral forums makes it clear that they are not acting 'in good faith' to achieve nuclear disarmament.

21 The NWSS have also agreed to an 'unequivocal undertaking' to eliminate their nuclear weapons.

22 The current upgrading of nuclear weapons by all NWSS simply fuels an ongoing arms race that threatens to continue escalating and could make the new systems obsolete before they are even deployed.

23 The nuclear disarmament which has taken place so far has involved removing mostly obsolete and useless weapons as well as the most unstable and dangerous ones.

24 We know nuclear disarmament is possible because it has already been done in places like South Africa.

25 Any NWS choosing to eliminate its nuclear arsenal would potentially have an electrifying effect on other countries and spur global efforts for the complete elimination of all nuclear weapons

26 Getting rid of all existing nuclear weapons and effectively monitoring all potential nuclear activity to prevent any country building a nuclear arsenal is perfectly doable and most of the mechanisms are already in place.

27 Nuclear weapons are morally indefensible according to all major world religions as well as from a humanist perspective. They cannot meet the test of a 'just war'.

28 Nuclear weapons are not a form of defence. All they can do is cause massive destruction and death in the aftermath of an attack, they cannot prevent such an attack.

29 War never has been an efficient or effective way to deal with conflicts between or within states. The sooner we commit to peaceful ways of resolving conflicts the safer we will all be.

30 The dictum 'if you want peace, prepare for war' has led to 25 centuries of war, not 25 centuries of peace. If we want peace, we must prepare for peace and rule out war – and especially nuclear war – as an option.

In a speech which went largely unnoticed, at the height of the Cold War in 1979, the late Admiral of the British Fleet, Lord Louis Mountbatten of Burma, made his views on this matter very clear:

> As a military man who has given half a century of active service, I say in all sincerity that the nuclear arms race has no military purpose. Wars cannot be fought with nuclear weapons. Their existence only adds to our perils because of the illusions which they have generated. There are powerful voices around the world who still give credence to the old precept, 'if you desire peace, prepare for war'. This is absolute nuclear nonsense...

'I am not asserting this without having deeply thought about the matter,' he added, going on to say:

> When I was Chief of the British Defence Staff, I made my views known. I have heard the arguments against this view but I have never found them convincing. So I repeat in all sincerity, as a military man I can see no use for any nuclear weapons which would not end in escalation, with consequences that no one can conceive.[1]

APPENDIX I

Treaty on the Non-Proliferation of Nuclear Weapons (NPT)

The States concluding this Treaty, hereinafter referred to as the Parties to the Treaty,

Considering the devastation that would be visited upon all mankind by a nuclear war and the consequent need to make every effort to avert the danger of such a war and to take measures to safeguard the security of peoples,

Believing that the proliferation of nuclear weapons would seriously enhance the danger of nuclear war,

In conformity with resolutions of the United Nations General Assembly calling for the conclusion of an agreement on the prevention of wider dissemination of nuclear weapons,

Undertaking to co-operate in facilitating the application of International Atomic Energy Agency safeguards on peaceful nuclear activities,

Expressing their support for research, development and other efforts to further the application, within the framework of the International Atomic Energy Agency safeguards system, of the principle of safeguarding effectively the flow of source and special fissionable materials by use of instruments and other techniques at certain strategic points,

Affirming the principle that the benefits of peaceful applications of nuclear technology, including any technological by-products which may be derived by nuclear-weapon States from the development of nuclear explosive devices, should be available for peaceful purposes to all Parties to the Treaty, whether nuclear-weapon or non-nuclear-weapon States,

Convinced that, in furtherance of this principle, all Parties to the Treaty are entitled to participate in the fullest possible exchange of scientific information for, and to contribute alone or in co-operation with other States to, the further development of the applications of atomic energy for peaceful purposes,

Declaring their intention to achieve at the earliest possible date the cessation of the nuclear arms race and to undertake effective measures in the direction of nuclear disarmament,

Urging the co-operation of all States in the attainment of this objective,

Recalling the determination expressed by the Parties to the 1963 Treaty banning nuclear weapons tests in the atmosphere, in outer space and under water in its Preamble to seek to achieve the discontinuance of all test explosions of nuclear weapons for all time and to continue negotiations to this end,

Desiring to further the easing of international tension and the strengthening of trust between States in order to facilitate the cessation of the manufacture of nuclear weapons, the liquidation of all their existing stockpiles, and the elimination from national arsenals of nuclear weapons and the means of their delivery pursuant to a Treaty on general and complete disarmament under strict and effective international control,

Recalling that, in accordance with the Charter of the United Nations, States must refrain in their international relations from the threat or use of force against the territorial integrity or political independence of any State, or in any other manner inconsistent with the Purposes of the United Nations, and that the establishment and maintenance of international peace and security are to be promoted with the least diversion for armaments of the world's human and economic resources,

Have agreed as follows:

Article I

Each nuclear-weapon State Party to the Treaty undertakes not to transfer to any recipient whatsoever nuclear weapons or other nuclear explosive devices or control over such weapons or explosive devices directly, or indirectly; and not in any way to assist, encourage, or induce any non-nuclear-weapon State to manufacture or otherwise acquire nuclear weapons or other nuclear explosive devices, or control over such weapons or explosive devices.

Article II

Each non-nuclear-weapon State Party to the Treaty undertakes not to receive the transfer from any transferor whatsoever of nuclear weapons or other nuclear explosive devices or of control over such weapons or explosive devices directly, or indirectly; not to manufacture or otherwise acquire nuclear weapons or other nuclear explosive devices; and not to seek or receive any assistance in the manufacture of nuclear weapons or other nuclear explosive devices.

Article III

1. Each non-nuclear-weapon State Party to the Treaty undertakes to accept safeguards, as set forth in an agreement to be negotiated and concluded with the International Atomic Energy Agency in accordance with the Statute of the International Atomic Energy Agency and the Agency's safeguards system, for the exclusive purpose of verification of the fulfilment of its obligations assumed under this Treaty with a view to preventing diversion of nuclear energy from peaceful uses to nuclear weapons or other nuclear explosive devices. Procedures for the safeguards

required by this Article shall be followed with respect to source or special fissionable material whether it is being produced, processed or used in any principal nuclear facility or is outside any such facility. The safeguards required by this Article shall be applied on all source or special fissionable material in all peaceful nuclear activities within the territory of such State, under its jurisdiction, or carried out under its control anywhere.

2. Each State Party to the Treaty undertakes not to provide: (a) source or special fissionable material, or (b) equipment or material especially designed or prepared for the processing, use or production of special fissionable material, to any non-nuclear-weapon State for peaceful purposes, unless the source or special fissionable material shall be subject to the safeguards required by this Article.

3. The safeguards required by this Article shall be implemented in a manner designed to comply with Article IV of this Treaty, and to avoid hampering the economic or technological development of the Parties or international co-operation in the field of peaceful nuclear activities, including the international exchange of nuclear material and equipment for the processing, use or production of nuclear material for peaceful purposes in accordance with the provisions of this Article and the principle of safeguarding set forth in the Preamble of the Treaty.

4. Non-nuclear-weapon States Party to the Treaty shall conclude agreements with the International Atomic Energy Agency to meet the requirements of this Article either individually or together with other States in accordance with the Statute of the International Atomic Energy Agency. Negotiation of such agreements shall commence within 180 days from the original entry into force of this Treaty. For States depositing their instruments of ratification or accession after the 180-day period, negotiation of such agreements shall commence not later than the date of such deposit. Such agreements shall enter into force not later than eighteen months after the date of initiation of negotiations.

Article IV

1. Nothing in this Treaty shall be interpreted as affecting the inalienable right of all the Parties to the Treaty to develop research, production and use of nuclear energy for peaceful purposes without discrimination and in conformity with Articles I and II of this Treaty.

2. All the Parties to the Treaty undertake to facilitate, and have the right to participate in, the fullest possible exchange of equipment, materials and scientific and technological information for the peaceful uses of nuclear energy. Parties to the Treaty in a position to do so shall also co-operate in contributing alone or together with other States or international organizations to the further development of the applications of nuclear energy for peaceful purposes, especially in the territories of non-nuclear-weapon States Party to the Treaty, with due consideration for the needs of the developing areas of the world.

Article V

Each Party to the Treaty undertakes to take appropriate measures to ensure that, in accordance with this Treaty, under appropriate international observation and through appropriate international procedures, potential benefits from any peaceful applications of nuclear explosions will be made available to non-nuclear-weapon States Party to the Treaty on a non-discriminatory basis and that the charge to such Parties for the explosive devices used will be as low as possible and exclude any charge for research and development. Non-nuclear-weapon States Party to the Treaty shall be able to obtain such benefits, pursuant to a special international agreement or agreements, through an appropriate international body with adequate representation of non-nuclear-weapon States. Negotiations on this subject shall commence as soon as possible after the Treaty enters into force. Non-nuclear-weapon States Party to the Treaty so desiring may also obtain such benefits pursuant to bilateral agreements.

Article VI

Each of the Parties to the Treaty undertakes to pursue negotiations in good faith on effective measures relating to cessation of the nuclear arms race at an early date and to nuclear disarmament, and on a treaty on general and complete disarmament under strict and effective international control.

Article VII

Nothing in this Treaty affects the right of any group of States to conclude regional treaties in order to assure the total absence of nuclear weapons in their respective territories.

Article VIII

1. Any Party to the Treaty may propose amendments to this Treaty. The text of any proposed amendment shall be submitted to the Depositary Governments which shall circulate it to all Parties to the Treaty. Thereupon, if requested to do so by one-third or more of the Parties to the Treaty, the Depositary Governments shall convene a conference, to which they shall invite all the Parties to the Treaty, to consider such an amendment.

2. Any amendment to this Treaty must be approved by a majority of the votes of all the Parties to the Treaty, including the votes of all nuclear-weapon States Party to the Treaty and all other Parties which, on the date the amendment is circulated, are members of the Board of Governors of the International Atomic Energy Agency. The amendment shall enter into force for each Party that deposits its instrument of ratification of the amendment upon the deposit of such instruments of ratification by a majority of all the Parties, including the instruments of ratification of all nuclear-weapon States Party to the Treaty and all other Parties which, on the date the amendment is circulated, are members of the Board of Governors of the International Atomic Energy Agency. Thereafter, it shall enter into force for any other Party upon the deposit of its instrument of ratification of the amendment.

3. Five years after the entry into force of this Treaty, a conference of Parties to the Treaty shall be held in Geneva, Switzerland, in order to review the operation of this Treaty with a view to assuring that the purposes of the Preamble and the provisions of the Treaty are being realised. At intervals of five years thereafter, a majority of the Parties to the Treaty may obtain, by submitting a proposal to this effect to the Depositary Governments, the convening of further conferences with the same objective of reviewing the operation of the Treaty.

Article IX

1. This Treaty shall be open to all States for signature. Any State which does not sign the Treaty before its entry into force in accordance with paragraph 3 of this Article may accede to it at any time.

2. This Treaty shall be subject to ratification by signatory States. Instruments of ratification and instruments of accession shall be deposited with the Governments of the United Kingdom of Great Britain and Northern Ireland, the Union of Soviet Socialist Republics and the United States of America, which are hereby designated the Depositary Governments.

3. This Treaty shall enter into force after its ratification by the States, the Governments of which are designated Depositaries of the Treaty, and 40 other States signatory to this Treaty and the deposit of their instruments of ratification. For the purposes of this Treaty, a nuclear-weapon State is one which has manufactured and exploded a nuclear weapon or other nuclear explosive device prior to 1 January 1967.

4. For States whose instruments of ratification or accession are deposited subsequent to the entry into force of this Treaty, it shall enter into force on the date of the deposit of their instruments of ratification or accession.

5. The Depositary Governments shall promptly inform all signatory and acceding States of the date of each signature, the date of deposit of each instrument of ratification or of accession, the date of the entry into force of this Treaty, and the date of receipt of any requests for convening a conference or other notices.

6. This Treaty shall be registered by the Depositary Governments pursuant to Article 102 of the Charter of the United Nations.

Article X

1. Each Party shall in exercising its national sovereignty have the right to withdraw from the Treaty if it decides that extraordinary events, related to the subject matter of this Treaty, have jeopardized the supreme interests of its country. It shall give notice of such withdrawal to all other Parties to the Treaty and to the United Nations Security Council three months in advance. Such notice shall include a statement of the extraordinary events it regards as having jeopardized its supreme interests.

2. Twenty-five years after the entry into force of the Treaty, a conference shall be convened to decide whether the Treaty shall continue in force indefinitely, or shall

be extended for an additional fixed period or periods. This decision shall be taken by a majority of the Parties to the Treaty.

Article XI

This Treaty, the English, Russian, French, Spanish and Chinese texts of which are equally authentic, shall be deposited in the archives of the Depositary Governments. Duly certified copies of this Treaty shall be transmitted by the Depositary Governments to the Governments of the signatory and acceding States.

IN WITNESS WHEREOF the undersigned, duly authorized, have signed this Treaty.

DONE in triplicate, at the cities of London, Moscow and Washington, the first day of July, one thousand nine hundred and sixty-eight.

Note: On 11 May 1995, in accordance with Article X, paragraph 2, the Review and Extension Conference of the Parties to the Treaty on the Non-Proliferation of Nuclear Weapons decided that the Treaty should continue in force indefinitely (see Decision 3).

APPENDIX II

Summary of Advisory Opinion of the International Court of Justice on the Legality of the Threat or Use of Nuclear Weapons, 8 July 1996

THE COURT
(1) By thirteen votes to one,
Decides to comply with the request for an advisory opinion;
IN FAVOUR: President Bedjaoui; Vice-President Schwebel; Judges Guillaume, Shahabuddeen, Weeramantry, Ranjeva, Herczegh, Shi, Fleischhauer, Koroma, Vereshchetin, Ferrari Bravo, Higgins;
AGAINST : Judge Oda;
Replies in the following manner to the question put by the General Assembly:
A. Unanimously,
There is in neither customary nor conventional international law any specific authorization of the threat or use of nuclear weapons;
B. By eleven votes to three,
There is in neither customary nor conventional international law any comprehensive and universal prohibition of the threat or use of nuclear weapons as such;
IN FAVOUR President Bedjaoui; Vice-President Schwebel; Judges Oda, Guillaume, Ranjeva, Herczegh, Shi, Fleischhauer, Vereshchetin, Ferrari Bravo, Higgins;
AGAINST Judges Shahabuddeen, Weeramantry, Koroma;
C. Unanimously,
A threat or use of force by means of nuclear weapons that is contrary to Article 2, paragraph 4, of the United Nations Charter and that fails to meet all the requirements of Article 51, is unlawful;
D. Unanimously,
A threat or use of nuclear weapons should also be compatible with the requirements of the international law applicable in armed conflict, particularly those of the principles and rules of international humanitarian law, as well as with specific obligations under treaties and other undertakings which expressly deal with nuclear weapons;
E. By seven votes to seven, by the President's casting vote,
It follows from the above-mentioned requirements that the threat or use of nuclear weapons would generally be contrary to the rules of international law applicable in

armed conflict, and in particular the principles and rules of humanitarian law;
However, in view of the current state of international law, and of the elements of fact at its disposal, the Court cannot conclude definitively whether the threat or use of nuclear weapons would be lawful or unlawful in an extreme circumstance of self-defence, in which the very survival of a State would be at stake;
IN FAVOUR: President Bedjaoui; Judges Ranjeva, Herczegh, Shi, Fleischhauer, Vereshchetin, Ferrari Bravo;
AGAINST: Vice-President Schwebel; Judges Oda, Guillaume, Shahabuddeen, Weeramantry, Koroma, Higgins;

APPENDIX III

Treaty on the Prohibition of Nuclear Weapons

The States Parties to this Treaty,

Determined to contribute to the realization of the purposes and principles of the Charter of the United Nations,

Deeply concerned about the catastrophic humanitarian consequences that would result from any use of nuclear weapons, and recognizing the consequent need to completely eliminate such weapons, which remains the only way to guarantee that nuclear weapons are never used again under any circumstances,

Mindful of the risks posed by the continued existence of nuclear weapons, including from any nuclear-weapon detonation by accident, miscalculation or design, and emphasizing that these risks concern the security of all humanity, and that all States share the responsibility to prevent any use of nuclear weapons,

Cognizant that the catastrophic consequences of nuclear weapons cannot be adequately addressed, transcend national borders, pose grave implications for human survival, the environment, socioeconomic development, the global economy, food security and the health of current and future generations, and have a disproportionate impact on women and girls, including as a result of ionizing radiation,

Acknowledging the ethical imperatives for nuclear disarmament and the urgency of achieving and maintaining a nuclear-weapon-free world, which is a global public good of the highest order, serving both national and collective security interests,

Mindful of the unacceptable suffering of and harm caused to the victims of the use of nuclear weapons (hibakusha), as well as of those affected by the testing of nuclear weapons,

Recognizing the disproportionate impact of nuclear-weapon activities on indigenous peoples,

Reaffirming the need for all States at all times to comply with applicable international law, including international humanitarian law and international human rights law,

Basing themselves on the principles and rules of international humanitarian law, in particular the principle that the right of parties to an armed conflict to choose methods or means of warfare is not unlimited, the rule of distinction, the prohibition against indiscriminate attacks, the rules on proportionality and precautions in attack, the prohibition on the use of weapons of a nature to cause superfluous injury or unnecessary suffering, and the rules for the protection of the natural environment,

Considering that any use of nuclear weapons would be contrary to the rules of international law applicable in armed conflict, in particular the principles and rules of international humanitarian law,

Reaffirming that any use of nuclear weapons would also be abhorrent to the principles of humanity and the dictates of public conscience,

Recalling that, in accordance with the Charter of the United Nations, States must refrain in their international relations from the threat or use of force against the territorial integrity or political independence of any State, or in any other manner inconsistent with the Purposes of the United Nations, and that the establishment and maintenance of international peace and security are to be promoted with the least diversion for armaments of the world's human and economic resources,

Recalling also the first resolution of the General Assembly of the United Nations, adopted on 24 January 1946, and subsequent resolutions which call for the elimination of nuclear weapons,

Concerned by the slow pace of nuclear disarmament, the continued reliance on nuclear weapons in military and security concepts, doctrines and policies, and the waste of economic and human resources on programmes for the production, maintenance and modernization of nuclear weapons,

Recognizing that a legally binding prohibition of nuclear weapons constitutes an important contribution towards the achievement and maintenance of a world free of nuclear weapons, including the irreversible, verifiable and transparent elimination of nuclear weapons, and determined to act towards that end,

Determined to act with a view to achieving effective progress towards general and complete disarmament under strict and effective international control,

Reaffirming that there exists an obligation to pursue in good faith and bring to a conclusion negotiations leading to nuclear disarmament in all its aspects under strict and effective international control,

Reaffirming also that the full and effective implementation of the Treaty on the Non-Proliferation of Nuclear Weapons, which serves as the cornerstone of the nuclear disarmament and non-proliferation regime, has a vital role to play in promoting international peace and security,

Recognizing the vital importance of the Comprehensive Nuclear-Test-Ban Treaty and its verification regime as a core element of the nuclear disarmament and non-proliferation regime,

Reaffirming the conviction that the establishment of the internationally recognized nuclear-weapon-free zones on the basis of arrangements freely arrived at among the States of the region concerned enhances global and regional peace and security, strengthens the nuclear non-proliferation regime and contributes towards realizing the objective of nuclear disarmament,

Emphasizing that nothing in this Treaty shall be interpreted as affecting the inalienable right of its States Parties to develop research, production and use of nuclear energy for peaceful purposes without discrimination,

Recognizing that the equal, full and effective participation of both women and men is an essential factor for the promotion and attainment of sustainable peace and security, and committed to supporting and strengthening the effective participation of women in nuclear disarmament,

Recognizing also the importance of peace and disarmament education in all its aspects and of raising awareness of the risks and consequences of nuclear weapons for current and future generations, and committed to the dissemination of the principles and norms of this Treaty,

Stressing the role of public conscience in the furthering of the principles of humanity as evidenced by the call for the total elimination of nuclear weapons, and recognizing the efforts to that end undertaken by the United Nations, the International Red Cross and Red Crescent Movement, other international and regional organizations, non-governmental organizations, religious leaders, parliamentarians, academics and the hibakusha,

Have agreed as follows:

Article 1 Prohibitions

1. Each State Party undertakes never under any circumstances to:

    a. Develop, test, produce, manufacture, otherwise acquire, possess or stockpile nuclear weapons or other nuclear explosive devices;

    b. Transfer to any recipient whatsoever nuclear weapons or other nuclear explosive devices or control over such weapons or explosive devices directly or indirectly;

c Receive the transfer of or control over nuclear weapons or other nuclear explosive devices directly or indirectly;

d Use or threaten to use nuclear weapons or other nuclear explosive devices;

e Assist, encourage or induce, in any way, anyone to engage in any activity prohibited to a State Party under this Treaty;

f Seek or receive any assistance, in any way, from anyone to engage in any activity prohibited to a State Party under this Treaty;

g Allow any stationing, installation or deployment of any nuclear weapons or other nuclear explosive devices in its territory or at any place under its jurisdiction or control.

Article 2 Declarations

1 Each State Party shall submit to the Secretary-General of the United Nations, not later than 30 days after this Treaty enters into force for that State Party, a declaration in which it shall:

   a Declare whether it owned, possessed or controlled nuclear weapons or nuclear explosive devices and eliminated its nuclear-weapon programme, including the elimination or irreversible conversion of all nuclear-weapons-related facilities, prior to the entry into force of this Treaty for that State Party;

   b Notwithstanding Article 1 (a), declare whether it owns, possesses or controls any nuclear weapons or other nuclear explosive devices;

   c Notwithstanding Article 1 (g), declare whether there are any nuclear weapons or other nuclear explosive devices in its territory or in any place under its jurisdiction or control that are owned, possessed or controlled by another State.

2 The Secretary-General of the United Nations shall transmit all such declarations received to the States Parties.

Article 3 Safeguards

1 Each State Party to which Article 4, paragraph 1 or 2, does not apply shall, at a minimum, maintain its International Atomic Energy Agency safeguards obligations in force at the time of entry into force of this Treaty, without prejudice to any additional relevant instruments that it may adopt in the future.

2 Each State Party to which Article 4, paragraph 1 or 2, does not apply that has not yet done so shall conclude with the International Atomic

Energy Agency and bring into force a comprehensive safeguards agreement (INFCIRC/153 (Corrected)). Negotiation of such agreement shall commence within 180 days from the entry into force of this Treaty for that State Party. The agreement shall enter into force no later than 18 months from the entry into force of this Treaty for that State Party. Each State Party shall thereafter maintain such obligations, without prejudice to any additional relevant instruments that it may adopt in the future.

Article 4 Towards the total elimination of nuclear weapons

1. Each State Party that after 7 July 2017 owned, possessed or controlled nuclear weapons or other nuclear explosive devices and eliminated its nuclear-weapon programme, including the elimination or irreversible conversion of all nuclear- weapons-related facilities, prior to the entry into force of this Treaty for it, shall cooperate with the competent international authority designated pursuant to paragraph 6 of this Article for the purpose of verifying the irreversible elimination of its nuclear-weapon programme. The competent international authority shall report to the States Parties. Such a State Party shall conclude a safeguards agreement with the International Atomic Energy Agency sufficient to provide credible assurance of the non-diversion of declared nuclear material from peaceful nuclear activities and of the absence of undeclared nuclear material or activities in that State Party as a whole. Negotiation of such agreement shall commence within 180 days from the entry into force of this Treaty for that State Party. The agreement shall enter into force no later than 18 months from the entry into force of this Treaty for that State Party. That State Party shall thereafter, at a minimum, maintain these safeguards obligations, without prejudice to any additional relevant instruments that it may adopt in the future.

2. Notwithstanding Article 1 (a), each State Party that owns, possesses or controls nuclear weapons or other nuclear explosive devices shall immediately remove them from operational status, and destroy them as soon as possible but not later than a deadline to be determined by the first meeting of States Parties, in accordance with a legally binding, time-bound plan for the verified and irreversible elimination of that State Party's nuclear-weapon programme, including the elimination or irreversible conversion of all nuclear-weapons-related facilities. The State Party, no later than 60 days after the entry into force of this Treaty for that State Party, shall submit this plan to the States Parties or to a competent international authority designated by the States Parties. The plan shall then be negotiated with the competent international authority, which shall submit it to the subsequent meeting of States Parties or

review conference, whichever comes first, for approval in accordance with its rules of procedure.

3. A State Party to which paragraph 2 above applies shall conclude a safeguards agreement with the International Atomic Energy Agency sufficient to provide credible assurance of the non-diversion of declared nuclear material from peaceful nuclear activities and of the absence of undeclared nuclear material or activities in the State as a whole. Negotiation of such agreement shall commence no later than the date upon which implementation of the plan referred to in paragraph 2 is completed. The agreement shall enter into force no later than 18 months after the date of initiation of negotiations. That State Party shall thereafter, at a minimum, maintain these safeguards obligations, without prejudice to any additional relevant instruments that it may adopt in the future. Following the entry into force of the agreement referred to in this paragraph, the State Party shall submit to the Secretary-General of the United Nations a final declaration that it has fulfilled its obligations under this Article.

4. Notwithstanding Article 1 (b) and (g), each State Party that has any nuclear weapons or other nuclear explosive devices in its territory or in any place under its jurisdiction or control that are owned, possessed or controlled by another State shall ensure the prompt removal of such weapons, as soon as possible but not later than a deadline to be determined by the first meeting of States Parties. Upon the removal of such weapons or other explosive devices, that State Party shall submit to the Secretary-General of the United Nations a declaration that it has fulfilled its obligations under this Article.

5. Each State Party to which this Article applies shall submit a report to each meeting of States Parties and each review conference on the progress made towards the implementation of its obligations under this Article, until such time as they are fulfilled.

6. The States Parties shall designate a competent international authority or authorities to negotiate and verify the irreversible elimination of nuclear-weapons programmes, including the elimination or irreversible conversion of all nuclear-weapons-related facilities in accordance with paragraphs 1, 2 and 3 of this Article. In the event that such a designation has not been made prior to the entry into force of this Treaty for a State Party to which paragraph 1 or 2 of this Article applies, the Secretary-General of the United Nations shall convene an extraordinary meeting of States Parties to take any decisions that may be required.

Article 5 National implementation

1. Each State Party shall adopt the necessary measures to implement its obligations under this Treaty.

2. Each State Party shall take all appropriate legal, administrative and other measures, including the imposition of penal sanctions, to prevent and suppress any activity prohibited to a State Party under this Treaty undertaken by persons or on territory under its jurisdiction or control.

Article 6 Victim assistance and environmental remediation

1. Each State Party shall, with respect to individuals under its jurisdiction who are affected by the use or testing of nuclear weapons, in accordance with applicable international humanitarian and human rights law, adequately provide age- and gender-sensitive assistance, without discrimination, including medical care, rehabilitation and psychological support, as well as provide for their social and economic inclusion.

2. Each State Party, with respect to areas under its jurisdiction or control contaminated as a result of activities related to the testing or use of nuclear weapons or other nuclear explosive devices, shall take necessary and appropriate measures towards the environmental remediation of areas so contaminated.

3. The obligations under paragraphs 1 and 2 above shall be without prejudice to the duties and obligations of any other States under international law or bilateral agreements.

Article 7 International cooperation and assistance

1. Each State Party shall cooperate with other States Parties to facilitate the implementation of this Treaty.

2. In fulfilling its obligations under this Treaty, each State Party shall have the right to seek and receive assistance, where feasible, from other States Parties.

3. Each State Party in a position to do so shall provide technical, material and financial assistance to States Parties affected by nuclear-weapons use or testing, to further the implementation of this Treaty.

4. Each State Party in a position to do so shall provide assistance for the victims of the use or testing of nuclear weapons or other nuclear explosive devices.

5. Assistance under this Article may be provided, inter alia, through the United Nations system, international, regional or national organizations

or institutions, non-governmental organizations or institutions, the International Committee of the Red Cross, the International Federation of Red Cross and Red Crescent Societies, or national Red Cross and Red Crescent Societies, or on a bilateral basis.

6 Without prejudice to any other duty or obligation that it may have under international law, a State Party that has used or tested nuclear weapons or any other nuclear explosive devices shall have a responsibility to provide adequate assistance to affected States Parties, for the purpose of victim assistance and environmental remediation.

Article 8 Meeting of States Parties

1 The States Parties shall meet regularly in order to consider and, where necessary, take decisions in respect of any matter with regard to the application or implementation of this Treaty, in accordance with its relevant provisions, and on further measures for nuclear disarmament, including:

   a The implementation and status of this Treaty;

   b Measures for the verified, time-bound and irreversible elimination of nuclear-weapon programmes, including additional protocols to this Treaty;

   c Any other matters pursuant to and consistent with the provisions of this Treaty.

2 The first meeting of States Parties shall be convened by the Secretary-General of the United Nations within one year of the entry into force of this Treaty. Further meetings of States Parties shall be convened by the Secretary-General of the United Nations on a biennial basis, unless otherwise agreed by the States Parties. The meeting of States Parties shall adopt its rules of procedure at its first session. Pending their adoption, the rules of procedure of the United Nations conference to negotiate a legally binding instrument to prohibit nuclear weapons, leading towards their total elimination, shall apply.

3 Extraordinary meetings of States Parties shall be convened, as may be deemed necessary, by the Secretary-General of the United Nations, at the written request of any State Party provided that this request is supported by at least one third of the States Parties.

4 After a period of five years following the entry into force of this Treaty, the Secretary-General of the United Nations shall convene a conference to review the operation of the Treaty and the progress in achieving the purposes of the Treaty. The Secretary-General of the United Nations

shall convene further review conferences at intervals of six years with the same objective, unless otherwise agreed by the States Parties.

5   States not party to this Treaty, as well as the relevant entities of the United Nations system, other relevant international organizations or institutions, regional organizations, the International Committee of the Red Cross, the International Federation of Red Cross and Red Crescent Societies and relevant non-governmental organizations, shall be invited to attend the meetings of States Parties and the review conferences as observers.

Article 9 Costs

1   The costs of the meetings of States Parties, the review conferences and the extraordinary meetings of States Parties shall be borne by the States Parties and States not party to this Treaty participating therein as observers, in accordance with the United Nations scale of assessment adjusted appropriately.

2   The costs incurred by the Secretary-General of the United Nations in the circulation of declarations under Article 2, reports under Article 4 and proposed amendments under Article 10 of this Treaty shall be borne by the States Parties in accordance with the United Nations scale of assessment adjusted appropriately.

3   The cost related to the implementation of verification measures required under Article 4 as well as the costs related to the destruction of nuclear weapons or other nuclear explosive devices, and the elimination of nuclear-weapon programmes, including the elimination or conversion of all nuclear-weapons-related facilities, should be borne by the States Parties to which they apply.

Article 10 Amendments

1   At any time after the entry into force of this Treaty, any State Party may propose amendments to the Treaty. The text of a proposed amendment shall be communicated to the Secretary-General of the United Nations, who shall circulate it to all States Parties and shall seek their views on whether to consider the proposal. If a majority of the States Parties notify the Secretary-General of the United Nations no later than 90 days after its circulation that they support further consideration of the proposal, the proposal shall be considered at the next meeting of States Parties or review conference, whichever comes first.

2   A meeting of States Parties or a review conference may agree upon amendments which shall be adopted by a positive vote of a majority of

two thirds of the States Parties. The Depositary shall communicate any adopted amendment to all States Parties.

3   The amendment shall enter into force for each State Party that deposits its instrument of ratification or acceptance of the amendment 90 days following the deposit of such instruments of ratification or acceptance by a majority of the States Parties at the time of adoption. Thereafter, it shall enter into force for any other State Party 90 days following the deposit of its instrument of ratification or acceptance of the amendment.

Article 11 Settlement of disputes

1   When a dispute arises between two or more States Parties relating to the interpretation or application of this Treaty, the parties concerned shall consult together with a view to the settlement of the dispute by negotiation or by other peaceful means of the parties' choice in accordance with Article 33 of the Charter of the United Nations.

2   The meeting of States Parties may contribute to the settlement of the dispute, including by offering its good offices, calling upon the States Parties concerned to start the settlement procedure of their choice and recommending a time limit for any agreed procedure, in accordance with the relevant provisions of this Treaty and the Charter of the United Nations.

Article 12 Universality

Each State Party shall encourage States not party to this Treaty to sign, ratify, accept, approve or accede to the Treaty, with the goal of universal adherence of all States to the Treaty.

Article 13 Signature

This Treaty shall be open for signature to all States at United Nations Headquarters in New York as from 20 September 2017.

Article 14 Ratification, acceptance, approval or accession

This Treaty shall be subject to ratification, acceptance or approval by signatory States. The Treaty shall be open for accession.

Article 15 Entry into force

1   This Treaty shall enter into force 90 days after the fiftieth instrument of ratification, acceptance, approval or accession has been deposited.

2   For any State that deposits its instrument of ratification, acceptance, approval or accession after the date of the deposit of the fiftieth instrument of ratification, acceptance, approval or accession, this Treaty shall

enter into force 90 days after the date on which that State has deposited its instrument of ratification, acceptance, approval or accession.

Article 16 Reservations

The Articles of this Treaty shall not be subject to reservations.

Article 17 Duration and withdrawal

1. This Treaty shall be of unlimited duration.
2. Each State Party shall, in exercising its national sovereignty, have the right to withdraw from this Treaty if it decides that extraordinary events related to the subject matter of the Treaty have jeopardized the supreme interests of its country. It shall give notice of such withdrawal to the Depositary. Such notice shall include a statement of the extraordinary events that it regards as having jeopardized its supreme interests.
3. Such withdrawal shall only take effect 12 months after the date of the receipt of the notification of withdrawal by the Depositary. If, however, on the expiry of that 12-month period, the withdrawing State Party is a party to an armed conflict, the State Party shall continue to be bound by the obligations of this Treaty and of any additional protocols until it is no longer party to an armed conflict.

Article 18 Relationship with other agreements

The implementation of this Treaty shall not prejudice obligations undertaken by States Parties with regard to existing international agreements, to which they are party, where those obligations are consistent with the Treaty.

Article 19 Depositary

The Secretary-General of the United Nations is hereby designated as the Depositary of this Treaty.

Article 20 Authentic texts

The Arabic, Chinese, English, French, Russian and Spanish texts of this Treaty shall be equally authentic.

DONE at New York, this seventh day of July, two thousand and seventeen.

References

Ainslie, John, 'Sharpening Trident', 2009: [www.swordofdamocles.org].
Ainslie, John, 'Unacceptable Damage: Damage criteria in British nuclear planning', February 2013.
Ainslie, John, 'If Britain fired Trident: the humanitarian consequences of a nuclear attack by a Trident submarine on Moscow', *Scottish CND*, Glasgow, February 2013.
Ainslie, John, 'Substandard: The Trident Whistleblower and the Safety of British Submarines', *Scottish CND*, Glasgow, May 2015.
Ainslie, John 'United Kingdom: Status of UK's Nuclear Forces,' in *Assuring Destruction Forever Reaching Critical Will*, March 2012, (www.reachingcriticalwill.org).
Ainslie, John, 'No place for Trident', *Scottish CND*, Glasgow, 2014.
All Saints Church Kings Heath Social Action Group *The Replacement of Trident* briefing paper, Birmingham (undated).
Aldridge, Robert, *Counterforce Syndrome*, 1978.
Arkin, WM and Handler, Joshua, 'Naval Accidents 1945–1988', *Neptune Papers*, No. 3, IPC, London, 1989.
Brehm, Maya, Moyes, Richard and Nash, Thomas 'Banning Nuclear Weapons' *Article 36* London, February 2013 [www.article36.org/wp-content/uploads/2013/02/Report_web_23.02.13.pdf].
Baker, Rt Rev John Austin, Bishop of Salisbury et al, *The Church and the Bomb*, Hodder and Stoughton, London, 1982.
Baum, Seth D, 'Winter-Safe Deterrence: The Risk of Nuclear Winter and Its Challenge to Deterrence' in *Contemporary Security Policy* 36(1), 14 March 2015.
Baylis, John and Stoddal, Kristian, *The British Nuclear Experience, The Roles of Beliefs, Culture and Identity*, Oxford University Press, Oxford, 2014.
Baylon, Caroline, Brunt, Roger and Livingstone, David, 'Cyber Security at Civil Nuclear Facilities: Understanding the Risks,' *Chatham House, The Royal Institute of International Affairs*, London, September 2015.
Blunt Crispin, 'Figures show crippling costs of renewing Trident' 25 October 2015 [http://www.blunt4reigate.com/news/figures-show-crippling-costs-renewing-trident].
Borrie, John 'A Limit to Safety: Risk, 'normal accidents' and nuclear weapons' *ILPI-UNIDIR Vienna Conference series*, 2014.
Boulton, Frank 'Dangers associated with civil nuclear power programmes' in *Medicine Conflict and Survival*, 31 (1) 2016 p. 6, pps 100–132.

British Bombing Survey Unit, *The Strategic Air War Against Germany 1939–45*, BBS, 1945.
Burroughs, John, *(Il)legality of Threat or Use of Nuclear Weapons: Guide to the Historic Opinion of the ICJ*, LIT, Munster, 1997.
Church of Scotland, *Taking Out Moscow: Conversations About Trident*, St Andrew Press, 1991. ISBN 9780861531486 (out of print).
Campaign for Nuclear Disarmament, *Trident Mythbuster* CND Briefing May 2015.
Chalmers, Malcolm and Walker, William, *Unchartered water: UK, nuclear weapons and the Scottish Question*, Tuckwell Press, 2001.
Church of England Board for Social Responsibility, *Church and the Bomb*, Hodder and Stoughton, London, 1982.
Churchill, Winston, *The Iron Curtain speech* Fulton, Missouri 5 March 1946.
Coates, Ken, ed., *The Carnage Continues, and Now for Trident*, Spokesman, 2006.
Corbyn, Jeremy 'Defence Diversification' August 2015.
Cox, John, *Overkill*, Penguin, Harmondsworth, 1977.
Darnton, Geoffrey Ed., *The Bomb and The Law, London Nuclear Warfare Tribunal; Evidence, Commentary and Judgment*, Alva and Gunnar Myrdal Foundation, Stockholm, 1989.
Fenwick, Toby, 'Trident: An alternative proposal for UK nuclear deterrence' *CentreForum*, February 2015.
Fromkin, David, 'The Strategy of Terrorism' in *Foreign Affairs*, July 1975, Council on Foreign Relations, USA.
Gaddis, John, *The Cold War: A New History*, Penguin, London, 2005.
Gill, David, *Britain and the Bomb*, Stanford University Press, California, 2014.
Glasstone, Samuel and Dolan, Philip J. eds *The Effects of Nuclear Weapons* Third Edition, United States Department of Defense Washington DC, 1977.
Green, Robert, *The Naked Nuclear Emperor*, DSc, Christchurch, NZ, 2000.
Green, Robert, *Security Without Nuclear Deterrence*, Second Edition, Disarmament and Security Centre, Christchurch, NZ, 2014.
Hall, Xanthe, 'Time for Nuclear Sharing to End' *OpenDemocracy.net*, 8 October 2015 (www.opendemocracy.net /can-europe-make-it/xanthe-hall/time-for-nuclear-sharing-to-end).
Hallett, Graham, *European Security in the Post-Soviet Age*, 2007.
Hambling, David, *The Inescapable Net: Unmanned Systems in Anti-Submarine Warfare*, BASIC, 2016
Hammond, Jeremy 'Rogue State: Israeli Violations of UN Security Council Resolutions', in *Foreign Policy Journal*, 27 January 2010: [http://www.foreignpolicyjournal.com/2010/01/27/rogue-state-israeli-violations-of-u-n-security-council-resolutions/].
Hasegawa, Tsuyoshi, *Racing the Enemy: Stalin, Truman and the Surrender of Japan*, Harvard University Press, Boston, 2005.
HM Government 'National Security Strategy and Strategic Defence and Security Review 2015: A Secure and Prosperous United Kingdom' November 2015.
HM Treasury, Spending Review and Autumn Statement, Cm 9162, November 2015:

[https://www.gov.uk/government/uploads/system/uploads/attachment_data/file/479749/52229_Blue_Book_PU1865_Web_Accessible.pdf].
Hennessy, Peter, *Silent Deep* London, Allen Lane, 2015.
Holy See *Pacem In Terris* Encyclical of Pope John XXIII on establishing universal peace in truth, justice, charity and liberty, 11 April 1963.
Holy See *Laudato Si'* Encyclical letter of the Holy Father Francis on Care for our Common Home, 24 May 2015.
House of Bishops, *Who is My Neighbour*, 2015.
Ingram, Paul, *Trident: the need for comprehensive risk assessment* BASIC 23, November 2015.
Ingram, Paul 'Measuring the Financial Costs,' in *Background Papers to the Trident Commission*, BASIC, 2014.
International Law and Policy Institute, 'NATO and a Treaty Banning Nuclear Weapons', [nwp.ilpi.org/?p=2317].
Jamison, Brian, *Britannia's Sceptre: Scotland and the Trident System* Argyll, 2006.
Johnson, Rebecca and Zelter, Angie, *Trident and International Law: Scotland's Obligations*, Luath Press, Edinburgh, 2011.
Kile, Shannon and Kristensen, Hans, 'British Nuclear Forces' in *SIPRI Yearbook 2015*, SIPRI, Stockholm, 2015.
Kristensen, Hans M, Norris, Robert S, Oelrich, I 'From Counterforce to Minimal Deterrence: A New Nuclear Policy on the Path Toward Eliminating Nuclear Weapons *Federation of American Scientists & The Natural Resources Defense Council*, April 2009.
Kristensen, Hans 'British submarines to receive upgraded US nuclear warhead,' *Federation of American Scientists*, 1 April 2011 [http://blogs.fas.org/security/2011/04/britishw76-1/].
Kristensen, Hans and Robert Norris, 'Chinese Nuclear Forces, 2016' in *Bulletin of Atomic Scientists*, 72:4.
Lewis, Patricia, Williams, Heather, Pelopidas, Benoît and Aghlani, Sasan, 'Too Close for Comfort: Cases of Near Nuclear Use and Options for Policy' *Chatham House, The Royal Institute of International Affairs* London, April 2014.
Mills, Claire, *Replacing the UK's Nuclear Deterrent*, House of Commons Library, Briefing Paper, No. 7353, 1 March 2016.
Myritten, Henri, 'Disarming Masculinities' *Disarmament Forum*, 4, UNIDIR: Geneva 2003.
NATO, 'Strategic Concept for the Defence and Security of the Members of the North Atlantic Treaty Organization' Adopted by Heads of State and Government at the NATO Summit in Lisbon 19–20 November 2010.
Norris, Robert S., Burrows Andrew S., and Fieldhous, Richard W, *Nuclear Weapons Data Book*, Westview Press, Boulder, July/August 1994.
Oertel, Janka 'The United Nations and NATO' unpublished draft paper prepared for the ACUNS 21st Annual Meeting, Bonn, Germany, 5–7 June 2008.
Ogilvie-White, Tanya, *On Nuclear Deterrence: The Correspondence of Sir Michael Quinlan*, International Institute of Strategic Studies, London, 2011, p. 11.

Parliamentary Office for Science and Technology, 'Chernobyl Fallout', *Information for Members Briefing Note 45*, July 1993, POST, London.
Pinker, Steven, *The Better Angels of Our Nature: Why Violence Has Declined*, Viking, New York, 2011.
Quinlan, Michael *Thinking about nuclear weapons*, RusI, London, 1997.
Religions for Peace, *Resource Guide on Nuclear Disarmament for Religious Leaders and Communities*, NY, 2013.
Republic of the Marshall Islands *Application Instituting Proceedings Against the United Kingdom*, International Court of Justice, 24 April 2014.
Ritchie, Nick, *Trident in UK Politics and Public Opinion* British American Security Information Council July 2013.
Richie, Nick, *A Nuclear Weapons Free World? Britain, Trident and the Challenge Ahead*, Palgrave MacMillan, London, 2012.
Ritchie, Nick *Response to the Trident Commission Concluding Report* University of York, 23 July 2014.
Rogers, Paul, *Guide to Nuclear Weapons*, Berg, Oxford, 1988.
Rogers, Paul, *The Role of British Nuclear Weapons After The Cold War*, British American Security Information Council, 1995.
Rowe, Dorothy, *Living With the Bomb*, Routledge and Kegan Paul, London, 1985.
Sandia National Laboratories, *Official List of Underground Nuclear Explosions (UNEs) in Nevada*, July 1994, [http://nuclearweaponarchive.org/Usa/Tests/Nevada.html].
Schell, Jonathan, *The Fate of the Earth*, Stamford University Press, 1982.
Schell, Jonathan, *The Unfinished Twentieth Century: The Crisis of Weapons of Mass Destruction*, Verso, London, 2011.
Schlosser, Eric, *Command and Control*, Penguin, London, 2013.
Scientists for Global Responsibility, *Newsletter 35*, Winter 2008.
Schneidmiller, Chris, 'Limited Nuclear War Could Deplete Ozone Layer, Increasing Radiation' *Global Security* Newswire 24, February 2011 [http://www.nti.org/gsn/article/limited-nuclear-war-could-deplete-ozone-layer-increasing-radiation/].
Sebald, WG *On the Natural History of Destruction*, Modern Library, New York, 1999.
Simon, Steven, Bouville, Andre, Land, Charles, 'Fallout from Nuclear Weapons Tests and Cancer Risks' in *American Scientist*, Jan-Feb 2006, vol. 94, no. 1, pp 48ff.
Simma, Bruno, 'NATO, the UN and the Use of Force: Legal Aspects' *EJIL* 10 (1) 1999.
Simpson, Tony, ed, 'Trident Undone', *The Spokesman*, Vol. 127, 2015.
Siracusa, Joseph M, *Nuclear Weapons: A Very Short Introduction*, OUP, Oxford, 2015.
Solomon, Fredric and Marston, Robert Q., *The Medical Implications of Nuclear War*, National Academy Press, Washington, 1986.

Speech at Brookings Institute, quoted in 'Scottish Independence would be Cataclysmic for the West' *Herald Scotland*, 8 April 2014, [http://www.heraldscotland.com/news/13154575.George_Robertson__Scottish_independence_would_be_cataclysmic_for_the_west/].
Stein, Walter Ed., *Nuclear Weapons: A Catholic Response*, Burns and Oates, London, 1963.
Street, Tim, 'Politics of British Nuclear Weapons', Oxford Research Group
Trident Commission, *Concluding Report*, BASIC, 2014 [www.basicint.org/tridentcommission].
Trenin, Dmitri, 'The Drivers of Russia's Foreign Policy' *APPG Global Security and Non-Proliferation* meeting held 3 November 2015.
Twigge, Stephen and Scott, Len, 'The Other Other Missiles of October: The Thor IRBMs and the Cuban Missile Crisis' in *Electronic Journal of International History* (3) 2000.
UK Government, *The Future of the United Kingdom's Nuclear Deterrent* HMSO Norwich December 2006.
UK Ministry of Justice '2012 Compendium of re-offending statistics and analysis' *Ministry of Justice Statistics bulletin* 12 July 2012.
UK Ministry of Defence, FOI Request ICO Case Reference FD50444068, 27 February 2013.
UK Ministry of Defence, FOI Request by Nukewatcher May 2006.
UK Ministry of Defence, *The Future of the United Kingdom's Nuclear Deterrent*, Fact Sheet Four, 1 December 2006.
UK Mission to the UN, *Intervention at Vienna Conference on the Humanitarian Impact of Nuclear Weapons* 8–9 December 2014 [www.gov.uk/government/world-location-news/uk-intervention-at-the-vienna-conference-on-the-humanitarian-impact-of-nuclear-weapons].
United Nations GA 53rd session, 79th plenary meeting, 4 December 1998, New York.
United Nations GA 70th session, Promotion of multilateralism in the area of disarmament and non-proliferation A/C.1/70/L.9, 15 October 2015, New York.
United States Department of Energy, *United States Nuclear Tests July 1945 through September 1992*, DOE/NV--209-REV 15, December 2000.
US NRC, *Reactor Safety Study: An Assessment of Accidental Risks in US Commercial Nuclear Power Plants*, 1975. WASH-1400, NUREG 75/014 [http://www.barringer1.com/mil_files/NUREG-75–014-Report-&-Executive-Summary.pdf].
US Strategic Bombing Survey (USSBS), *Overall Report: European War*, 30 Sept 1945.
Vinthagen, Stella and Kenrick, Justin, *Tackling Trident*, Irene, 2012.
Walker, William, 'Trident – not in our backyard' in *Surging for Oil* eds Lykiard, A, Gorbachev, M and Rogers, P, Spokesman Books, Nottingham, 2007.
Walker, William, 'Trident's Replacement and the Survival of the United Kingdom' *Survival* 57 (5) October – November 2015.

Webber, Phil and Parkinson, Stuart, *UK Nuclear Weapons: A Catastrophe in the Making?* Scientists for Global Responsibility, 2015.

Webber, Phil, 'Could one Trident submarine cause nuclear winter?' 2008 [http://www.sgr.org.uk/climate/NuclearWinterTrident_NL35.pdf].

Wilson, Richard, 'Resource Letter EIRLD-2: Effects of Ionizing Radiation at Low Doses *American Journal of Physics* 80 (1) 2012.

Wilson, Ward, *Five Myths About Nuclear Weapons*, Houghton Mifflin Harcourt, 2013.

YouGov/*The Times Trident Survey* results 25–26 January 2015 [https://d25d2506sfb94s.cloudfront.net/cumulus_uploads/document/ksx1tw2rj8/TimesResults_150126_Trident_Website.pdf].

Zelter, Angie, *Trident on Trial: The Case for People's Disarmament*, Luath Press, Edinburgh, 2001.

Zelter, Angie, ed, *World in Chains*, Luath Press, Edinburgh, 2014.

Stephen Zunes [http://fpif.org/united_nations_security_council_resolutions_currently_being_violated_by_countries_other_than_iraq/].

Endnotes

Chapter 1

1. Fissile materials capable of exploding through 'fission' in a nuclear weapon include highly-enriched uranium-235 (HEU) and plutonium-239. Uranium ore is mined in a number of countries but this contains very little uranium-235, so it must go through a process of 'enrichment' to be concentrated enough to be fissile. Plutonium cannot be mined but must be artificially created in a nuclear power station, where it is a by-product of producing electricity.

2. The largest conventional weapon in the US military is the Massive Ordnance Aerial Bomb, MOAB, or 'Mother of All Bombs'. This causes a blast equivalent to about 11 tonnes of TNT. The smallest nuclear weapons that have been successfully tested were in the region of 10–20 tonnes of TNT (0.01–0.02 KT).

3. The largest nuclear weapon ever tested was the Soviet's 'Tsar Bomba', which was a 50 Megaton bomb, ie 50 million tonnes of TNT. Both the US and Soviets deployed nuclear weapons in the 20–25 Megaton range during the Cold War, although the largest nuclear weapons today are around 8 Megatons.

4. These were Sweden, Japan, Brazil, Argentina, South Korea, Taiwan, Iraq, Libya, Syria, Egypt and Algeria.

5. The NewSTART Treaty, signed by the US and Russian presidents in 2010, sets targets for reducing certain categories of nuclear warheads and delivery vehicles, for both sides to achieve by 2018.

6. See Federation of American Scientists: https://fas.org/issues/nuclear-weapons/status-world-nuclear-forces/

7. See Hans Kristensen and Robert Norris, "Chinese Nuclear Forces, 2016" in Bulletin of Atomic Scientists, 72:4, pp205-211. http://www.tandfonline.com/doi/pdf/10.1080/00963402.2016.1194054

8. Earlier, the figure of 12.5 KT was used as an estimate but it is more common now to use the figure of 15 KT, which is the average of 12–18 KT. The truth is no one knows the exact figure.

9. In 1997, the official register claimed 202,118 killed from the Hiroshima bomb. See http://www.warbirdforum.com/hirodead.htm

10. Temperature of the interior of the sun is estimated to be 7–10 million degrees C, while the interior of a nuclear weapon fireball is estimated to be between 30–100 million degrees C.

11. See Samuel Glasstone and Philip Dolan, eds, *Effects of Nuclear Weapons*, US Department of Defense, Washington, DC, 1977, p 390. Chapter 3 goes into much more detail about the radiological effects of a nuclear explosion.

12. John Ainslie, *Unacceptable Damage*, Feb 2013: [http://www.banthebomb.org/images/stories/pdfs/UnacceptableDamage.pdf].

13 Normal air pressure at sea level is 14.7 psi, so overpressure is how much pressure is applied additional to that.
14 http://www.cdc.gov/niosh/docket/archive/pdfs/niosh-125/125-ExplosionsandRefugeChambers.pdf.
15 Glasstone and Dolan op cit, p. 78.
16 Ainslie, op cit.
17 See Webber, Phil and Parkinson, Stuart, 'UK Nuclear Weapons: A Catastrophe in the Making?' *Scientists for Global Responsibility*, 2015, p. 6. Also Webber, Phil, 'Could one Trident submarine cause nuclear winter?' 2008 [http://www.sgr.org.uk/climate/NuclearWinterTrident_nl35.pdf].
18 See Hefland, Ira, *Nuclear Famine: Two Billion People at Risk?*, International Physicians for the Prevention of War, 2013.
19 Webber, 2008, op cit.

Chapter 2

1 In the US, the 'rad' is still used as a unit of radiation dose. In the rest of the world this has largely been replaced by the 'Gray'. One rad is 1/100th of a Gray. 240
2 The equivalent unit in the US is the 'rem', which is 1/100th of a Sievert.
3 US Dept of Defense, *Effects of Nuclear Weapons*, 1977, p. 607.
4 See Dennis Heresi, 'Dr Louise Reiss, Who Helped Ban Atomic Testing, Dies at 90', in *New York Times*, 10 January 2011 [www.nytimes.com/2011/01/10/science/10reiss.html?r=0].
5 Glasstone and Dolan op cit.
6 Glasstone and Dolan op cit.
7 [http://www.telegraph.co.uk/news/uknews/9156393/Chernobyl-sheep-movement-restrictions-finally-lifted.html].
8 International Physicians for the Prevention of Nuclear Weapon estimate that 430,000 people have already died as a result of nuclear tests, and a further two million will eventually die as a result of cancers and other long-term effects, based on data from US National Research Council and UN Committee on the Effects of Atomic Radiation. See ippnw, *Radioactive Heaven and Earth*, p. 164.
9 Boulton, Frank, 'Dangers associated with civil nuclear power programmes: weaponisation and nuclear waste' in *Medicine, Conflict and Survival*, Vol. 31, 2015, pp. 100–122.

Chapter 3

1 UK Mission to the UN, Intervention at Vienna Conference on the Humanitarian Impact of Nuclear Weapons 8–9 December 2014 [www.gov.uk/government/world-location-news/uk-intervention-at-the-vienna-conference-on-the-humanitarian-impact-of-nuclear-weapons].
2 'To talk about a 'nuclear deterrent' implies acceptance of the doctrine of deterrence, which not all do. Referring to a 'nuclear weapons programme' might be a suitable alternative,' from BBC *News Style Guide*: [http://www.bbc.co.uk/academy/journalism/article/art20130702112133560].
3 US Department of Defence, dictionary of military terms: [www.militaryfactory.com/dictionary/military-terms-defined.asp?term_id=1657].

4   There is considerable controversy around the figures used, but for example, see [http://news.bbc.co.uk/1/hi/uk/4457402.stm].
5   See Ministry of Justice, *Compendium of Re-Offending Statistics and Analysis*, 12 July 2012.
6   Then French President Francois Mitterrand, in his memoirs, said that Mrs Thatcher threatened to nuke Argentina if he did not give her the codes for the French-made missiles threatening British ships. Quoted in Tony Simpson, ed, Trident Undone, p. 34.
7   Ogilvie-White, Tanya, *On Nuclear Deterrence: The Correspondence of Sir Michael Quinlan*, International Institute of Strategic Studies, London, 2011, p. 11.
8   See chapter 6 for examples.

Chapter 4

1   Russia also has mobile ICBM launchers that can be moved between different secret locations on land to achieve the same purpose.
2   Richard Moyes, Phil Webber and Greg Crowther, *Humanitarian Consequences*, Article 36, London, 2013.
3   At present, the main concern is that North Korea might get even a single nuclear missile through US defences, which could have catastrophic consequences on a major US city, for instance, but this would still be a long way from causing the assured destruction of the United States as a country.

Chapter 5

1   General MacArthur estimated Operation Olympic would cost the US 23,000 lives in the first 30 days. Admiral Nimitz estimate was 49,000 and General Norstad claimed it would cost 'half a million' US lives. In his memoirs, President Truman claimed it would have cost at least 250,000 lives but perhaps that was meant to include Japanese military and civilian deaths.
2   Figures vary, but these are generally accepted numbers. See, for instance, [http://www.historynet.com/battle-of-okinawa-operation-iceberg.htm].
3   US Strategic Bombing Survey, *Summary Report: Pacific War*, 1946.
4   The RAF was already a separate wing of the British military, but during WWII all US bombing was conducted by the US Army Air Force (USAAF) and only in 1947 was the USAF established.
5   Statistics from Ward Wilson, *Five Myths About Nuclear Weapons*, Houghton Mifflin Harcourt, 2013.
6   Hasegawa, Tsuyoshi, *Racing the Enemy: Stalin, Truman and the Surrender of Japan*, Harvard University Press, Boston, 2005, p37. See also Wilson, op cit, Chapter 1 and Weber, Mark, 'Was Hiroshima Necessary', *Institute for Historical Review*, Vol. 16, no 3, p4: [http://www.ihr.org/jhr/v16/v16n3p-4_Weber.html].
7   Hasegawa, op cit, p. 108.
8   *Ibid*, p. 71.
9   Truman did not let Stalin sign the Potsdam Proclamation demanding that Japan surrender unconditionally or 'face devastating consequences' because at this point he was hoping the atom bomb would end the war and leave the Soviets out of it.
10 *Ibid*, p. 73.

11 'The evidence is compelling that Soviet entry into the war had a strong impact on the peace party. Indeed, Soviet attack, not the Hiroshima bomb, convinced political leaders to end the war by accepting the Potsdam Proclamation', Hagesawa, p. 198.
12 Wilson, op cit, p. 58.
13 USSBS, Overall Report: European War, 30 Sept 1945, p. 72.
14 *Ibid*, p. 166.
15 Chapter 15 of British Bombing Survey Unit, *The Strategic Air War Against Germany 1939–45, 1945*.
16 Quoted in Gian Gentile, 'Advocacy or Assessment? The US Strategic Bombing Survey of Germany and Japan' in *Pacific Historical Review*, vol 66, no 1, Feb 1997, p. 53.
17 As is usual when it comes to war casualties, the numbers vary enormously.
18 See [http://www.gallup.com/poll/4924/bush-job-approval-highest-gallup-history.aspx]
19 From Wilson, op cit, p77.

Chapter 6

1 As quoted by Margaret Thatcher at Soviet State banquet in Moscow, 30 March, 1987.
2 The Peace Research Institute Oslo (PRIO) counts any violent conflict with more than 1,000 killed in a given year as a 'war' and has totted up more than 258 of these since 1945.
3 Between them, US, UK, France, Russia/Soviet Union, China, Israel, India, Pakistan and North Korea have been involved in at least 44 wars since 1945.
4 The Franco-Prussian War of 1870–71 included a seige of Paris and the deaths of nearly 170,000 combatants. It also sowed the seeds of WWI. But in terms of the length of the war and the number of countries involved, it can be classed as a 'small' war in comparison to the Napolean Wars before it and the World Wars that came after it.
5 Following the Russian revolution of 1917 and their withdrawal from WWI in March 1918, there was an Allied invasion of Russia to try to topple the Bolsheviks, involving troops from Britain, France, the USA, Greece, Japan, China, Poland and Italy.
6 Quoted in Rob Green, *The Naked Nuclear Emperor*, p. 65.
7 See Vladislav Zubok and Constantine Pleshakov, *Inside the Kremlin's Cold War*, Harvard University Press, Cambridge, Ma, 1996, p. 32. Also John Gaddis, *The Cold War: a New History*, Penguin, New York, 2005, p. 11 ff.
8 There was alleged Soviet support to the Spanish Civil War and to attempted coups in Greece and Italy.
9 Steven Pinker uses a formula to calculate war deaths, genocides and other historical data as a proportion of the total human population at the time. This gives a very different picture than looking at absolute figures, since 40 million dead in WWII is much more than two million dead at the hands of Genghis Khan, for instance. But since the world population at the time of Genghis Khan is estimated to have been only a fraction of what it was in the 20th century, Pinker calculates that Genghis Khan killed more of the world's population than Hitler did.
10 USA, UK, France, Russia, China, India, Pakistan, Israel and North Korea (although it is doubted that North Korea has the means to deliver one).
11 Spain did not join NATO until 1982.
12 Also Afghanistan, North Vietnam, North Korea as well as the Eastern European states, all allied to the Soviet Union and/or China.

13 There is no hard evidence that the mujahedeen were being funded by the CIA prior to the Soviet invasion, however the US was funding anti-Soviet forces in virtually every country of the world during the Cold War, so it seems unlikely that they would have avoided Afghanistan, where the pro-Soviet government was repressive and unpopular and there were armed groups already trying to overthrow it.
14 The UK eventually 'won' the Falklands War against Argentina, but that was also no thanks to having nuclear weapons.
15 One of the worrying features of the Chechen War is the fact that Chechen guerillas held out for many months against formidable Russian bombardment after occupying the reinforced bunkers and missile silos of a former Soviet nuclear missile base at Bamut in Chechnya. We must assume that no nuclear materials were still present at the time this site was being heavily bombed, but in fact large quantities of nuclear material went missing during the collapse of the Soviet Union.
16 In fact, Pakistan began testing nuclear weapons in 1983, but these tests did not involve a nuclear detonation and were kept secret until 2000, so they can hardly have acted as a 'deterrent' for Pakistan prior to the public nuclear test detonation in 1998.
17 President Singh of India was encouraged by the international community not to use nuclear weapons on Pakistan. This was not popular in India and he lost the following election.
18 This is disputed but the US installed intermediate range nuclear missiles in Turkey within easy reach of Moscow in 1960. These became operational in 1962 just prior to the Cuban missile crisis. See Ward Wilson, *Five Myths About Nuclear Weapons*, Houghton Mifflin Harcourt, 2013.

Chapter 7

1 BBC1, *Andrew Marr Show*, 8 November 2015. Transcript quoted.
2 NSS/SDSR, Cm9161, p. 24.
3 NSS/SDSR pp. 85–86.
4 [http://large.stanford.edu/courses/2015/ph241/holloway1/docs/si-v10-i1_Kesler.pdf].
5 [http://www.acq.osd.mil/dsb/reports/ResilientMilitarySystems.CyberThreat.pdf].
6 [http://www.theguardian.com/uk-news/2015/nov/24/trident-could-be-vulnerable-to-cyber-attack-former-defence-secretary-says].
7 [http://www.computing.co.uk/ctg/news/2436369/yes-trident-really-could-be-vulnerable-to-a-cyber-attack-warn-experts].
8 UK NSS/SDSR, op cit, p.16
9 See for example [https://zgeography.wordpress.com/2014/02/19/geographic-and-demographic-cleavages-ukraine/].
10 US funding for pro-Western Ukrainian organisations came from USAID, the National Endowment for Democracy, the Open Society Foundation, the US embassy and big name US backers like John McCain. Some have claimed CIA involvement. See 'Brokering Power: us role in Ukraine coup hard to overlook' in *RT*, 19 Feb 2015: [https://www.rt.com/news/233439-us-meddling-ukraine-crisis/].
11 There could now be another contender for this dubious distinction, but it is perhaps too early to say.
12 Some say his only priority is his own survival or that of his family, or of the regime. But neither he nor his regime can survive if his country does not.

Chapter 8

1. See David Hambling, *The Inescapable Net: Unmanned Systems in Anti-Submarine Warfare*, basic, 2016.

Chapter 9

1. Tony Blair, *A Journey*, Hutchinson, London, 2010, pp. 635–636.
2. This number does not include all the resolutions about Israel that have been vetoed by the US over the years. Well over half of all US vetoes in the UN Security Council have been about Israel. Stephen Zunes in his report lists 32 Israeli violations of UN Security Council resolutions (up to 2002): [http://fpif.org/united_nations_security_council_resolutions_currently_being_violated_by_countries_other_than_iraq/], while Jeremy Hammond lists 80 security resolutions ignored by Israel in 'Rogue State: Israeli Violations of UN Security Council Resolutions', in *Foreign Policy Journal*, 27 January 2010: [http://www.foreignpolicyjournal.com/2010/01/27/rogue-state-israeli-violations-of-u-n-security-council-resolutions/].
3. See full text of the NPT treaty in Appendix I.
4. Referring to the N5 recognised by the NPT would then allow us to refer to the N9 as the currently known actual NWS, the N8 as the 'declared' NWS, etc. just as we have the G7, G8 etc.
5. It was the G7 before Russia was invited to join, and Russia's membership was suspended in 2014 so it may revert to being called G7 again. The OECD is the Organisation for Economic Cooperation and Development. See definition of other acronyms at the front of the book.

Chapter 11

1. See Janka Oertel, 'The United Nations and NATO' unpublished draft, 3/6/08, pg 2 and Bruno Simma, 'NATO, the UN and the Use of Force: Legal Aspects', *European Journal of International Law*, Vol. 10, No. 1, 1999, pp. 1–22.
2. International Law and Policy Institute, 'NATO and a Treaty Banning Nuclear Weapons', [http://nwp.ilpi.org/?p=2317], accessed 15 December 2015.
3. See [http://www.flanderstoday.eu/politics/federal-parliament-joins-call-ban-nuclear-weapons].
4. [http://www.thelocal.de/20120905/44779].

Chapter 12

1. Most recently in reference to the bombing of Syria, claimed by David Cameron as an act of self-defence under Article 51 when in fact Article 51 allows for no such thing.
2. International Court of Justice, *Legality of the Threat or Use of Nuclear Weapons, Advisory Opinion*, 8 July, 1996 [http://www.icj-cij.org/docket/files/95/7495.pdf], p. 258.
3. *Ibid*, p. 258.
4. *Ibid*, p. 259.
5. Under the Criminal Justice Act of 2003, the threat to kill 'where the defendant intends the victim to fear it will be carried out' carries a maximum life sentence.
6. ICJ, op cit, p. 246.

7   *Ibid*, p. 264.
8   There was also a second element to this bargain, which was the promise to share peaceful nuclear power generation technology with all countries so they could also benefit from this.
9   See full text of NPT in Appendix I.
10 Speech by Lord Mulley, UK Minister for Disarmament, at Geneva during plenary of Eighteen Nation Disarmament Committee, 1968.
11 See Appendix II.

Chapter 13

1   Written statement to the House of Commons, HCWS4, Safety at HM Naval Base Clyde, 28 May 2015: [http://www.parliament.uk/documents/commons-vote-office/May%20 2015/28%20May/1-Defence-Clyde.pdf].
2   See Eric Schlosser, *Command and Control*, Penguin, London, 2013. Also Lewis, Patricia, Williams, Heather, Pelopidas, Benoît and Aghlani, Sasan, 'Too Close for Comfort: Cases of Near Nuclear Use and Options for Policy' Chatham House, The Royal Institute of International Affairs London, April 2014.
3   [http://www.theguardian.com/world/2013/may/08/us-airforce-nuclear-missiles].
4   Schlosser, op cit, p. 472.
5   According to papers released in 2013 under a FOI request.
6   Schlosser, op cit, p. 246.
7   See Thule Forum, 'Broken Arrow: the B-52 Accident...' [http://www.thuleforum.com/broken_arrow/].
8   [http://www.aerospaceweb.org/question/weapons/q0268.shtml].
9   [http://www.theguardian.com/world/2001/apr/05/kursk.russia].
10 See [www.pravdareport.com/russia/politics/09-10-2012/122396-submarine_reagan_gorbachev-0].
11 Quoted in Chatham House, 2014. [http://www.publications.parliament.uk/pa/cm200809/cmhansrd/cm090402/text/90402w0024.htm].
12 *Ibid*.
13 See Schlosser, op cit, pp. 470–471.
14 Ainslie, op cit, p. 19–20.
15 [http://www.bbc.co.uk/news/uk-politics-26463923].
16 [http://robedwards.typepad.com/files/the-nuclear-secrets.pdf].
17 Quoted in [http://www.savetheroyalnavy.org/parliamentary-debate-in-wake-of-trident-safety-allegations/].
18 Patricia Lewis et al, op cit.
19 *Ibid*, pp. 16–17.
20 This is evident from Reagan's memoirs and other Western intelligence reports, although no archives have been forthcoming from the Russian side to confirm what Soviet leaders were thinking. See Chatham House, op cit, pp. 13–16.
21 *Ibid*.
22 [http://thebulletin.org/three-minutes-and-counting7938].

23 US NRC, *Reactor Safety Study: An Assessment of Accidental Risks in US Commercial Nuclear Power Plants*, 1975. wash-1400, nureg 75/014. [http://www.barringer1.com/mil_files/nureg-75-014-Report-&-Executive-Summary.pdf].

Chapter 14

1 Paul Ingram, 'Measuring the Financial Costs' in *Background Papers to the Trident Commission*, basic, 2014, p. 21.
2 See Ritchie, op cit, p. 22.
3 Ibid.
4 These are broken down for 2005–2006 in a written parliament answer by then Defence Secretary Des Browne. *Hansard*, Written Questions, 24 July 2006, column 776w.

Chapter 15

1 From HM Government, National Security Strategy and Strategic Defence Review, 2015, Cm 9161, p. 36.
2 This was in answer to questions during launch of the Trident Commission report, House of Commons, 1 July 2014.
3 [https://www.gov.uk/government/uploads/system/uploads/attachment_data/file/28423/120426_2011_ukni_workshop_final_rpt.pdf].
4 See Frank Boulton 'Dangers associated with civil nuclear power programmes' in *Medicine Conflict and Survival*, 31 (1) 2016 pg 6, pgs 100–132 (forthcoming). 249
5 Ibid.
6 See [http://www.nti.org/treaties-and-regimes/conference-on-disarmament/] for a complete breakdown of what the CD has done in each of its sessions since 1998.
7 [http://reachingcriticalwill.org/images/documents/Disarmament-fora/1com/1com15/ eov/L13_n5.pdf].
8 [http://reachingcriticalwill.org/images/documents/Disarmament-fora/1com/1com12/ eov/l46_France-uk-us.pdf].
9 [http://www.nuclearinfo.org/article/non-proliferation/vienna-conference-maintains-momentum-humanitarian-initiative-nuclear].
10 See http://cpr.unu.edu/why-the-2015-npt-review-conference-fell-apart.html.
11 Many countries opposed an 'indefinite extension' of the NPT when this came up at the 1995 review conference, since it would mean leaving the situation in situ where five countries have nuclear weapons and the other 182 countries do not. Since the five NWS had made little progress towards fulfilling their Article VI obligation to disarm, the 1995 conference sought a number of assurances from them that this would happen if they allowed the NPT to be extended indefinitely. The Middle East NFZ was part of that bargaining which took place.

Chapter 16

1 See Rob Green, *The Naked Nuclear Emperor*, DSC Christchurch 2000, p. 10.
2 This is apparently only possible through the use of real time weather and other targeting data from US satellites.
3 Nick Richie, *A Nuclear Weapons Free World? Britain, Trident and the Challenge Ahead*, Palgrave MacMillan, London, 2012 p. 12.

4   In the 1974–79 Labour government, David Owen argued that the ability to kill one million Russians ought to be sufficient as a deterrent. He was outnumbered by those in cabinet who pointed out that Russia lost more than 20 million in WWII and still survived as state. Therefore, it was argued that 1 million dead was not enough.
5   Ritchie, p. 310.
6   See Aldrich, op cit.

Chapter 18

1   Ward Wilson, op cit.
2   See, for instance, Mike Bowker and Robin Brown, eds, *From Cold War to Collapse*, Cambridge University Press, Cambridge, 1993, p. 102.
3   Tony Blair, op cit, pp. 635–636.

Chapter 19

1   Quinlan, Michael, *Thinking about nuclear weapons*, RUSI, London, 1997, pp. 45–47.
2   Church of England Board for Social Responsibility, *Church and the Bomb*, Hodder and Stoughton, London, 1982.
3   *Ibid*, p. 160.
4   *Ibid*, p. 143.
5   St Petersburg Declaration of 1868 [http://www.weaponslaw.org/instruments/1968-saint-petersburg-declaration].
6   As outlawed by the Hague Declaration of 1899, which was not signed by the UK until 1907 and was never signed by the US.
7   Geneva Protocol, 1925, came into force in 1928. Further treaties prohibiting all biological weapons came into force in 1972 and chemical weapons in 1993.
8   [https://w2.vatican.va/content/francesco/en/messages/pont-messages/2014/documents/papa-francesco_20141207_messaggio-conferenza-vienna-nucleare.html]
9   Quran, 2:190.
10 According to the Sunni tradition, these are the instructions which Abu Bakr al-Siddiq, the first Caliph, gave to his armies. See [http://www.juancole.com/2013/04/islamic-forbids-terrorism.html].
11 Quran, 2:190.
12 Quran 8:61.
13 Shevuot 35b. See [http://www.jlaw.com/Articles/war3.html].
14 'Purity of Arms' doctrine of the Israeli Defence Force (IDF).
15 Hinduism, Buddhism, Jainism, Sikhism, Taoism, Confucianism and Shintoism.
16 Religions for Peace, *Resource Guide on Nuclear Disarmament for Religious Leaders and Communities*, NY, 2013, p. 6.
17 http://endnuclearweapons.org.uk.
18 Quoted in Ogilvie-White, p. 125.
19 Michael Quinlan, *Thinking About Nuclear Weapons*, RUSI, London, 1997.

Chapter 20

1. Quoted in Hennesey, op cit, p. 678.
2. Rotblat, Joseph Ed., *Nuclear Weapons: Road to Zero*, Westview Press, Boulder CO, 1998, pg. 4.
3. Letter to *The Times*, 21 April 2010.

Chapter 21

1. Speech by Admiral of the Fleet, Earl Mountbatten of Burma, on the occasion of the award of the Louise Weiss Foundation Prize to the Stockholm International Peace Research Institute, Strasbourg, 11 May, 1979. Reproduced in pamphlet form by CND, London, 1979.

Quakers in Britain

The Quaker commitment to peace arises from the conviction that love is at the heart of existence and that all human beings are unique and equal. This leads Quakers to put their faith into action by working locally and globally to change the systems that cause injustice and violent conflict.

Quakers share a way of life, not a set of beliefs. Their unity is based on shared understanding and a shared practice of silent worship, where they seek a communal stillness. Quakers seek to experience the Spirit directly, within themselves and in their relationships with others and the world around them. They meet together for worship in local meetings, which are open to all who wish to attend. Quakers try to live with honesty and integrity. This means speaking truth to all, and engaging actively and creatively with decision-makers.

Since the 17th century, Quakers have worked to bring this world into conformity with the Kingdom of God as they understand it. This has meant being at the forefront of campaigns to abolish the transatlantic slave trade, to find peaceful alternatives to war, for restorative justice, to achieve equal rights for women and to build a fairer and more sustainable society for all.

Website: http://www.quaker.org.uk/
Twitter: @BritishQuakers
Facebook: facebook.com/QuakersinBritain/
Email: enquiries@quaker.org

Some other books published by **Luath Press**

World in Chains – the impact of nuclear weapons and militarisation from a UK perspective
Angie Zelter
ISBN 978-1-910021-03-3 PBK £12.99

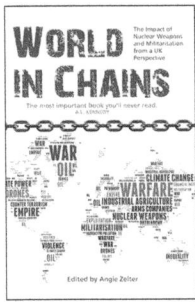

World in Chains is a collection of essays from well-reputed experts in their field, all of which deliver engaging and analytical critiques of nuclear warfare. They point to the changes needed to re-structure society, so that it is based on compassion, co-operation, love and respect for all. Their words inspire us to resist the growing militarisation and corporatisation of our world.

In the past I have often wondered why obviously unethical or inhumane horrors were able to take place, what people were doing at the time to prevent them or what kind of resistance was happening, how many people knew and tried to stop the genocide, slavery, poverty and pollution... I want those who come after my generation to know that, yes, we do know of the dangers of nuclear war, of climate chaos, of environmental destruction. This book will show you that there were many people working to change the structures that keep our world in chains. ANGIE ZELTER

The most important book you'll never read. AL KENNEDY

Faslane 365: A year of anti-nuclear blockades
Edited by Angie Zelter
ISBN: 978-1-906307-61-5 PBK £12.99

The Faslane campaign has been fantastic, it has encouraged people to act as the opposition to a government of false consensus and arrogance. Trident is an expensive stupid nuclear toy that creates an arms race, threatens to destabilise arms reduction treaties and lurches us into an uncertain future. It is a redundant dinosaur of the cold war era that has no place and serves no purpose, other than to aggrandise the military prowess of Britain's rulers. So when a state is uncivil, civil disobedience to the state becomes merely good manners. To everyone who locked themselves to the gates of Faslane, who blocked the roads, who dressed as pixies or swam across the loch to reach the submarines, I salute your lessons in civic etiquette. MARK THOMAS, comedian and political activist

Faslane 365 is the story of the people and ideas that embodied the 365 day blockade of Fasland Naval Base, home of Britain's nuclear submarines. Combining poems, anecdotes, articles and observations, it details the preparation and demonstration of the blockades, documents Scotland's history of anti-nuclear resistance, analyses Britain's nuclear policy, examines the campaign's impact on Faslane's local community, and considers the international ramifications of disarmament. With contributions from AL Kennedy, Adrian Mitchell, Eurig Scandrett and many others.

Trident on Trial: The case for the people's disarmament
Angie Zelter
ISBN: 978–1-906307–61–5 PBK £12.99

Trident and international Law: Scotland's Obligations
Edited by Rebecca Johnson and Angie Zelter
ISBN: 978–1-906817–24–4 PBK £12.99

This is the story of global citizenship in action, a story of people's power and the right of individuals to prevent their state from committing very great wrongs. This book is about the women and men who are taking responsibility to prevent mass murder. It is about people's disarmament. I hope it will inspire you to join us. ANGIE ZELTER

When three women – Ellen Moxley, Ulla Roder and Angie Zelter – boarded a research laboratory barge responsible for the concealment of Trident when in operation, they emptied all the computer equipment into Loch Goil. Their subsequent trial ended with acquittal for the 'The Trident Three' on the basis that they were acting as global citizens preventing nuclear crime. This led to what is thought to be the world's first High Court examination of the legality of an individual state's deployment of nuclear weapons. However the High Court failed to answer a number of significant questions.

Trident on Trial is Angie Zelter's personal account of Trident Ploughshares, the civil-resistance campaign of People's Disarmament. The book also includes profiles of and contributions by people and groups who have pledged to prevent nuclear crime in peaceful and practical ways… This fine book should be read by everyone, especially those who have the slightest doubt that the world will one day be rid of nuclear weapons. JOHN PILGER

As a further generation of nuclear-armed submarines is developed, *Trident and International Law* challenges the legality of UK nuclear policy, and asks who is really accountable for Coulport and Faslane.

Although controlled by the Westminster Government, and to some extent by the US Government, all of the UK's nuclear weapons are based in Scotland. The Scottish Government therefore has responsibilities under domestic and international law relating to the deployment of nuclear weapons in Scotland.

Public concern expressed over these responsibilities led to the Acronym Institute for Disarmament Diplomacy, the Edinburgh Peace and Justice Centre and Trident Ploughshares organising an international conference, 'Trident and International Law: Scotland's Obligations'. This book presents the major documents and papers, with additional arguments from renowned legal scholars. The conclusions deserve careful consideration.

Gross violations of international obligations are not excluded from the purview of the Scottish Parliament.
HE JUDGE CHRISTOPHER WEERAMANTRY

Details of books published by Luath Press can be found at:
www.luath.co.uk

Luath Press Limited
committed to publishing well written books worth reading

LUATH PRESS takes its name from Robert Burns, whose little collie Luath (*Gael.*, swift or nimble) tripped up Jean Armour at a wedding and gave him the chance to speak to the woman who was to be his wife and the abiding love of his life. Burns called one of 'The Twa Dogs' Luath after Cuchullin's hunting dog in Ossian's *Fingal*. Luath Press was established in 1981 in the heart of Burns country, and now resides a few steps up the road from Burns' first lodgings on Edinburgh's Royal Mile.

Luath offers you distinctive writing with a hint of unexpected pleasures.

Most bookshops in the UK, the US, Canada, Australia, New Zealand and parts of Europe either carry our books in stock or can order them for you. To order direct from us, please send a £sterling cheque, postal order, international money order or your credit card details (number, address of cardholder and expiry date) to us at the address below. Please add post and packing as follows: UK – £1.00 per delivery address; overseas surface mail – £2.50 per delivery address; overseas airmail – £3.50 for the first book to each delivery address, plus £1.00 for each additional book by airmail to the same address. If your order is a gift, we will happily enclose your card or message at no extra charge.

Luath Press Limited
543/2 Castlehill
The Royal Mile
Edinburgh EH1 2ND
Scotland

Telephone: 0131 225 4326 (24 hours)
email: sales@luath.co.uk
Website: www.luath.co.uk